ACTOR:
Key to Efficient Reading

Victoria M. Rey

Kendall Hunt
publishing company

Kendall Hunt
publishing company

www.kendallhunt.com
Send all inquiries to:
4050 Westmark Drive
Dubuque, IA 52004-1840

Copyright © 2017 by Kendall Hunt Publishing Company

ISBN 978-1-5249-5560-1

Published in the United States of America

Brief Contents

Detailed Contents

chapter 3
Sentence Relationships   *41*

chapter 4
Main Idea   *61*

chapter 5
Supporting Details   *83*

chapter 6
Paragraph Patterns   *101*

Preface

ACTOR: Key to Efficient Reading is designed to help you to become a focused, an engaged and a productive reader before, during, and after reading. This book is divided into 12 chapters that include the skills and strategies that can help you cope with the demands of reading college materials and completing reading assignments. The first chapter helps you to examine the causes of poor comprehension and the steps that you can follow to become an efficient reader. The rest of the chapters show you how to use ACTOR in reading different types of materials that college students encounter. Most of the informational texts that are included in this book were derived from newspapers, magazines, and college textbooks such as Psychology, Sociology, Philosophy, Criminal Justice, Architecture, Dance, Literature, Music, Biology, Health, Archaeology, Music, Sustainability, Women Studies, Astronomy, Arts, Digital Literacy, and Career Planning. This book also includes stories that can inspire you in your life journey.

Rationale for Different Chapters

You read the material that has been written by a writer who uses previous knowledge and experiences, vocabulary, and writing skills and strategies to achieve a purpose. Since you read materials that have been written by others who may introduce unfamiliar top-ics and vocabulary, you need to devise a way to relate to these materials. Lack of prior knowledge about a topic or vocabulary, ineffective reading strategies, and insufficient reading skills may result in poor reading comprehension.

The writer usually considers a purpose, a thesis or the main point of the article and supporting details in the materials that you read. These details may include ideas that are true or false and beliefs of the writer. Ideas may also be clearly stated or suggested. Reading assignments in some college courses may require you to analyze a text or book chapter and summarize or write an argument. Therefore, you need to learn how to deal with these situations by using an effective method that will help you better understand what you read. ACTOR is a method that includes different steps and accompanying strategies to fully understand what you read, and it can help you to acquire the reading skills to satisfactorily complete the reading requirements or tasks in content courses. This book, *ACTOR: Key to Efficient Reading*, is divided into 12 chapters. It shows you how to acquire the skills and strategies that will help you to become an efficient reader. The chapters include the following:

1. Using ACTOR in Reading
2. Vocabulary Enhancement
3. Sentence Relationships
4. Main Idea
5. Supporting Details
6. Paragraph Patterns
7. Inference
8. Fact and Opinion
9. Purpose
10. Tone
11. Argument
12. Summing Up

After showing how ACTOR is used in Chapter 1, this is further demonstrated in Chapters 2–11 in applying the different skills that will help you to better understand what you read. These skills are crucial in understanding written materials. Chapter 12 explains different reading test–taking strategies that can be helpful to you in taking reading mastery or standardized tests.

Chapter Features

This book is designed to help you realize the causes of poor reading comprehension and lack of interest in reading and poor performance in reading tests or other exams that require reading. An awareness of these factors leads you to a path of dealing with these situations. As a result, you will find out that you will be able to better understand, remember, and enjoy what you read.

In every chapter, the information that will help you become an efficient reader is provided. It also shows you how to use this information to better understand what is explicitly stated and suggested in reading materials with varying difficulty and interest levels. This is followed by practice exercises and mastery tests. It also shows the strategies that will enable you to evaluate if your answers to these exercises are correct or wrong. If you find out that your answers are wrong, strategies are presented to correct your mistakes. Mastery tests and interesting and informative materials are provided at the end of every chapter.

Acknowledgments

ACTOR: Key to Efficient Reading is a research-based book that has been developed through the years. After teaching developmental reading courses for several years, using different textbooks in teaching these courses, and conducting research relating to reading and learning, I developed ACTOR, a method that is designed to help you to become a focused, engaged, and productive reader before, during, and after reading.

I have used ACTOR in helping my students to better understand what they read. Their comments have inspired me to write this book. I also appreciate the support of the following who have helped me to finish this book.

1. My students, who used ACTOR, gave me very positive feedback and suggestions which are found on page 11.
2. Kean University foundation, granted funding for the tests that were administered to students in the duration of my research on the use of ACTOR.
3. Drs. Joan Kastner, Ethel Young, and Davida Schuman, Kean University professors, supported me in my studies that contributed to the development of ACTOR. Dr. Davida Schuman, who used the instructor's edition of the book and accompanying test bank and PowerPoint slides, gave valuable comments and suggestions.
4. Ms. Sue Saad, Acquisitions Editor, and Ms. Kim Schmidt and Ms. Torrie Johnson, Project Coordinators of Kendall Hunt Publishing Company, guided me during the production of this book.
5. Mr. Solomon Rey, my supportive husband, reviewed this book and answered all exercises therein.

Using ACTOR in Reading

Reading is very important to college students. They have to read in order to learn new information, complete reading assignments and take tests. However, there are some students who become sleepy, get bored, or do not fully understand what they are reading. This chapter will help you examine the causes of poor comprehension and the steps that you can follow to become an efficient reader.

Topics

Importance of Reading

Causes of Poor Reading Comprehension

The Reading–Writing Connection

ACTOR and Efficient Reading

Reading Skills

Reading Strategies

Importance of Reading

Reading plays an important role in life. One way to know what is going on around you is to read the news articles online or in newspapers. When you order food in a restaurant, you may need to read the menu. To fill out applications, you must read instructions and questions. In college, you read to acquire information that is related to your field. Assignments, projects, tests, and other tasks require you to read. There are many benefits of reading.

Andrey_Popov/Shutterstock.com

1. Broadens Knowledge and Experiences

You gain information on different subjects through reading. So, the more you read, the more information you acquire. You will be able to use this prior knowledge in relating to what you will read later on. Also, it may give you a good feeling that you are knowledgeable on various topics. You may be able to use this information in the future. Furthermore, you may learn from the experiences of others. For example, reading the characteristics of academically successful students may lead you to examine your goals as a student and make plans to reach your goal.

2. Expands Vocabulary

When you read, you learn new vocabulary that will be helpful to you. There are times that you may not be familiar with the meanings of the words. However, if you use some techniques to figure out the meanings of these words, you are likely to make sense of these words in order to understand written materials. Later, you may find these helpful when you encounter these words in reading related topics.

3. Stimulates Thinking

To make sense of what you are reading, you have to think to figure out what a sentence in the paragraph means. You have to connect the idea of this sentence to the next sentence. As you repeatedly connect ideas, you process the information in your mind to figure out what you are reading. You think in a logical or in an organized way. This logical way of thinking helps you in everyday life situations. The more you think logically, the more you become organized in the way you deal with a situation, solve a problem, and consider possible consequences of alternative solutions to this problem.

4. Improves Communication Skills

To express your ideas, you speak and write. Previous knowledge that you have gathered in reading constitutes what you say and write about. Prior knowledge also helps you to understand the new information that you receive in listening. The thinking skills that you apply to comprehend what you are reading also help you in listening, speaking, and writing. Applying the thinking skills that you acquire in reading helps you in listening comprehension. Like in reading, you connect and make sense of what the speaker is saying. Similarly, in speaking, you make sure that what you say makes sense. All sentences must relate or connect to each other. You also do this in writing by including logical and cohesive sentences.

5. Boosts Self-Confidence

The information that you have acquired in reading will help you boost your self-confidence in conversing with friends and others during formal and informal gatherings. In class discussions, the thinking skills that you have applied in reading will also guide you to participate, whether you ask questions or give comments, because you can easily follow the direction or flow of ideas in the conversation.

6. Increases Job Opportunities

Companies follow different policies in selecting job applicants. Usually, applicants are interviewed. To do well in the interview, you use the thinking skills and information pertaining to the field or job that you have acquired in reading. Appropriate answers to questions and depth of knowledge on the topic are important. In some situations, applicants are required to take a reading comprehension test.

7. Leads to Creativity

Reading may lead to creativity such as inventions; writing poems, stories, novels, or biography; and other forms of productivity. Reading may stir a person's imagination to create something. For example, a person who is interested in machines has read the need for a motor or a mechanism to make something to move. This could lead to a creation of motorized toy boats, kites, or other helpful moving objects. Reading may be a source of inspiration for writing poems or stories. For example, a news article about a homeless student who graduated with the highest honor may be the basis for writing a poem, a story, or an essay.

Reading is a very important tool for learning and dealing with everyday life situations. Why is reading important to you? Write five reasons.

1. _____
2. _____
3. _____
4. _____
5. _____

Causes of Poor Reading Comprehension

Since reading is important, you want to be sure that you understand what you are reading. However, you may find some materials to be difficult to understand. Finding out the causes of poor comprehension will be helpful. Sometimes, do you become sleepy and bored while you are reading? Do you feel that you do not understand what you are reading? If so, what do you think are the reasons? Perhaps, you are not interested in the topic. Another reason is the complicated presentation of the ideas. There are long, compound, or complex sentences. Also, you do not have a clear goal or purpose for reading an article. In addition, there are words that you do not understand. Furthermore, you cannot maintain concentration while you are reading. Your mind wanders—you are thinking of something.

Examine the following causes of poor reading comprehension. Which of these have you experienced?

1. Lack of interest in the topic—You are not interested in the topic and you find the material boring or hard to understand.
2. Complicated presentation of ideas—You become overwhelmed due to very long and complicated sentences.
3. Unclear goal or lack of purpose—You are not sure why you are reading or what you are looking for in the reading material. This is similar to the situation where a person is driving to an unknown place. It takes you longer than usual to understand what you are reading.
4. Unfamiliar words—The reading material does not make sense because you are not familiar with some words.
5. Poor concentration—Internal distractors such as hunger, thirst, sleepiness, or daydreaming, and external distractors that include cell phones or noise prevent you from understanding the material.

What are other causes of poor comprehension?

1. _____
2. _____
3. _____

Recognizing the causes of poor reading comprehension is very important because you can find ways to deal with this situation. To further understand the causes of poor comprehension and how to deal with these, let us examine the reading–writing connection.

The Reading–Writing Connection

Sometimes, you cannot understand what you are reading because you are not familiar with the topic or some words. It happens because you read what a writer has written. The writer considers his or her knowledge and experience, writing skills, and strategies to communicate ideas. When you read, do you also use your knowledge and experience? What happens when you do not have the same knowledge and experience as the writer? Perhaps, you may not easily relate to the material. Or, you may find difficulty comprehending the text. So, what will you do in order to relate to and understand the text? What does the writer consider during the writing process? What does the reader do during the reading process?

Copyright © Kendall Hunt Publishing Company.

Study the chart and answer the questions that follow.

Writer–Reader Connection

Writer	Reader

1. Prior knowledge and experience
   a. direct
   b. indirect or vicarious
     1) read
     2) listen
     3) see
	1. Prior knowledge and experience
	   a. direct
	   b. indirect or vicarious
	     1) read
	     2) listen
	     3) see

2. Writing skills
   a. Includes a main idea in a paragraph
   b. Supports the main idea with details
   c. Connects ideas through transitional words
   d. Has a purpose
   e. Uses punctuation marks
   f. Other writing skills
	2. Reading skills
	   a. Identifies the main idea in a paragraph
	   b. Recognizes supporting details
	   c. Identifies transitional words that connect ideas
	   d. Has a purpose
	   e. Recognizes use of punctuation marks
	   f. Other reading skills

3. Writing techniques to show skills	3. Reading techniques to show skills
4. Vocabulary	4. Vocabulary

Questions

1. How are the writer and the reader similar?

   _____

   _____

2. How are the writer and the reader different?

   _____

   _____

3. What happens if the reader and the writer have common knowledge and experiences?

_____

_____

4. What happens if the reader does not have the knowledge and experience that the writer uses in the written material?

_____

_____

5. What happens when the reader does not understand what is being read?

_____

_____

_____

_____

_____

6. What can help the reader to understand what is being read?

_____

_____

7. What can help the reader to figure out the meanings of unfamiliar words?

_____

_____

8. Writers use different punctuation marks. What is the purpose of each of the following punctuation marks?

   a. Comma

_____

_____

_____

_____

   b. Period

_____

_____

   c. Dash

_____

_____

d. Colon

_____

_____

You read the material that has been written by a writer who uses previous knowledge and experiences, vocabulary, punctuation marks, and writing skills and strategies to achieve a purpose. Lack of prior knowledge about the topic or vocabulary may lead to poor comprehension.

> **ACTOR**—A method that shows explicit steps and strategies, helps you to acquire the skills that are necessary to understand complex texts in college, and helps you to improve your reading comprehension

ACTOR and Efficient Reading

If you want to become a good reader, you have to read. You may read materials that are easy to understand as well as materials that are difficult to understand. As a college student, you may be assigned to read something that is challenging. Since you have to read this material, you have to apply reading skills and strategies that will help you understand what you are reading. ACTOR can help you become an efficient reader. A skill is something that you are able to do. In reading, for example, you are able to state the main idea of a paragraph or what the paragraph is telling you. Being able to figure out the meaning of an unfamiliar word

Jacob Lund/Shutterstock.com

ACTOR: Activate, Connect, Trigger strategies, Organize ideas and Respond = Efficient Reading

is also an important vocabulary skill. A strategy is something that you will do to acquire the skill. For instance, to get the main idea, ask the following questions. (1) What is the paragraph about? (2) What do all or most of the sentences in the paragraph tell you? (3) What is the most general sentence? (4) Do the rest of the sentences tell about the most general sentence? Being efficient means that the reader understands what is being read in a reasonable time and shows proof of understanding. After reading, you are able to summarize what you have read. Also, you do not read the material several times to understand the material.

ACTOR is designed to help you become an efficient reader because this method includes steps and strategies that will enable you to become focused, engaged, and productive readers, before, during, and after reading. The steps in ACTOR are *activate* prior knowledge, *connect* to new information in the text, *trigger* appropriate strategies to understand what is being read, *organize* ideas that are generated from the text, and *respond* to what has been read.

During the <u>activate</u> step, readers recall prior knowledge by reading the title and headings, asking questions on what the title and headings suggests and thinking about what is known about the expected ideas based on the title and major headings. They also reasonably activate prior knowledge on content and vocabulary while reading. They <u>connect</u> previous knowledge (vocabulary or ideas) to the new information in order to relate or to make sense of what is being read. During the third stage, <u>trigger</u>, students derive meanings or make sense of printed texts by choosing a combination of strategies from the list in Table 3 ensure engagement with the text and comprehension. In the fourth stage, students think about what they have read, recall and <u>organize</u> in their minds or on paper the ideas that they generate from the text. Finally, they <u>respond</u> to what they have read to show proof of comprehension by reciting, writing, or creating something. Answering and asking questions about the texts during class and group discussions or written assignments can measure readers' comprehension. Responding helps the readers to determine if what is read is understood. In independent reading, readers use their own words to recite or think about what has been read.

Reading Skills

A writer uses prior knowledge that is drawn from personal experience and secondary information and considers writing skills. For example, to write a good paragraph, a writer uses appropriate vocabulary, states or implies the main idea and includes related supporting details. To understand this paragraph, the reader has to apply vocabulary and comprehension skills such as inferring word meanings, activating prior knowledge, and identifying the main idea and supporting details. Being able to correctly summarize and sensibly react to the information in the paragraph may prove the reader's comprehension. A list of skills that can help a reader to facilitate and to show signs of comprehension is shown in Table 1. This book will explain and show you how to acquire these skills. Reviewing the charts that follow and examining your vocabulary and comprehension skills will help you recognize your strengths and identify steps that you may do to improve your reading comprehension (Table 2).

How well do you rate your skill of using each of the following? Mark X in the appropriate column.

Table 1

Vocabulary	Very Good	Good	Needs Improvement
1. Infer the meaning of an unfamiliar word through its surrounding words in a sentence.			
2. Figure out the meaning of an unfamiliar word through its prefix, suffix, or root word.			
3. Infer the meaning of an unfamiliar word through punctuation clues.			

Explain your answer for each item. Why is your answer very good, good, or needs improvement?

1. _____

_____

2. _____

_____

3. _____

_____

Comprehension

Examine your reading comprehension skills. How well do you find your skill of using each of the following? Mark X in the appropriate column.

Table 2 Survey on Reading

Skills	Good	Very Good	Needs Improvement
1. Connect ideas in sentences through transitional words.			
2. Sense a smooth flow of ideas between sentences.			
3. Identify the main idea of a paragraph.			
4. Identify details that support the main idea of a paragraph.			
5. Connect ideas between paragraphs in an article.			
6. Identify the main thesis of an article.			
7. Identify the details that support the main thesis of an article.			
8. Recognize paragraph patterns.			
9. Make an outline of what is read.			
10. Summarize what is read.			
11. Distinguish between a fact and an opinion.			
12. Make an inference.			
13. Identify the purpose of an article.			
14. Recognize the tone of an article.			
15. Identify an argument.			
16. Identify the point and supports in an argument.			

Rey. Survey on Reading Skills. 2017.

Reading Strategies

In using ACTOR (Activate, Connect, Trigger, Organize, and Respond), readers use appropriate meta-cognitive, cognitive, and reading strategies before, during, and after reading to develop or improve their vocabulary and comprehension skills. In using metacognitive strategies, you know if you are understanding the material that you are reading and you are aware that you have to do something to understand the material. Cognitive strategies are things that you do to understand the material. In reading, you have to apply strategies before, during, and after reading to relate and understand the written material and show proof of comprehension.

Which of the strategies that are listed in Table 3 do you usually use? Mark X in the appropriate column.

Table 3

Strategies	X
1. Have a purpose for reading.	
2. Read the title and/or headings.	
3. Think about what the title and/or headings in the article suggest.	
4. Connect related knowledge about the title or headings to the reading material.	
5. Concentrate or stay focused while reading.	
6. Use context clues in the sentence or paragraph to figure out the meanings.	
7. Use prefixes, suffixes, or roots to figure out the meanings of unfamiliar words.	
8. Use punctuation clues such as commas, colons, parentheses, or dashes to figure out the meanings of unfamiliar words.	
9. Use word definition clues such as <u>is, means, refers to, or is defined as</u> to figure out the meanings of unfamiliar words.	
10. Break apart or chunk down ideas in sentences.	
11. Say the first sentence without looking at it.	
12. Imagine or make a picture in mind of what is being read.	
13. Ask questions while reading.	
14. Underline or highlight information that is important.	
15. Adjust reading speed or slow down when needed.	
16. Study given charts, tables, maps, or pictures in the text.	
17. Know if what is read is understood.	
18. Change the strategy if what is being read is not understood.	

(Continued)

Table 3 (Continued)	
Strategies	**X**
19. Connect the idea in one sentence to the next sentence.	
20. Connect all ideas in a paragraph.	
21. Say what the whole paragraph says.	
22. Connect the idea in the first paragraph to the next paragraph.	
23. Organize in mind the ideas that are read from the text.	
24. Say the information that is understood from the article.	
25. Write about what is understood from the reading material.	

Which of the strategies on the list do you find the three most helpful in understanding what you are reading? Explain your answers.

Strategies

    1. Strategy 1 _____

       Reason _____

       _____

    2. Strategy 2 _____

       Reason _____

       _____

    3. Strategy 3 _____

       Reason _____

       _____

I developed ACTOR because I wanted to help students to improve their reading comprehension of complex texts and enjoy reading. My experience in teaching reading in the elementary, secondary, and college students and conducting substantial research have helped me designed the skills and strategies in ACTOR. I also conducted a research on the effects of ACTOR on college students' reading performance and perceptions of their reading skills and comprehension. The results of my study showed that students have improved their reading comprehension and have found ACTOR to be beneficial.

Students who have used ACTOR gave the following comments.

    1. It helps give me a boost while reading, and I don't become bored.
    2. I feel as though the ACTOR method overall, gave me a way to better understand a lot of whatever I read which caused me to score higher than usual in tests or quizzes in my classes.

3. The concept allows me as a reader to understand and memorize what I am reading. It also keeps me intrigued, so I do not fall to boredom while reading a "boring" writing piece.

4. I find the ACTOR method helpful in understanding what I am reading because it helps me to better comprehend the meaning of the text. It makes me take time to think about what I am reading and what I get out of it.

5. As I read a passage, I look to think if I have any prior knowledge, as well as creating images in my head and breaking down each supporting detail.

6. It is helpful because it helps me connect my ideas and understand them better.

7. It is helpful because it reminds me to be aware of every aspect that I should be getting when I am reading.

8. The ACTOR method has significantly improved my reading skills because while reading, I follow the steps and my mind is able to process information more carefully. I am also able to trigger strategies such as visualization, auditory, and kinesthetic. Overall, I feel like I improved a lot in reading skills.

9. I never used it before, but now it is starting to help me understand what I am reading.

10. It helps me organize ideas and gather my thoughts before reading, during reading, and after reading. It's easier for me to understand what I'm reading about because things make more sense.

11. It helps me to not just understand what I'm reading, but also how to apply if to life if it comes to situations or even answering questions on homework or writing a response/ reflection.

12. I have been able to study more and understand better since I started using the ACTOR method. I no longer lose interest or feel sleepy while reading, not just the books in English, but all other books even the not-so-interesting ones.

You can also benefit from using ACTOR. It can help you become an efficient reader if you consistently follow the steps and accompanying strategies. Examples on how to follow the steps in this method and use appropriate techniques are explained and demonstrated in each chapter. Be patient because it takes time and practice to feel confident in using ACTOR. This will be helpful to you in reading, listening, speaking, and writing. You will also find the strategies beneficial to you in studying in other courses. Most of the reading materials in this book have been chosen from college texts, magazines, and news articles because the purpose of this book is to help you cope with the demands of understanding the materials that you read in print and digital forms.

Chapter Review Questions

Answer the following questions.

1. Why is reading important?

2. What are the causes of poor reading comprehension?

3. What is ACTOR?

4. What are the benefits of using ACTOR?

5. What is the difference between a reading skill and a strategy?

6. What are five of the reading skills that students need to acquire?

7. Why do readers use reading strategies?

8. What are five of the strategies that may help readers to improve comprehension?

2

Vocabulary Enhancement

One way to help you improve your reading comprehension is to pay attention to clues that will enable you to figure out the meaning of an unfamiliar word. Clues include definition words, punctuation marks, context clues, and word parts. This chapter will show you how to

1. identify the clues that will help you to figure out the meanings of unfamiliar words,
2. use these clues to understand what you are reading, and
3. follow the steps in ACTOR.

Topics

Definition Clues

Punctuation Clues

Context Clues

Word Parts

In reading, vocabulary plays an important role. If you cannot recognize a given word and its meaning, the printed words may not mean anything to you. Sometimes, sounding out an unfamiliar word and later saying the word orally or aloud in your mind may help you make the word sound familiar and make sense to you. If the meaning is not clear, apply some techniques that can help you get the meanings of these words. Pay attention to definition clues, punctuation marks, context clues, and word parts. These will help you to figure out the meanings of unfamiliar words. Since some words have multiple meanings, be sure to consider what the sentence is telling you.

Definition Clues

When you are reading, pay attention to words that are used to state the definitions of words. Usually, a word that is written in boldface, underlined, or italicized is followed by definition words such as or, is, means, is defined as, refers to, and is called. Any of these signal words may be followed by a definition.

Study the examples below.

1. *Psychology* is the scientific study of the human mind and its functions, especially those affecting behavior in a given context.

   Word *Psychology*

   Definition word *is*

   Meaning *study of the human mind and its functions*

2. According to the Merriam-Webster's Dictionary, an *artwork* is defined as a "painting, sculpture, photograph, etc., that is created to be beautiful or to express an important idea or feeling."

   Word _____

   Definition word _____

   Meaning _____

Practice

Read each sentence. Identify the word that is defined, the definition word(s) and the meaning. Write your answers in the blanks for each number.

1. *Beauty* refers to an aesthetic quality in a person or object that appeals to one's physical or spiritual senses.

   a. Word _____

   b. Definition word _____

   c. Meaning _____

2. **Idealism,** or the concept of physical perfection, was not just about proportion.

   a. Word _____

   b. Definition word _____

   c. Meaning _____

3. Cardiac arrest is a sudden stop in effective blood flow due to the failure of the heart to contract effectively.

   a. Word _____

   b. Definition word _____

   c. Meaning _____

Limitations of definition clues

Be aware that a word that is followed by or, is, means, is defined as, refers to, or is called does not necessarily give the meaning of a word. Ask yourself if the sentence gives you the word meaning. You may also use other clues to figure out the meaning of the word.

Punctuation Clues

Writers sometimes use punctuation marks to show definitions. These include comma, dash, semi colon, and parenthesis. A word that is preceded or followed by any of these punctuation marks may be the word that is being defined.

Let us examine the following examples.

1. A term that most definitions of art reference is aesthetics, a branch of philosophy traditionally concerned with the study of beauty in all of its forms.

   a. Word __**aesthetics**_____

   b. Punctuation clue _____**, (comma)**_____

   c. Definition _____**study of beauty in all its forms**_____

2. Body mass index—a method of measuring a person's degree of overweight or obesity— is thought to be a more sensitive indicator than traditional height–weight charts.

   a. Word _____

   b. Punctuation clue _____

   c. Definition _____

Practice

Identify the word that is defined, the punctuation clue for the meaning, and the definition of the word. Write your answers in the blanks under each sentence.

1. Art is described as the human ability to make things; creativeness.

   a. Word _____

   b. Punctuation clue _____

   c. Definition _____

2. His body is in a contrapposto stance, or counter pose, a posture that is natural and comfortable.

   a. Word _____

   b. Punctuation clue _____

   c. Definition _____

3. Sociology—the study of social behavior or society, including its origins, development, organization, networks, and institutions—uses various methods of investigation and critical analysis.

   a. Word _____

   b. Punctuation clue _____

   c. Definition _____

Limitations of punctuation clues

Be aware that a word that follows a punctuation mark is not always the meaning of a word. Ask yourself if the sentence is giving you a definition. You may use other clues to figure out the meaning of this word.

Context Clues

Sometimes, you come across a word that does not sound familiar to you. Paying attention to context clues or surrounding words can help you figure out the meaning of this word. Clues include words that show examples, comparison, contrast, and cause and effect. If you do not find these clues, figuring out the general sense of the sentence or what the sentence is saying can also help you.

Examples

When you are reading, you may notice words that include **for example, for instance, including, such as, to illustrate, and other words that suggest examples**. These are signal words that may help you figure out the meanings of unfamiliar words.

Let us study the example below and figure out how we can get the meaning of the italicized word.

Example: Usually, several people help victims of natural *calamities* that include earthquakes, snowstorms, and tornadoes.

To get the meaning of the word, follow the steps in ACTOR.

1. Activate your previous knowledge—Scan the sentence. The example clue is <u>include</u>. What are the given examples? What other words do you know? What do these words mean to you? Examples of calamities are earthquakes, snowstorms, and tornadoes. Do these words suggest a positive, negative, or neutral feeling?
2. Connect your answer to the idea of the sentence as you read.
3. Trigger strategies—Ask questions or make a picture in your mind. Break the sentence if necessary. Who are we talking about in the sentence? What do they do? Why do they do it? Talk to yourself or make a picture in your mind.
4. Organize the idea in your mind—Based on your answers to these questions, which of the given choices make sense when you use that choice in the place of the calamities? Say it to yourself. Does the sentence sound right?
5. What is the meaning of the italicized word? The meaning is disaster.

_____1. Usually, several people help victims of natural *calamities* that include earthquakes, snowstorms, and tornadoes.

Word: calamities
Example clue: include
Examples: earthquakes, snowstorms, and tornadoes
Meaning: disasters

a. situations
b. conditions
c. disasters
d. tendencies

_____2. My *mentor* guided me to do well in my chosen career. For example, she carefully explains to me after class the topics that are not clear to me.

Word _____
Example clue _____
Examples _____
Meaning _____

a. mother
b. teacher
c. nurse
d. guidance counselor

Using ACTOR

In the beginning, it takes willpower, concentration, time, and patience to use ACTOR. Through constant practice, you will notice that steps come automatically and your comprehension improves. With this improvement, you tend to understand what you read in less time. Eventually, you will read and will enjoy more what you are reading because you will gain something from reading.

Practice

Directions: Each of the sentences below uses an example clue. Following the steps in ACTOR, write the example clue, and select the best meaning of the italicized word.

_____1. Damon was allowed to come back to class with certain *provisions*. These include coming to class regularly, observing acceptable behavior, and completing requirements.

Example clue _____   Example(s) _____
a. warning   c. conditions
b. statements   d. regulations

_____2. My cousin was so *egocentric* when the family got together. For example, he said that he should be served first and with the best wine.

Example clue _____   Example(s) _____
a. proud   c. kind
b self-centered   d. pleased

_____3. The professor gives *incentives* to encourage students to complete requirements on time. For instance, she adds 5% to the average on quizzes if a student completes the required reading lab hours three weeks before the deadline.

Example clue _____   Example(s) _____
a. rewards   c. warnings
b. announcement   d. lab hours

_____4. Students in this class are *homogeneous*. For example, almost every student gets an **A** on tests and assignments.

Example clue _____   Example(s) _____
a. different   c. alike
b. nice   d. attentive

_____5. There are many *benevolent* people around the world. Their projects include donating their monies to build hospitals, schools, and water facilities to benefit the poor in several countries and paying for tuitions of needy students.

Example clue _____   Example(s) _____
a. wealthy   c. proud
b. kindhearted   d. successful

Comparison

When you are reading, notice words that include **similarly, in like manner, also, likewise, in a similar way, and other words that suggest comparison or similarity**. These comparison words or clues may give you the meanings of unfamiliar words.

In the example below, the italicized word is *deviance*. Use the steps in ACTOR.

The protesters were in *deviance* with the senator's decision to allow marijuana for recreational purposes. They were in disagreement with the mayor's suggestion to build a casino in the city also.

To get the meaning of the word, follow the steps in ACTOR.

1. Activate your previous knowledge—Scan the sentence. The comparison word is <u>also</u>. What other words do you know? What do these mean to you?
2. Connect your answer to the idea of the sentence as you read.
3. Trigger strategies—Ask questions or make a picture in your mind. Break the sentence if necessary. Who are we talking about in the sentence? What do they do? Why do they do it? Talk to yourself or make a picture in your mind. What are being compared?
4. Organize the idea in your mind—Based on your answers to these questions, which of the given choices makes sense when you use that choice in the place of *deviance*? Say it to yourself. Does the sentence sound right?
5. Respond—What is the meaning of the italicized word? The meaning of deviance is disagreement.

Following the steps in ACTOR, write this clue and select the best meaning of the italicized word.

_____1. The protesters were in *deviance* with the senator's decision to allow marijuana for recreational purposes. They were in disagreement with the mayor's suggestion to build a casino in the city also.

Comparison clue: __also__
a. agreement
b. consultation
c. disagreement
d. doubt

_____2. The lone survivor's family was so *euphoric* when he came out from the pile of debris. This is the same feeling which you experience when your favorite team won the football championship game.

Comparison clue: _____
a. anxious
b. happy
c. nervous
d. relaxed

Practice

Directions: Each of the sentences below uses a comparison clue. Following the steps in ACTOR, write this clue and select the best meaning of the italicized word.

_____1. This current government program seems to be *fruitful* like the previous projects that were successful.

Comparison clue: _____
a. easy
b. productive
c. difficult
d. fearless

21

_____2. In a recent *replication* of the study with fifty students who smoked, the results were the same as those in the first and second studies.

Comparison clue: _____
a. discussion
b. result
c. repeat
d. program

_____3. Whether there are aliens in Mars is an *enigma*. In like manner, there is no answer if there is life in the newly discovered Earth-like planet.

Comparison clue: _____
a. doubt
b. exploration
c. mystery
d. excitement

_____4. Rita's house is *embellished* with colorful balloons, banners, and flowers just like Lauren's house that is decorated with so many things.

Comparison clue: _____
a. decorated
b. pinned
c. written
d. displayed

_____5. This letter is *ambiguous* just like the first one that is not clear.

Comparison clue: _____
a. good
b. graded
c. unclear
d. clear

Contrast

When you are reading, pay attention to words that include **but, although, however, on the other hand, nevertheless, and other words that suggest contrast or difference**. These contrast words may help you figure out the meanings of unfamiliar words.

In the example below, the italicized word is <u>impressive</u>.

His accomplishment is *impressive* to me even though it is disgusting to the interviewer.

> ## To get the meaning of the word, follow the steps in ACTOR.
>
> 1. Activate your previous knowledge. Scan the sentence. The contrast clue is <u>even though</u>. What other words do you know? What do these mean to you?
> 2. Connect your answer to the idea of the sentence as you read.
> 3. Trigger strategies—Ask questions or make a picture in your mind. Break the sentence if necessary. Who are we talking about in the sentence? What do they do? Why do they do it? Talk to yourself or make a picture in your mind. What are being compared?
> 4. Organize the idea in your mind—Based on your answers to these questions, which of the given choices makes sense when you use that choice in the place of *impressive*? Say it to yourself. Does the sentence sound right?
> 5. Respond—What is the meaning of the italicized word? The meaning of impressive is <u>admirable</u>.

Examples

Following the steps in ACTOR, write the contrast clue and select the best meaning of the italicized word.

_____1. His accomplishment is *impressive* to me even though it is disgusting to the interviewer.

Contrast clue: _even though_   Meaning: _admirable_
a. questionable   c. admirable
b. average   d. welcome

_____2. The president *condemns* his enemies while he praises his friends.

Contrast clue: _while_   Meaning: _____
a. likes   c. commends
b. speaks against   d. speaks for

Practice

Directions: Each of the sentences below uses a contrast clue. Following the steps in ACTOR, write the contrast clue and select the best meaning of the italicized word.

_____1. In the first movie, Rachel played a minor role. However in *subsequent* movies, her role became very important.

Contrast clue: _____   Meaning: _____
a. several   c. following
b. second   d. successful

_____2. The *surrogate* mother has learned to love Jane very much although they are not related to each other.

Contrast clue: _____   Meaning: _____
a. loving   c. hopeful
b. substitute   d. sad

_____3. Peter kept on bullying Nathan both in and off campus. However, Nathan *steadfastly* ignored Peter.

Contrast clue: _____   Meaning: _____
a. constantly   c. silently
b. wrongly   d. carelessly

_____4. They *withstood* so many snowstorms. This time though, they could not do anything except to gather their belongings that were displaced by the tornado.

Contrast clue: _____   Meaning: _____
a. recognized   c. resisted
b. witnessed   d. understood

_____5. Harry is so *inhibited* in the classroom. However, he is very relaxed and talkative with his friends after class.

Contrast clue: _____   Meaning: _____
a. responsive   c. unfriendly
b. controlled   d. kind

Cause and Effect

When you are reading, notice words that show cause or reason. These include **because, due to, for this reason, and other words that show cause or reason.** Also, pay attention to words such as **therefore, so, consequently, as a result, and other words that that suggest effect or result.** Cause and effect word clues may help you figure out the meanings of unfamiliar words. In the example below, the italicized word is *deprived*.

The naughty boy has been *deprived* of watching television for a week due to his unacceptable behavior.

To get the meaning of the word, follow the steps in ACTOR.

1. Activate your previous knowledge—Scan the sentence. The cause and effect clue is <u>due to</u>. What other words do you know? What do these mean to you?
2. Connect your answer to the idea of the sentence as you read.
3. Trigger strategies—Ask questions or make a picture in your mind. Break the sentence, if it is necessary. Who are we talking about in the sentence? What do they do? Why do they do it? Talk to yourself or make a picture in your mind. What is the cause? What is the effect?
4. Organize the idea in your mind—Based on your answers to these questions, which of the given choices makes sense when you use that choice in the place of *deprived*? Say it to yourself. Does the sentence sound right?
5. Respond—What is the meaning of the italicized word? The meaning of deprived is <u>denied</u>.

Examples

Following the steps in ACTOR, write the word clue and select the best meaning of the italicized word.

_____1. The naughty boy has been *deprived* of watching television for a week due to his unacceptable behavior.

Cause/Effect clue: __**due to**__   Meaning: __**denied**__
a. warned   c. denied
b. cared   d. scared

_____2. The doctor is *optimistic* that she will recover from cancer because all signs show that everything is under control.

Cause/Effect clue: _____   Meaning: _____
a. hopeless   c. hopeful
b. sad   d. doubtful

Practice

Directions: Each of the sentences below uses a cause or an effect clue. Following the steps in ACTOR, write the word clue and select the best meaning of the italicized word.

_____1. Overcrowding in factories provided an ideal environment for the *proliferation* of bacteria, resulting in an epidemic.

Cause/Effect clue: _____   Meaning: _____
a. excessive spread   c. rapid elimination
b. production   d. reduction

_____2. She spoke *incessantly* in thirty minutes. As a result, I became annoyed for not having a chance to explain my point.

Cause/Effect clue: _____   Meaning: _____
a. effectively   c. clearly
b. continuously   d. slowly

_____3. Robert has to take calcium supplements because he is *deficient* in calcium.

Cause/Effect clue: _____   Meaning: _____
a. missing   c. sufficient
b. lacking   d. allergic

_____4. A manufactured brain, a *novel* idea, has been creating a lot of discussions in the medical field because it has never existed.

Cause/Effect clue: _____   Meaning: _____
a. questionable   c. new
b. possible   d. productive

_____5. The employer *terminated* her contract because she was always absent, sleepy while working, or uncooperative.

Cause/Effect clue: _____   Meaning: _____
a. renewed   c. negotiated
b. ended   d. cleared

General Sense

Sometimes, you do not see clues that show examples, comparison, contrast, or cause and effect. Making inference or figuring out what the general sense or message of the sentence will help you. In the example that follows, the italicized word is *retaliate*.

The lawyer cautioned the man not to *retaliate* against the murderer and promised him that justice would come. What is the meaning of retaliate? Use ACTOR to figure out the meaning of this word.

Examples

____1. The lawyer cautioned the man not to *retaliate* against the murderer and promised that justice would come.

Who are we talking about? <u>Lawyer</u>
What did he do? <u>Cautioned the man not to retaliate against the murderer</u>
What was the logic of doing it? <u>The man did not have to do anything because the</u>
<u>lawyer would find ways to make the murderer pay for his crime,</u>
a. file a complaint   c. do not do something bad
b. make promise   d. curse

____2. This hurricane really brought *havoc* to this town. Look at the flipped houses and cars.

What are we talking about? _____
What did it do? _____
What is the logic or reason of saying what it did? _____
a. surprise   c. destructions
b. rain   d. question

Practice

Directions: Following the steps in ACTOR, select the best meaning of the italicized word.

_____1. The verbal exchanges between the two passengers in the airplane *escalated* to a fistfight until a military escort came to break them apart.
a. broke   c. returned
b. intensified   d. followed

____2. The final result is *consistent* with all the studies that were conducted in several countries that produced the same results.
a. unchangeable   c. questionable
b. coincidence   d. complete

____3. The *ingenious* solution to the problem has given the teachers and students a sign of relief.
a. intelligent   c. careful
b. difficult   d. questionable

_____4. The *spectrum* of brilliant and colorful stars fascinated the children.
   a. shape
   b. size
   c. array
   d. height

_____5. Her success in the election was *buoyed* by supporters who have been helping her since she announced her candidacy.
   a. announced
   b. questioned
   c. briefed
   d. made possible

Limitations of context clues

Be aware that context clues may not give you the complete or exact definition of a word. You may need to use punctuation clues, definition clues, word parts, relationships between parts of a sentence or ideas in a paragraph, and other skills that will be explained in succeeding sections of this book.

Mastery Test 1

Choose the best meaning of the italicized word. Pay attention to context clues such as example, comparison, contrast, cause and effect, and general sense of the sentence.

_____I. I think there is a *trade deficit* between China and United States because US is flooded with Chinese goods. There is a disparity between import and export of goods between these two countries.
   a. trade question
   b. trade gap
   c. trade profit
   d. trade loss

_____2. I do not want to live in a *remote* area that is surrounded by several tall trees and a mile away from neighbors and twenty miles from the city.
   a. isolated
   b. spacious
   c. quiet
   d. underdeveloped

_____3. I know that I might die any time because I am always exposed to *hazardous* chemicals.
   a. gaseous
   b. various
   c. liquid
   d. unhealthy

_____4. Don't you think you should have *aspirations*, so you know what you really want?
   a. college education
   b. money
   c. ambition
   d. relationships

_____5. Of course, I want my business to be *lucrative*. This is my only source of income.
   a. sweet
   b. profitable
   c. continuous
   d. noticeable

_____6. She shows *hypocrisy* because she tells people to do good things, but she does so many unpleasant things thinking that people do not notice her misdeeds.
   a. secrecy
   b. dishonesty
   c. difference
   d. sympathy

_____7. He will not be able to join the trip because he is still sick. His condition might *regress* if he goes out.
    a. improve   c. progress
    b. worsen   d. stop

_____8. Because I had witnessed the accident, one driver asked me to *corroborate* his claim that the other driver had gone through a red light.
    a. confirm   c. hide
    b. state   d. check

_____9. Cars in the street are *ubiquitous* during heavy traffic just like the cell phones in the hands of the passengers on the train.
    a. rare   c. common
    b. bright   d. rushing

_____10. The building was evacuated immediately because it had been *contaminated* with deadly chemicals.
    a. cleaned   c. cleared
    b. infected   d. contagious

Mastery Test 2

When you are reading, you are not given choices from which you select the meaning of a word. You create your choices by figuring out the meanings of unfamiliar words through the help of context clues. You activate your prior knowledge on any word or phrase and connect this to the new information. You trigger strategies that will help you make sense of the sentence. Organize the ideas in your mind to be sure that the meaning that you get makes sense. Substitute this word for the given word. Say the sentence to yourself. Does it sound right? If it sounds awkward, perhaps your answer is wrong. Write the meaning of each italicized word and the reason for the answer.

1. The boy *goaded* his mother to buy him a big motorized car. He did not stop crying until he got it.

    goaded _____

    reason _____

2. The president will *monitor* the war in that country to be sure that all attacks will be synchronized.

    Monitor _____

    Reason _____

3. Anyone can gain *access* to his accounts because there is no password.

    Access _____

    Reason _____

4. For me, it is wrong and *lethal* to sleep with a pet snake.

   Lethal _____

   Reason _____

5. She has been recuperating from the head injuries that she *sustained* in a helicopter crash.

   Sustained _____

   Reason _____

6. The soldiers who were bombarded with continuous fire were lucky to escape *unscathed*.

   Unscathed _____

   Reason _____

7. His agony over the death of his mother was *compounded* by the fact that he lost his job and his house.

   Compounded _____

   Reason _____

8. The attack on the innocent children and women during the war angered the president who ordered a *reprisal* to the attackers.

   Reprisal _____

   Reason _____

9. I promise to perform my duties well because I do not want others to *demean* my capability.

   Demean _____

   Reason _____

10. When driving to Melissa's house, go left at the end of the road, the point where the street *diverges* into two.

    Diverges _____

    Reason _____

Word Parts

In addition to definition and context clues, paying attention to parts of a word may help you figure out the meaning of a word. Word parts include a prefix, root or base word, and suffix. In the word successful, success, a noun, is the root and ful is a suffix. The word impolite consists of im, a prefix, and polite, a root word. Let us review some common prefixes, roots, and suffixes.

Root word

A root is a word or part of a word where a prefix or a suffix nay be added. A prefix is a *letter* or a group of letters attached to the beginning of a word while a suffix is a letter or group of letters added to the end of a word or root. The root of the word, export, for example, is port, which means carry outside. Understanding the meanings of common roots can help you figure out the meanings of unfamiliar words.

Common Roots and Meanings

1. anni, annu-year
2. bio-life
3. brev-short
4. cord, cor, cardi-heart
5. dict-say, speak
6. doc, dokein-teach
7. luc-light
8. man-hand
9. ped, pod-foot
10. scrib, script-write
11. simil, simul-like, resembling
12. solus-alone
13. vid-see
14. vac-empty

Practice

With the help of your knowledge about roots, the general sense of the sentence, and other clues, figure out the missing word or word part and write it in the space provided.

1. Due to his bad conduct, the prisoner was placed in soli_____ confinement.

2. The veteran pilot was able to man_____ the plane to a safety ground in spite of the bad weather.

3. I need to see a pod_____ because of my swollen feet.

4. Although the solar eclipse will be vis_____, you need to wear dark glasses to protect your eyes.

5. During this training, we shall use a sim_____ instead of an actual airplane to train you to fly safely.

6. The secretary typed the instructions that the supervisor dic_____.

7. She is very cor_____ to her friends in spite of suffering from cancer.

8. The _____ was given a ticket for jaywalking.

Common Prefixes and Meanings

Review the prefixes below and figure out the missing words or word parts in the sentences that follow.

1. an, il, in, im, ir-not
2. ad-toward
3. ambi-both sides
4. ante-before
5. anti-against
6. inter-between, among
7. mis-wrongly

8. over-too much, above
9. pre-before
10. re-again
11. semi-half
12. sub-under, lower
13. trans-across
14. under-too little, below

Practice

With the help of your knowledge about prefixes, the general sense of the sentence, and other clues, figure out the missing word or word part and write it in the space provided.

1. The underground electric railroad beneath the surface of the ground is called the _____.

2. Salamanders, toads, and frogs are called am _____.

3. Projects such as training workers, giving affordable houses to the poor, providing clean drinking water, educating children, improving transportation, and other useful activities will help people in under _____ countries.

4. Please re _____ your make-up because some marks on your face are still visible.

5. Peter is _____ because he can write with both hands.

6. Please ad _____ to the reading journal report guidelines in order to avoid grade deductions.

7. A person who considers the fetus to be alive is usually anti _____.

8. Penicillin is an _____ because it can treat infections.

Common Suffixes and Meanings

Review the suffixes and figure out the missing words or word parts in the sentences that follow.

1. able, ible-able, capable
2. age-act of, state of, result of
3. al-relating to
4. an, ian-native of, relating to
5. ance, ancy-action, process, state
6. cian-possessing a specific skill or art
7. cule, ling-very small

8. dom-quality, realm
9. ful-full of
10. fy-make
11. hood-order, condition, quality
12. ly-like, manner
13. ment-act of, state
14. ure-state of, act, process, rank

Practice

With the help of your knowledge about suffixes, word parts, the general sense of the sentence, and other clues, infer the missing word or word part and write it in the space provided.

1. Before you eat fruits that you find in the mountain, make sure these are _____ ble because there are fruits that are poisonous.

2. Wow, the m _____ transformed the flower into a lion!

3. It is okay to ask for _____ ance if you need help.

4. Be _____ not to break the glass because it is very expensive.

5. Please do not _____ ule him because he has the same rights that we have.

6. He _____ ly fought with his opponent because he is not afraid of anyone.

7. There should be an _____ ment to the constitution to protect the rights of different groups.

8. The man showed his _____ ude to the person who helped him by taking care of his pet dog.

Mastery Test 1

Use clues such as definition, punctuation, context, and word parts to get the meaning of each italicized word.

_____1. The manager has to pay close attention to very important concerns, not the *trivial* ones.
    a. serious   c. insignificant
    b. difficult   d. enjoyable

_____2. Please *amplify* the volume of the television because I cannot hear well.
    a. lower   c. raise
    b. turn on   d. turn of

_____3. The *prominent* candidate won the election with a big margin because several thousands of people in town liked him.
    a. cheating   c. actor
    b. well-known   d. presidential

_____4. The prisoner could not be *hostile* because his hands and feet could hardly move.
    a. composed   c. dangerous
    b. moved   d. talkative

_____5. Some people who reach the *zenith*, on top of their careers, find that it is lonely there.
    a. success   c. problem
    b. peak   d. end

_____6. The president should *relinquish* his job because he has been found guilty of the charges against him.
- a. keep
- b. fight for
- c. shorten
- d. vacate

_____7. Guards want to be sure that the big boys do not *abet* the kids who have a hard time defending themselves.
- a. follow
- b. provoke
- c. teach
- d. call

_____8. The mayor appealed to the federal government for help because the rate of crime in the neighborhood became *disproportionately* high.
- a. too
- b. likely
- c. equally
- d. suddenly

_____9. Some of the strongest storms in recent memory have *pummeled* California this past month. The rains have done much to overflow the water in the California's lakes and reservoirs and flooded the streets.
- a. visited
- b. crushed
- c. helped
- d. strengthened

_____10. The war in my country has continued to *escalate* while the war in the neighboring country has ended.
- a. stop
- b. lessen
- c. return
- d. grow

Mastery Test 2

Use clues such as definition, punctuation, context, and word parts to get the meaning of each italicized word.

_____1. He has *extraordinary* strength because he can lift a car by himself.
- a. normal
- b. amazing
- c. believable
- d. questionable

_____2. The vice president on Wednesday made a surprise visit to a historic cemetery to *condemn* the recent vandalism that took place there.
- a. announce
- b. criticize
- c. blame
- d. take picture

_____3. His enemy has been a harsh critic of the president's worldview, declaring that his administration is in *disarray* because there is no clear leader who is placing things in order.
- a. disorder
- b. order
- c. shame
- d. shape

_____4. Combined with the recent vandalism at cemeteries, the calls have stoked fears that a *virulent* anti-Semitism has increasingly taken hold in the early days of the independence.
    a. harmful   c. common
    b. harmless   d. questionable

_____5. The baby *persisted* to cry for 10 minutes because she was very hungry.
    a. liked   c. continued
    b. stopped   d. began

_____6. Many people work in an unnoticeable, *clandestine* factory of illegal drugs to earn extra money.
    a. hidden   c. far away
    b. huge   d. glass

_____7. According to reports, the smuggler's private resort is *impeccable* with wood cabin rooms, a spa, a huge swimming pool, a man-made lake, and 100 miles of ski slopes.
    a. remote   c. dirty
    b. immaculate   d. stolen

_____8. Presidents, kings, queens, and prime ministers follow *protocols*, or accepted guidelines, when they meet leaders of other countries.
    a. obligations   c. procedures
    b. set of rules   d. orders

_____9. Her baby is *prone* to getting sick in the day care when some children cough.
    a. recovering   c. likely
    b. about   d. trying

____10. James is *intimidated* to participate in class while his twin brother is eager to lead the group discussion.
    a. likely   c. afraid
    b. willing   d. bullied

INTRODUCTION TO THE DIGITAL LITERACY JOURNEY

What is Digital Literacy?

[1]Literacy is an important skill in our society because many of our activities depend on our ability to read and write. Literacy is invaluable; let's take a moment to look closer at the activity of reading. Imagine picking up a book, scanning the chapters with your eyes, processing the concepts in your mind, and preserving the ideas in your memory. Life would be nearly impossible without this skill. However, we must also master other types of literacy in order to get the most from our lives. One example is digital literacy, which at its most basic level, means understanding how and why computers work, and knowing the best way to use them to accomplish our career and personal

goals. Although both types of literacy are important, a further relationship exists between reading and computers. Everything you do when you read a book has a corresponding process in the world of computing. The way you interact with words on a page is similar to the way a computer processes data. Let's investigate this similarity.

ESB Professional/Shutterstock.com

2A book is really a storage device for letters, words, paragraphs, and chapters. Computers rely on many such devices, including hard drives or disk drives that store bits (a bit is a BInary digiT) of information. The marks in a book are called words, and the bits of information in a computer are called data. Your eyes are the path by which words travel to your brain; for computers, the process is called input. Inside your head is a brain, and inside a computer is a processor (the brain is infinitely more complex than even our more advanced computer processor). In the real world, you communicate by writing or speaking; in computer terminology, this is known as output. Just as your brain has memory from which you can recall certain aspects of your life, a computer has various types of memory where it stores all of its data. The preceding computer terms are familiar to us in our daily lives and are present each time we read a book, but they are also terms used to describe the functions of computers.

3Our society is in the midst of a revolutionary transformation—from a literary society (where information is stored in books) to a digital one (where information is stored on computers). Being digitally literate means having the skills to search, understand, use, and share information on a computer (Rivoltella, 2008). Being digitally literate also means learning how to become a productive and ethical citizen in the information society and a member of the virtual communities that are blossoming every day.

4Everyone has experienced the necessity of computer and digital literacy. It is important to note that the terms computer literacy and digital literacy are sometimes used interchangeably. While these terms can have a similar meaning, computer literacy focuses more on the hardware. In contrast, digital literacy focuses more on mastering the entire environment of electronic information such as the Web, databases, applications, and searching.

5In either sense, knowledge of computer or digital literacy is critical for professional and personal success in the 21st century. You need to look only as far as the words you are reading right now on the screen. They are digital—not printed on traditional paper. You are also not in a physical classroom but in one that exists online. In this new world, we rarely take out a pen to write a letter; instead, we open our smartphone to text or log onto our computer to email. We also less frequently visit a physical library to search for information; instead, we search the Internet and electronic libraries online.

Vocabulary

The italicized words below are based on *Introduction to the Digital Literacy Journey*. Use clues to get the meaning of each word. Write the letter of the word in the space provided.

_____1. It is the teachers' responsibility to enable first grade students to be *literate* because they need this to perform basic communication and numerical skills in succeeding grades.
    a. performers   c. knowledgeable
    b. good   d. test takers

_____2. Literacy is *invaluable* in reading and writing in all grade levels.
    a. not valuable   c. validated
    b. useful   d. taught

_____3. In the twenty-first century, *digital* literacy is used to acquire information online.
    a. computer   c. nonprint
    b. print   d. visual

_____4. Our society is in the midst of a *revolutionary* transformation—from a literary society (where information is stored in books) to a digital one (where information is stored on computers).
    a. partial   c. new
    b. needed   d. debatable

_____5. Being digitally literate also means learning how to become a productive and ethical citizen in the information society and a member of the virtual communities that are *blossoming* every day.
    a. growing   c. making
    b. learning   d. deciding

_____6. In either sense, knowledge of computer or digital literacy is *critical* for professional and personal success in the 21st century.
    a. mandatory   c. legal
    b. necessary   d. contrary

Vocabulary Clues

Choose the vocabulary clue that the writer used for the given terminology in each paragraph. Write the letter of the answer in the space provided.

_____1. digital literacy—paragraph 1
    a. example   c. comma
    b. definition   d. contrast

_____2. digitally literate—paragraph 3
    a. example   c. definition
    b. comparison   d. addition

_____3. digital and computer literacy—paragraph 4
    a. example   c. dash
    b. comparison   d. contrast

_____4. critical—paragraph 5
    a. definition   c. dash and commas
    b. examples and contrast   d. addition and comparison

_____5. digital—paragraph 5
    a. example   c. dash
    b. comparison   d. contrast

WHAT IS CRIMINOLOGY?

1Turn to almost any television station and you are likely to see a program that involves crime and the criminal justice system. *Dateline, 48 Hours, Law and Order: Special Victims, NCIS: Los Angeles, NCIS: New Orleans, Castle, Criminal Minds, CSI: Crime Scene Investigation, CSI: Cyber, CSI: New York, CSI: Miami, The Shield, The Good Wife, The Mentalist, Sherlock, True Detective, Law and Order, Blue Bloods, COPS*, etc. all are popular shows that deal with crime. The public's interest in crime can't seem to be satisfied. Every newspaper and television news program spends an excessive amount of column inches or airtime covering stories about crime. In fact most TV news programs lead with a story on crime. In the last year, the airwaves have been overtaken with stories of police shootings, with the police as both perpetrators and victims.

Criminology vs. Criminal Justice

2Depending on to whom one is talking, there are often two general responses to the question "what are the differences between criminology and criminal justice?" One approach to answering the question is that criminology is a component of the broader field of criminal justice, while the second approach suggests just the opposite, criminal justice is a component of the broader field of criminology. A case can be made for both approaches. However, it is generally agreed that the primary focus of criminology is the understanding of crime and its causes, whereas the primary focus of criminal justice is on understanding the systems that exist to address transgressions of law.

Laws

3Laws are binding customs on members of a community and have been approved by a legislative body that has the authority to create laws. Often, mores become laws, moving from informal to formal, when a community feels strongly enough to go through the process of creating a written piece of codified legislation approved by a governing body in which the citizenry has invested its authority. Laws are binding customs on members of a community and have been approved by a legislative body that has the authority to create laws. Laws are being enforced by an official law enforcement agency that represents the state. Violation of laws can result in sanctions including fines, imprisonment, or execution. When a law has been violated, a crime has occurred.

Law Breaking

4Crimes can occur in one of two ways, either through an act of commission, or an act of omission. An act of commission occurs when an individual actively engages in a behavior that is a violation of a law. For example, when an individual commits a robbery or shoplifts, she/he is committing a crime by an act of commission. In contrast, a crime committed by an act of omission occurs when an individual fails to do something the law requires her/him to do. An example of a crime of omission in the United States would be the failure to file a federal income tax return if your income requires you to do so. In all instances, for a crime to actually occur, a law must exist that has been violated.

Reaction to Law Breaking

5A system of criminal justice has been developed, in part, to respond to the societies' need to address the breaking of laws. The preference would be for agencies of the justice system to prevent violations of law and enforce the laws as a last resort. In other words, crime prevention is preferable to having to apprehend and process individus through the system. The criminal justice system is often characterized as consisting of three parts such as law enforcement, courts, and corrections.

Source:Mutchnick, Criminology. Kendall Hunt. 2017.

Vocabulary

Choose the word/phrase that best completes the idea of each sentence. Write the letter of your answer in the space provided

_____1. The *perpetrator* who was found guilty of a crime was sent to prison. The italicized word most likely means _____.
   a. prey   c. criminal
   b. murderer   d. robber

___ 2. Which of the following is an example of criminal justice? The jurors find _____.
   a. the complainant guilty of a crime   c. someone to be guilty of a crime
   b. the plaintiff guilty of a crime   d. the perpetrator guilty of a crime

_____3. An example of an act of commission is _____.
   a. attempting to rob a person   c. studying how to murder a person
   b. asking money at gunpoint   d. making a map of the house to rob

_____4. An example of an act of omission in the United States is _____
   a. voting by an immigrant   c. failure to vote by a citizen
   b. failure by a corporation to file taxes d. stealing money from the corporation

_____5. The criminal justice system least likely consists of _____.
   a. criminal justice education   c. courts
   b. law enforcement   d. corrections

_____6. The meaning of laws in the third paragraph is given through a/an _____.
   a. antonym   c. definition
   b. example   d. word part

_____7. To clarify the two types of crimes that are stated in the fourth paragraph, _____
       are given.
   a. contrast and comparison   c. contrast and examples
   b. definition and comparison   d. contrast and addition

3

Sentence Relationships

One way to help you improve your reading comprehension is to pay attention to transition words that show relationships between parts of a sentence, ideas between sentences, and ideas between paragraphs. This chapter will help you to

1. identify the transitions that show relationships between ideas,
2. use transition words in understanding what you are reading, and
3. follow the steps in ACTOR.

Topics

Example Words

Addition Words

Time Order Transitions

Comparison Words

Contrast Words

Cause and Effect Words

Chapter 2 explains the benefits of paying attention to signal words that show examples, addition, comparison, contrast, and cause and effect in order to figure out the meanings of unfamiliar words. These signal words are also important in comprehending what you are reading because these show relationships of ideas between parts of a sentence, between sentences, and among paragraphs. In addition to these clues, words that show addition and time are helpful to readers. Activate your prior knowledge on the purposes of these words. Connect this knowledge to the idea of the sentence. Trigger strategies to get the message of sentences or paragraphs. Organize the ideas that you get from the sentences or paragraphs. Recite to yourself what you understand from the reading material.

Example Words

Read the example words below and activate your prior knowledge on the purposes of using these words.

Example Words

for example	specifically	including
for instance	to illustrate	includes
to be specific	like	such as

Study the examples below. To guide you in using ACTOR, questions are provided.

1. Can you control involuntary actions like breathing and beating of the heart?

    a. What is the example clue in the sentence? <u>like</u>

    b. What is the purpose of the clue? <u>To give examples of involuntary actions</u>

    c. What are the examples? <u>breathing and beating of the heart</u>

2. This new camera tech can read your heart rate. To illustrate this, place this camera in front of you. It will read and tell you the number of your heart beats per minute.

    a. What is the example clue? _____

    b. What is the purpose of this clue? _____

    c. Example(s) _____

Practice

Using your knowledge of example words and the idea in the sentence, answer the questions for each number.

1. Thanks to their systematic observations, ancient priests were able to detect many regularities in the motions of the moon, planets, sun, and other stars. For example, from

sunrise to the next sunrise is one day; the interval of time for the moon to return to appear to be fully lit is one month, and so on.

   a. What is the example clue? _____

   b. What is the purpose of this clue? _____

   c. What are the examples? _____

2. Artistic standards and visual traditions may also be linked to a society's religious belief system or governmental structure. For instance, in the Ife region of Nigeria, beginning around 1100, artists produced an array of metal and terracotta figures, which are likely depictions of kings and other important members of the community.

   a. What is the example clue? _____

   b. What is the purpose of this clue? _____

   c. Example(s) _____

3. Attending college has many benefits such as a better chance of getting a good job, realizing your dream, and improving your self-confidence.

   a. What is the example clue? _____

   b. What is the purpose of this clue? _____

   c. Example(s) _____

Addition Words

Read the addition words below and recall the purposes of using these words.

Addition Words

One	to begin with	for one thing	first (of all)
Second(ly)	in addition	next	further
third(ly)	other	another	also
last (of all)	moreover	finally	furthermore

Examples

Study the examples below. To guide you in using ACTOR, questions are provided.

   1. According to records, Wilma Mankiller, the Cherokee Nation's first female chief transformed the nation-to-nation relationship between the Cherokee Nation and the

federal government. She also served as an inspiration to women in Indian Country and across America.

   a. What is the word that shows addition? <u>also</u>

   b. What is the purpose of this word? <u>To add information to what the first Cherokee first female did</u>

   c. What information is added? <u>Wilma Mankiller served as an inspiration to women in the Indian community.</u>

2. Completion of reading lab hours three weeks before the deadline will qualify you to receive an extra credit of 5% on your average on quizzes. In addition, you will be able to take the final exam.

   a. What is the word that shows addition? _____

   b. What is the purpose of this word? _____

   c. What information is added? _____

Practice

Using your knowledge of addition words and the idea in the sentence, answer the questions that follow each statement.

1. Research shows that intense physical activity reduces susceptibility to diseases. In addition, it helps in reducing weight.

   a. What is the word that shows addition? _____

   b. What is the purpose of this word? _____

   c. What information is added? _____

2. First, benign tumor stays in one place. Second, it is harmless.

   a. What is the word that shows addition? _____

   b. What is the purpose of this word? _____

   c. What information is added? _____

3. One way to do well in a course is to read your notes before coming to class. Another is process the information while you listen intently during the discussion.

   a. What is the word that shows addition? _____

   b. What is the purpose of this word? _____

   c. What information is added? _____

Time Order Transitions

Read the time words below and recall the purposes of using these.

Time Words

before	previously	first (of all)	until
immediately	next	second(ly)	then
following	eventually	final(ly)	later
whenever	while	when	last (of all)
third(ly)	during	often	by
frequently	now	after	currently

Examples

Study the examples below. To guide you in using ACTOR, questions are provided.

1. Three people were killed and two others are in critical condition after a small plane crashed into a California home on Monday, authorities said.

    Time word(s) <u>after; on Monday</u>

    Purpose of the word(s) <u>To state when things happened</u>

    What happened? <u>Three people were killed and two others were in critical condition.</u>

2. According to a report, Marie Curie won the prize for Physics after a research on radioactivity.

    Time word(s) _____

    Purpose of the word(s) _____

    What happened? _____

Practice

Using your knowledge of time words and the idea in the sentence, answer the questions that follow each statement.

1. Danica Patrick became the first woman to win an Indy Car Series in 2008 when she finished first at the Indy Japan 300.

    a. Time word(s) _____

    b. Purpose of the word(s) _____

    c. What happened? _____

2. He recalled that Edith Wharton was recognized for her work in the early 1900s. She then became the first woman to win the Pulitzer Prize for fiction in 1921.

   a. Time word(s) _____

   b. Purpose of the word(s) _____

   c. What happened? _____

3. To begin with, our understanding of climate change started with intense debates among 19th-century scientists about whether northern Europe had been covered by ice thousands of years ago. In the 1820s Jean Baptiste Joseph Fourier [a French mathematician and physicist] discovered that "greenhouse gasses" trap heat radiated from the Earth's surface after it has absorbed energy from the Sun.

   a. Time word(s) _____

   b. Purpose of the word(s) _____

   c. What happened? _____

Comparison Words

Read the comparison words below and recall the purpose of each.

Comparison Words

just as	both	in like manner	in a similar fashion
just like	common	in the same way	in a similar manner
similarly	alike	equally resemble	in like fashion
likewise	similarity	same	

Study the examples below. To guide you in using ACTOR, questions are provided.

1. Like his twin brother, Ralph shows great interest in exploring robotics.

   a. Comparison word(s) <u>like</u>

   b. Purpose of the word(s) <u>to compare Ralph's and his brother's interest</u>

   c. Who/what are compared? <u>Ralph and his brother</u>

2. Just as the tea ceremony is considered an important art form in Japan, in Indonesia the process of dyeing and weaving cloth is a long-practiced form of art.

a. Comparison word(s) _____

b. Purpose of the word(s) _____

c. Who/what are compared? _____

Practice

Using your knowledge of comparison words and the idea in the sentence, answer the questions that follow each statement.

1. Like adults, children recognize if their rights are not respected.
   a. Comparison word(s) _____
   b. Purpose of the word(s) _____
   c. Who/what are compared? _____

2. Children become able to sort using complex classification systems. They can also demonstrate the ability to see things from multiple perspectives.
   a. Comparison word(s) _____
   b. Purpose of the word(s) _____
   c. Who/what are compared? _____

3. Three to four thousand years ago, the ancient Chinese, Egyptians, and Mesopotamians were systematically studying the skies and keeping records of their observations. In later centuries, similar activities were carried out on the Indian subcontinent, and also by the great cultures of the New World that flourished in what is now Mexico.
   a. Comparison word(s) _____
   b. Purpose of the word(s) _____
   c. Who/what are compared? _____

Contrast Words

Read the contrast words below and recall the purpose of each. Activate your prior knowledge.

Contrast Words

however	instead	yet	in spite of	rather than
but	in contrast	as opposed to	even though	despite
while	on the contrary	unlike	although	
conversely	different	on the other hand	nevertheless	

Examples

Study the examples below. To guide you in using ACTOR, questions are provided.

1. Groundwater is water found underground in aquifers. On the other hand, surface water is water that flows or is impounded on the surface of the earth.

    a. Contrast word(s) <u>On the other hand,</u>

    b. Purpose of the word(s) <u>Show contrast between groundwater and surface water.</u>

    c. What is the difference? <u>Groundwater is found underground while surface water is found on the surface of the earth.</u>

2. Fine artists have traditionally been described in terms of "artistic genius" and "originality," whereas craftsmen were viewed as merely skilled artisans.

    a. Contrast word(s) _____

    b. Purpose of the word(s) _____

    c. What is the difference? _____

Practice

Using your knowledge of contrast words and the idea in the sentence, answer the questions that follow each statement.

1. Self-esteem refers to one's sense of self-respect or self-worth. In contrast, self-efficacy describes a person's belief about whether he or she can successfully engage or complete a specific behavior or task.

    a. Contrast word(s) _____

    b. Purpose of the word(s) _____

    c. What is the difference? _____

2. Studies of mobility have traditionally ignored the significance of gender, but research findings are now available that explore the relationship between gender and mobility.

    a. Contrast word(s) _____

    b. Purpose of the word(s) _____

    c. What is the difference? _____

3. Getting enough sleep helps you to become alert. Lack of sleep on the other hand, may lead to inattentiveness and distractions.

    a. Contrast word(s) _____

    b. Purpose of the word(s) _____

    c. What is the difference? _____

Cause and Effect Words

Read the cause and effect words below and activate your prior knowledge on the purpose of each.

Cause and Effect Words

due to	so	therefore	accordingly
because	as a result	effect	reason
as a consequence	results in	cause	thus
consequently	leads to	if . . . then	since

Study the examples below. To guide you in using ACTOR, questions are provided.

1. Guy S. Callender [a British engineer and inventor] suggested that the global warming trend revealed in the 19th century had been caused by a 10% increase in atmospheric carbon dioxide from the burning of fossil fuels.

   a. Cause/effect word(s) <u>caused</u>

   b. Purpose of the word(s) <u>To show a cause of global warming</u>

   c. What happened? <u>There was global warming trend in the 19th century</u>

   d. Why did it happen? <u>The atmospheric carbon dioxide increased by 10% due to burning of fossil fuel</u>

2. Excessive caffeine may result in insomnia, upset stomach, racing heartbeat, and nervousness.

   a. Cause/effect word(s) _____

   b. Purpose of the word(s) _____

   c. What happened? _____

   d. Why did it happen? _____

Practice

Using your knowledge of cause and effect words and the idea in the sentence, answer the questions that follow each statement.

1. Human beings are naturally curious, and each question one asks leads to another, then another, and then another.

   Cause/effect word(s) _____

   Purpose of the word(s) _____

   What happened? _____

   Why did it happen? _____

2. Philosophy involves the asking of questions and seeking answers to these questions. It is important because it can help us understand our own beliefs as well as beliefs of others.

   Cause/effect word(s) _____

   Purpose of the word(s) _____

   What happened? _____

   Why did it happen? _____

3. Since we draw conclusions that are based on certain assumptions, we engage in reasoning.

   Cause/effect word(s) _____

   Purpose of the word(s) _____

   What happened? _____

   Why did it happen? _____

Mastery Test 1

Using your knowledge of transition words and the idea in the sentence, choose the transition(s) that each statement shows. Write the letter of the answer in the space provided.

_____1. The term fine arts usually refers to art forms whose primary purpose is their aesthetic value or content. Additionally, fine artists have traditionally been described in terms of "artistic genius" and "originality," whereas craftsmen were viewed as merely skilled artisans.

    a. addition   c. contrast

    b. addition and contrast   d. addition and example

_____2. Three to four thousand years ago, the ancient Chinese, Egyptians, and Mesopotamians were systematically studying the skies and keeping records of their observations. In later centuries, similar activities were carried out on the Indian subcontinent, and also by the great cultures of the New World that flourished in what is now Mexico and most of Central America and in the South American regions we now call Bolivia and Peru.

    a. time and comparison   c. comparison

    b. time   d. addition

_____3. Usually it takes more than one resource to provide a thorough analysis of a topic, so you as a researcher will have to find a system that groups items of the same subject together. Your familiarity with organization systems will help you find resources grouped together on a topic.

    a. example   c. cause and effect

    b. addition   d. comparison

_____4. Two dwellings were destroyed when the plane went down in Riverside at about 4:45 PM.

    a. addition   c. time

    b. example   d. comparison

_____5. All of the victims had been flying in the aircraft, he said. Moore previously put the number of dead at four but later corrected the tally to three.
   a. time
   b. time and contrast
   c. addition
   d. example and time

_____6. According to reports, Aretha Franklin got mounds of praises and fame for her incredible contributions to the music world, but she tries her best to stay humble, claiming that she wasn't a big force for the feminism movement.
   a. contrast
   b. time
   c. example
   d. comparison

_____7. It is important to remember, however, that the distinction between fine arts and crafts is largely a Western philosophical and aesthetic construct.
   a. comparison
   b. cause and effect
   c. contrast
   d. comparison and example

_____8. Another Indonesian form of weaving is tenun-ikat, in which patterns are created on the threads by a tie-dyeing process prior to being woven on the loom.
   a. addition
   b. time and contrast
   c. addition and time
   d. addition and example

_____9. Utilitarian objects, particularly those used in religious ceremonies, are more highly praised and sought after than those that are not.
   a. comparison
   b. time
   c. contrast
   d. cause and effect

____10. Although much of Anatsui's art is made from everyday objects like bottle caps and cop-per wire, one would not mistake these beautiful hangings for anything but art when they are seen in the context of a museum or gallery.
   a. comparison
   b. contrast and example
   c. time and contrast
   d. time

Mastery Test 2

Using your knowledge of transition words and the idea in the sentence, choose the transition(s) that each statement shows. Write the letter of the answer in the space provided.

_____1. Despite the disparities between the twins' capabilities, both were able to win the competition.
   a. comparison
   b. comparison and contrast
   c. contrast
   d. example

_____2. In some cultures, the written word alone is considered a work of art. For example, in the early Islamic period, calligraphers beautified handwritten transcriptions of the Qur'an, the Muslim holy book that contains God's revelations to the Prophet Muhammad.
   a. addition
   b. time
   c. example
   d. comparison

_____3. The priests also became quite skilled in predicting certain astronomical events, such as eclipses.
- a. addition
- b. example
- c. addition and example
- d. cause and effect

_____4. Many agricultural states had sumptuary laws, or laws regulating the possession of particular items of wealth, such as fine cloth and jewelry.
- a. example
- b. addition and example
- c. addition
- d. cause and effect

_____5. In spite of being very wealthy and influential in the community, she insists that she does not want special treatment.
- a. addition
- b. addition and example
- c. contrast
- d. cause and effect

_____6. After graduating from law school, she said that at least 30 corporations denied her an interview because she was a woman with an ethnic background.
- a. time
- b. time and example
- c. time and cause and effect
- d. cause and effect

_____7. The famous building went in the dark yesterday while several tourists were touring the place. As a result, they were led by the guide to the entrance of the building.
- a. time
- b. cause and effect and time
- c. cause and effect
- d. example and time

_____8. Elizabeth Blackwell became the first woman to finish a medical degree in the United States. She was often told to disguise herself as a man or study elsewhere.
- a. example
- b. time
- c. time and example
- d. contrast

_____9. A patient who did not have the money to pay for a deposit was advised to look for another hospital. Now, everyone is admitted in this hospital.
- a. cause and effect
- b. example and time
- c. time
- d. comparison

____10. Due to the one child policy, the family has to pay for a fine of $3,000.00 to keep the baby.
- a. time
- b. example
- c. cause and effect
- d. contrast

MANAGING YOUR CAREER IN TODAY'S WORLD

1Do you know people who:

- Make career choices on the basis of their best talents and top interests?
- Align their career aspirations with the economic realities of the marketplace?
- Draw upon the best available resources for help in making career decisions?
- Manage their careers on the basic principles of good marketing practice?

If so, you know people who know themselves and are sufficiently knowledgeable about the realities of marketplace economics to enjoy career success and sustain employability in rapidly changing times.

> In this era of rapid change and uncertainty, our conventional, traditional career planning for success is archaic—as outdated as the slide rule or the typewriter.
>
> —Helen Harkness

A Brief History Lesson

2Career management has become a far more complicated process in the twenty-first century than at any previous time in history. In your grandparents' era, most people were employed in large corporations and probably spent their entire work lives with a single organization performing similar types of job functions the whole time. Career choice in those days was a matter of deciding what company to work for if you were "blue-collar" inclined or what profession to pursue if you had "white-collar" origins or aspirations. Getting ahead in those days meant promotion, and career development meant climbing a "career ladder." Back then, people were primarily concerned about job security, which meant staying employed with your organization until you could retire with a company pension supplemented by Social Security. But that was then, and that's history. If you're proceeding in your career aspirations as if this were still the twentieth century, you're preparing for the past rather than the world in which we now live.

3Significant numbers of working adults still do work in large organizations today, but recent trends show greater numbers of people working in smaller businesses. But whether employed in a large or small organization, managing your career in today's knowledge-based economy is decidedly different than in the industrial-based economy of yesteryear. In our twenty-first century world, there are few corporate ladders to climb, few people will spend an entire career within a single organization, and the old idea of job security is a

At last Kim realized what had gone wrong with her Internet job search. She had made a terrible mistake by leaving the "r" out of driver.

From *Your Career Planner*, Tenth Edition, by David Borchard, Cheryl Bonner, and Susan Musich. Copyright © 2009 by Kendall Hunt Publishing Company. Reprinted by permission.

Capitalizing on Career Chaos: Bringing Creativity and Purpose to Your Work and Life

fading concept. Change is a constant dynamic is today's workplace, and that requires being far more flexible, creative, and self-reliant than your grandparents ever dreamed of being. Career choice and career management in our twenty-first-century world is a new ballgame, and we all need to learn how to play it well. The change in employment patterns requires a shift in career-related mind-sets. In today's knowledge- and technology-based economy, we need to replace a preoccupation on job security with a focus on market-savvy employability.

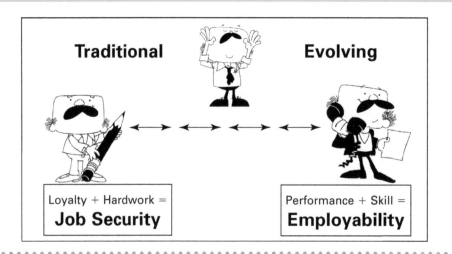

The Changing Employment Contract

From *Your Career Planner*, Tenth Edition, by David Borchard, Cheryl Bonner, and Susan Musich.
Copyright © 2009 by Kendall Hunt Publishing Company. Reprinted by permission.

Playing to Your Strengths

4How does anybody choose his or her profession and manage a career in today's world full of so many choices and in a state of constant change? Career counselors and personal coaches are often asked what are the best professions to pursue or what's the best course for advancing in one's career. The answer is, it depends. It depends less on organization-based job security and more upon who you are and your unique talents and interests and what role you want work to play in your life. Understanding what occupational and professional opportunities are available in the workplace of today and tomorrow is important. The key to personal success in work and life, however, is based in knowing yourself and in what arena you are best equipped to provide business-relevant value.

5Whether beginning or changing a career, we all need to become effective marketers. In this regard, it's important to understand the difference between advertising and marketing. Advertising is about promotion. It involves trying to convince someone to buy what you are selling. Advertising is what you do when you "pump up" your resume with high-falutin language in an attempt to make yourself look profoundly desirable. Marketing, on the other hand, involves assessing the needs of the marketplace and determining how to meet a real need with a viable product or service. While an exaggerated resume is a tactic used by some aspiring job seekers to get hired, staying employed depends on being able to perform well what you promote. A sure way to fail is to successfully advertise something you can't successfully deliver. Marketing, conversely, involves truthfully representing the "real thing" in the "right way" to the "right place."

6In effective marketing, you need to know your product and the market. In career management the product is what you bring to the market through your personal strengths, which we refer as motivated strengths. The "right place" is an employment niche that fits your particular brand of personal attributes and aspirations. Figure 3.1 conceptualizes the way in which talent unites with passion to produce "motivated strengths." In this perspective, talent is a combination of your

54

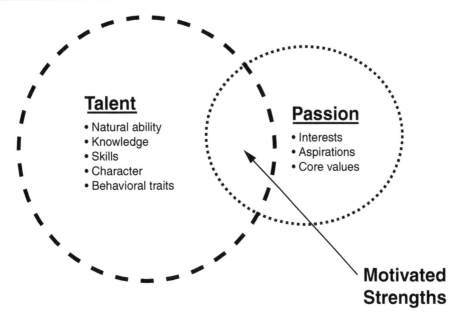

Figure 3.1

Talent + Passion = Motivated Strength

From *Your Career Planner*, Tenth Edition, by David Borchard, Cheryl Bonner, and Susan Musich.
Copyright © 2009 by Kendall Hunt Publishing Company. Reprinted by permission.

natural abilities, the knowledge you have acquired, the skills you have developed, and the positive aspects of your personality. Natural ability refers to your unique gifts of potentials. Some of us come into the world gifted musically, some athletically, some analytically, some linguistically, some creatively, and others with a broad array of capabilities rather than any standout, specific talent. Your natural abilities serve as the basis for what you can and can't excel in mentally, physically, and personality-wise.

7Because a talent represents a potential, it remains a latent ability, a dormant possibility, unless it's developed. What you are capable of today is a matter of which of your abilities you have developed into what you know (knowledge), what you have learned to do well (skill), your personality attributes (character), and how you have learned to manage yourself in the world (behavior).

8A personal strength, however, goes well beyond your talent to include your passion, or what motivates you. Passion includes your deep-seated personal interests, which are those things that energize you. Values are what you care about most deeply. To develop a talent into strength requires motivation, and that's where passion comes into the picture. You might, for example, be as gifted scientifically as Marie Currie or creatively as Frank Lloyd Wright but lack the motivation to develop and apply those particular talents. It is possible, of course, to have a passion to do something for which you lack a sufficient degree of god-given talent to succeed. Someone might, for example, aspire to be an astrophysicist but lack the requisite innate ability to master quantum physics or to think outside of the box and outside of the known universe for that matter.

9The key in successful career management is to find and define the place where your talents connect with your passion. Without the passion connection, you are like a car without a battery. Having a passion minus the right kind of talent is like a battery minus the vehicle. To be a high performer and to sustain that over time, you need both the engine (talent) and the battery (energizing power source).

A Quirk of Nature

10There are challenges to this process of defining your motivated strengths, one of which has to do with a peculiarity of nature. In the maturation process, a young person's talents develop well before his or her uniquely personal interests crystallize. By the age of 12 or 13, you can pretty much tell what a youth is going to be good at and where his or her talents lie. You can distinguish the gregarious extroverts from the quiet contemplatives. You can see who can shoot a basket through a hoop at 20 feet and who can make you laugh. You can see who is good at numbers, who is skilled at drawing, and who can tunefully sing the songs to the latest hit recordings. You can also see those who possess natural leadership traits, those who can follow, the lone wolves, and the crowd pleasers. What you can't see in a youthful adolescent, however, is who might enjoy high finance, who will aspire to elective office, and who will develop a passion for designing the architectural structures of our twenty-first-century lifestyle.

11Deep-seated interests and autonomously inspired personal aspirations evolve with maturity and are unlikely to fully crystallize until into one's 20s. It takes life experience and maturity to develop your unique nature and to appreciate the gifts of your distinctive intellectual and creative endowments. There are, of course, exceptions to this. Mozart knew at a young age that he was a composer, Ginger Rogers was born to dance, Michelangelo was no doubt drawing little masterpieces before reaching adolescence, Gladys Knight was performing at the age of four, and General George Patton may have been playing strategically with toy soldiers when barely out of diapers. For most of us, however, maturation develops like good wine, and great wines take time along with nurturing "aging" conditions. Individuals tend to grow their interests in their own time, and some of us just require longer to ferment into the full-bodied vintage self.

12The consequence of this quirk in nature is that many individuals often make career choices before their interests fully mature. Because talents gel before interests, many young people are encouraged to do what they are good at before they really come to know for themselves where their work-related passions might reside. That's why Stewart, a past client of ours, became a physician only to realize at the age of 48 that he would much preferred to have been a poet, a philosopher, or a professor of humanities. Regina, another of our past clients, became an accountant at her father's urgings because she was "good with numbers," only to realize in her 30s that she was energized far more in creative endeavor than in analytical activity. Learning about yourself is a life-long journey, and finding your way in life and career is an ongoing exploration. Some of us acquire accurate self-knowledge early in life and make choices that are consistent with the strengths we inherit and develop. Some of us think we know who we are and what we want before time and experience matures us. Some of us don't have a clue as to who we are and what we want and go forth into the world utterly confused and uncertain. No matter where you fall on the spectrum of self-knowledge and astute decision making, keep in mind that each of us possesses unique strengths and that there are far greater rewards in playing to your strengths than cruising through life on someone else's plan for you or overlooking your personal strengths in pursuit of fame, fortune, or soulless materialism.

13Realizing and defining your motivated strengths is challenging, but the satisfaction for doing so and creating a self-realizing vision for your future is well worth the investment. It's an endeavor that pays dividends through ongoing adventures in self-discovery and the sense of fulfillment that comes through applying your unique endowments and interests in a good marketplace fit. Believing that you are using and developing the best you have to offer in work worth doing is psychic pay that's hard to top.

Source: Borchard et al., Managing Your Career in Today's World. Kendall Hunt Publishing Company, 2008.

Vocabulary

The following statements are based on the article, *Managing Your Career in Today's World.* Choose the best meaning of the italicized word in each sentence.

_____1. In this era of rapid change and uncertainty, our conventional, traditional career planning for success is *archaic*—as outdated as the slide rule or the typewriter.
   a. interesting   c. old
   b. workable   d. new

_____2. The change in employment patterns requires a shift in career-related mind-sets. In today's knowledge- and technology-based economy, we need to replace an on-job security with a focus on *market-savvy* employability.
   a. research   c. possible
   b. smart   d. flexible

_____3. Advertising is what you do when you "*pump up*" your resume with high-falutin language in an attempt to make yourself look profoundly desirable.
   a. write   c. fired up
   b. force   d. revise

_____4. The "right place" is an employment *niche* that fits your personal qualifications and dreams.
   a. letter   c. dream
   b. position   d. application

_____5. In this *perspective*, talent is a combination of your natural abilities, the knowledge you have acquired, the skills you have developed, and the positive aspects of your life.
   a. personality   c. decision
   b. question   d. point of view

_____6. In the maturation process, a young person's talents develop well before his or uniquely personal interest *crystallizes*.
   a. cracks   c. goes
   b. forms   d. stops

_____7. Someone might, for example aspire to be an astrophysicist but lack the requisite *innate* ability to naturally master quantum physics or to think outside of the box and outside of the known universe for that matter.
   a. standard
   b. inborn
   c. common
   d. required

_____8. It's an *endeavor* that pays dividends through ongoing adventures in self-discovery and the sense of fulfillment that comes through applying your talents and interests in a good marketplace fit.
   a. interest
   b. dream
   c. undertaking
   d. success

Transitions

The following statements are based on the article, *Managing Your Career in Today's World*. Identify the type of transition word(s) in each sentence.

_____1. Career choice and career management in our twenty-first-century world is a new ballgame. As a result, we all need to learn how to play it well.
   a. comparison
   b. cause and effect
   c. example
   d. addition and cause and effect

_____2. The key to personal success in work and life, however, is based in knowing yourself and in what arena you are best equipped to provide business-relevant value.
   a. example
   b. contrast
   c. comparison and contrast
   d. comparison

_____3. Marketing, on the other hand, involves assessing the needs of the marketplace and determining how to meet a real need with a viable product or service.
   a. example
   b. contrast
   c. comparison
   d. addition

_____4. A sure way to fail is to successfully advertise something you can't successfully deliver. Marketing, conversely, involves truthfully representing the "real thing" in the "right way" to the "right place."
   a. contrast
   b. example
   c. addition
   d. cause and effect

_____5. Because a talent represents a potential, it remains a latent ability, a dormant possibility, unless it's developed.
   a. contrast
   b. example
   c. addition
   d. cause and effect

_____6. A personal strength, however, goes well beyond your talent to include your passion, or what motivates you.
   a. contrast
   b. example
   c. contrast and example
   d. cause and effect

_____7. Passion includes your deep-seated personal interests, which are those things that ener-
gize you.
   a. contrast   c. contrast and example
   b. example   d. cause and effect

_____8. You might, for example, be as gifted scientifically as Marie Currie or creatively as Frank
Lloyd Wright, but lack the motivation to develop and apply those particular talents.
   a. contrast   c. contrast and example
   b. example   d. cause and effect

_____9. Without the passion connection, you are like a car without a battery. Having a passion
minus the right kind of talent is like a battery minus the vehicle.
   a. contrast   c. comparison
   b. example and comparison   d. example

____10. Someone might, for example, aspire to be an astrophysicist but lack the requisite innate
ability to master quantum physics or to think outside of the box and outside of the
known universe for that matter.
   a. comparison and example   c. example
   b. contrast and example   d. contrast

Answer the following questions.

1. What is the difference between advertising and marketing?

2. Why is career today a new ballgame?

3. What is your major? What made you decide on your major?

4. What is the difference between a passion and talent?

5. Do you have the key to a possible successful career? Explain your answer.

4

Main Idea

A writer considers a topic and a main idea in writing a paragraph. Since the reader reads what has been written by the writer, recognizing the topic and the main idea will help a reader to understand what is being read. This chapter will show you the strategies and activities that will enable you to identify a topic, and a topic sentence that states the main idea in a paragraph and to figure out the main idea if it is not stated. Most of the reading materials that are used for reading applications are found in college textbooks because this chapter intends to help you better understand textbooks in other courses. Specifically, the objectives of this chapter are the following:

1. recognize the topic of a paragraph,
2. identify the sentence that states the main idea, and
3. state the implied or unstated main idea.

Topics

Topic

General and Specific Topics

Stated Main Idea at the Beginning of the Paragraph

Stated Main Idea between the First and Last Sentences

Stated Main Idea at the End of the Paragraph

Stated Main Idea at the Beginning and End of the Paragraph

Implied Main Idea

Topic

Identifying the topic and the topic sentence that states the main idea are reading skills that will help you understand what you read. A topic is a word or phrase that tells what the paragraph is about while a topic sentence is a sentence that states the main idea of a paragraph. It is the most general sentence. All or most of the sentences that come before or after it tell about it. The main idea may be found at the beginning, between the first and the last sentences, the last sentence or both at the beginning and the last sentences in a paragraph. Your knowledge of transitions, vocabulary enhancement, and ACTOR will help you recognize the topic and the main idea.

General and Specific Topics

Distinguishing the difference between a general word and a specific topic will later help you to recognize the difference between a general idea and specific details. Like the general word, the main idea is a general sentence. Let us examine the example below. Which is the general word? Why is it the general word?

Example
    1) vote   2) worship   3) speak   4) rights

Practice 1

Identify the general word in each group. Write the letter of your answer in the space provided.

1. _____
   a. bitter
   b. sour
   c. sweet
   d. tastes

2. _____
   a. psychology
   b. sociology
   c. philosophy
   d. disciplines

3. _____
   a. George W. Bush
   b. Ronald Reagan
   c. William Clinton
   d. Presidents

4. _____
   a. headings
   b. subheadings
   c. outline
   d. topics

5. _____
   a. yen
   b. money
   c. dollar
   d. peso

6. _____
   a. -ment
   b. suffixes
   c. -ish
   d. –ly

Practice 2

Write the topic for each group of words in the space provided.

1. _____
   a. sentimental
   b. sarcastic
   c. nostalgic

2. _____
   a. caring
   b. compassionate
   c. concerned

3. _____
   a. corporation
   b. partnership
   c. proprietorship

4. _____
   a. sea
   b. river
   c. lake

5. _____effects
   a. good
   b. beneficial
   c. advantageous

6. _____
   a. sharks
   b. whales
   c. humans

7. _____
   a. attendance
   b. quizzes
   c. assignments

8. _____
   a. Connecticut
   b. New York
   c. New Jersey

Stated Main Idea at the Beginning of the Paragraph

Usually, you find the main idea at the beginning of a paragraph in a textbook. Pay attention to this sentence and make sure that you understand what it is telling you. Determine what it is about—the subject of the sentence and what is being said about it—the predicate. If it is a long sentence, break it down or apply the strategies that we discussed in Chapter 1. This enables you to understand it because succeeding sentences flow from it or connect to it. In college textbooks, the first sentence usually states the main idea. The first sentence may give you a definition of a word while the next sentence may state an example or examples. The first sentence may also suggest a list of items, comparison, contrast, narration, or cause and effect.

Let us examine the example below.

[1]Completion of the required reading lab hours three weeks before the deadline has many benefits. [2]Five percent will be added to your average on quizzes. [3]You will also be able to take the final test. [4]In addition, you can attend to assignments and projects in other classes.

To help you fully understand this paragraph, use the steps in ACTOR. Following the steps may take time and patience at the beginning. However, continuous practice will enable you to use these naturally and automatically, better understand and remember what you are reading.

Using ACTOR

1. Read the first sentence. There is a deadline to complete reading lab hours. What or who is being talked about? (completion of reading lab hours three weeks before the deadline). What is being said about it? (has many benefits). **Activate** prior knowledge of the content or vocabulary. There is a deadline to complete reading lab hours. Benefit means good.
2. **Connect** this knowledge to the new information, so you can relate to what you are reading.
3. **Trigger strategies**: Break down the sentence, ask questions or visualize. Do these and other strategies to be sure that you understand every sentence. Connect the idea of each sentence to the preceding or succeeding sentence, so that everything makes sense or connects. Talk to yourself and analyze. In the second sentence, adding 5% to the average on quizzes is good—a benefit. In the third sentence, being able to take the final test is good—a benefit. In the fourth sentence, using your time to do assignments and tasks in other courses because you have completed the reading lab hours is good—a benefit.
4. Organize in your mind the ideas that you get from reading. There are benefits of completing the reading lab hours three weeks before the deadline. All the sentences show the benefits.
5. Respond by reciting or writing what you understand. State the main idea and details. Doing this enables you to find out if you understand and remember what you read. This information will later be a part of your prior knowledge that can help you in reading, writing, and other tasks in the future.

1Completion of the required reading lab hours three weeks before the deadline has many benefits. 2Five percent will be added to your average on quizzes. 3You will also be able to take the final test. 4In addition, you can attend to assignments and projects in other classes.

The diagram shows that the main idea is found at the beginning. It is the most general sentence. The details that follow answer this question, why is the first sentence the main idea? The three sentences that follow give the benefits of completing the reading lab hours three weeks before the deadline.

Main Idea
Specific Detail
Specific Detail
Specific Detail

Topic: _____ Benefits of completion of the reading lab hours three weeks before the deadline.
Main idea: Completion of the required reading lab hours three weeks before the deadline has many benefits.
Reasons for the main idea: Sentences 2, 3, and 4 tell about the benefits of completing the reading lab hours three weeks before the deadline.

Identify the topic and the reasons for the first sentence as the main idea. To help you fully understand this paragraph, use the steps in ACTOR. Write your answers in the spaces provided.

Group 1

1Wikipedia and some handbooks are reference sources that provide information that can help you on your research. 2These give you overviews of topics. 3These also present viewpoints of experts on different subjects. 4In addition, you find terminologies that are common to the field or subjects.

Topic: _____

Reasons for the main idea: _____

_____

_____

Group 2

1There is no one system that organizes the information on the Web. 2Webpage makers create their pages and put them on a server. 3Some Internet Service Providers (ISPs) include providing a server to host webpages as one of the services to their subscribers. 4Other webpages are hosted on the servers of corporations or educational institutions.

Source: List-Handley et al., Information Literacy and Technology, 5E.
Kendall Hunt Publishing Company, 2013.

Topic: _____

Reasons for the main idea: _____

_____

_____

Stated Main Idea between the First and Last Sentences

Sometimes, the topic is introduced at the beginning of the sentence. So, the topic sentence that states the main idea is found after the introductory sentence or sentences. Identify the most general sentence. Do all or most of the sentences that come before or after tell about it? This general sentence may give you a definition of a word and may be followed by an example or examples. It may also suggest a list of items. In addition, it may state information that shows similarities, differences, event, or cause and effect.

Let us examine the example below. To help you fully understand this paragraph, use the steps in ACTOR.

1The availability of freshwater has been a key factor in the rise and fall of ancient civilizations. 2Humans use water for numerous purposes. 3Obviously, we need water to drink. 4We use it to bathe ourselves, wash and cook our food, and dispose of human waste. 5We use it to irrigate our crops and raise animals. 6We use it to produce raw materials and goods, to produce electricity, and occasionally, to fight fires. 7We also use it for less critical activities such as for watering lawns and gardens, swimming pools, and fountains. 8It is estimated that for 2005 in the United States, 210 billion gallons of water per day were withdrawn from various sources of water for these activities.

Contributed by Quay, Sustainability in the 21st Century, Kendall Hunt Publishing Company, 2015

Using ACTOR

1. Read the first sentence. The availability of freshwater has been a key factor in the rise and fall of ancient civilizations. What or who is being talked about? (Availability of freshwater) What is being said about it? (A factor in the rise and fall of ancient civilization.) The first sentence is an introduction.
   Activate prior knowledge of the content or vocabulary.
2. **Connect** this knowledge to the new information, so you can relate to what you are reading. Water is important to people.
3. **Trigger strategies**: Break apart the sentence, ask questions, or visualize. What or who is being talked about? What is being said about it? Do these and other strategies to be sure that you understand every sentence. Connect the idea of each sentence to the preceding or succeeding sentence so that everything makes sense or connects. Talk to yourself and analyze. In the second sentence, humans use water for numerous purposes. The third sentence states that we need water to drink. The fourth sentence says that we use it to bathe ourselves, wash and cook our food, and dispose of human waste. The fifth sentence says that we use water to irrigate our crops and raise animals. The sixth sentence tells us that we use it to produce raw materials and goods, to produce electricity, and occasionally, to fight fires. The seventh states that we also use it for less critical activities such as for watering lawns and gardens, swimming pools, and fountains. It is estimated that for 2005 in the United States, 210 billion gallons of water per day were withdrawn from various sources of water for these activities. What do most of the sentences tell you?
4. **Organize** in your mind the ideas that you got from reading. Humans use water for numerous purposes. The details in sentences 3–8 give the uses of water. These show why the second sentence is the main idea. All of these sentences tell about the main idea.
5. **Respond** by reciting or writing what you understand. State the main idea and details. Doing this enables you to find out if you understand and remember what you read. This information will be a part of your prior knowledge that can help you in reading, writing, and other tasks in the future.

1The availability of freshwater has been a key factor in the rise and fall of ancient civilizations. 2Humans use water for numerous purposes. 3Obviously, we need water to drink. 4We use it to bathe ourselves, wash and cook our food, and dispose of human waste. 5We use it to irrigate our crops and raise animals. 6We use it to produce raw materials and goods, to produce electricity, and occasionally, to fight fires. 7We also use it for less critical activities such as for watering lawns and gardens, swimming pools, and fountains. 8It is estimated that for 2005 in the United States, 210 billion gallons of water per day were withdrawn from various sources of water for these activities.

Specific Detail

Main Idea

Specific Detail

Specific Detail

Specific Detail

Specific Detail

Specific Detail

Specific Detail

The diagram shows that the main idea is found after the first sentence. It is the most general sentence. The details in sentences 3–7 state the uses or purposes of water and not the importance of water for the rise and fall of civilization that is stated in the first sentence.

Topic: _____ Purposes of using water _____

Main idea: _____ Humans use water for numerous purposes _____

Reasons for the main idea: ___Sentence 3 states that we drink water. Sentence 4 tells about the use of water for bathing, cooking and disposing human waste. Sentence 5 states the use of water for irrigating crops and raising animals. Sentence 6 tells about the use of water for producing raw materials and goods. Sentence 7 states the use of water for less critical activities.___

Practice

Identify the topic, the main idea, and the reasons for the main idea in each group. Write your answers in the spaces provided.

Group 1

1The hospitality business has its origins in the ancient past. 2Over the centuries, the standards and practices of hospitality have evolved as civilization has progressed. 3Two patterns that have influenced the industry are particularly clear. 4First, the hospitality industry has been influenced by transportation technology and infrastructure such as roads, railroads, steamships, automobiles, and aircraft. 5Second, the hospitality industry has been influenced by the vast increase in the scale and distribution of wealth resulting from the Industrial Revolution.

Brymer et al., Hospitality: An Introduction, 16E. Kendall Hunt Publishing Company, 2017.

Topic: _____

Main idea: _____

Reasons for the main idea: _____

_____

Group 2

1Phytochemicals are found in the colorful parts of fruits and vegetables. 2Although they are not required for body functioning, they may have a very powerful impact on your health. 3For example, quercetin, which is found in red apples functions like an antihistamine and as an anti-inflammatory effect. 4Resveratrol, which is found in grape skins and seeds, is a powerful antioxidant.

5Antioxidants help protect your body from free radical damage that comes from the sun, pollution, smoke, and poor dietary choices. 6They are found in the phytochemicals of fruits and vegetables, as well as some vitamins and amino acids.

Topic: _____

Main idea: _____

Reasons for the main idea: _____

_____

Stated Main Idea at the End of the Paragraph

Sometimes, the details are found before the topic sentence. So, the main idea is stated at the end of the paragraph. It is the most general sentence and usually gives a conclusion or summarizes the details in a paragraph.

Let us examine the example below.

1Coming to class prepared, taking good lecture notes, paying attention in class, developing a stronger vocabulary, and reviewing notes are often good habits that can help you to survive academically in college. 2Slouching in your chair in the back of the class, procrastinating, and not completing the assigned readings before coming to class are bad habits that interfere with academic performance. 3Take an inventory of your academic habits, and differentiate between habits that can contribute to your academic success and ones that create barriers to success. 4Habits have a profound influence on the way we approach academia and future learning situations beyond college. 5Making a conscious decision to replace ineffective learning habits with more effective ones can have a powerful effect on your potential and capacity to process and retain vital information. 6Begin to change your behavior by initiating small changes to avoid overwhelming yourself. 7Achieving academic excellence requires that you consistently engage in the process of developing and strengthening good learning habits while eliminating poor habits that interfere with your academic performance.

Using ACTOR

1. Read the first sentence. Coming to class prepared, taking good lecture notes, paying attention in class, developing a stronger vocabulary, and reviewing notes are often good habits that can help you to survive academically in college. What or who are being talked about? (Coming to class prepared, taking good lecture notes, paying attention in class, developing a stronger vocabulary, and reviewing notes) What is being said about it? (These are good habits that can help you survive in college) **Activate** prior knowledge of the content or vocabulary. These are good habits that will help you in college.

2. Connect this knowledge to the new information, so you can relate to what you are reading.
3. Trigger strategies: Break down the sentence, ask questions, or visualize. Do these and other strategies to be sure that you understand every sentence. Connect the idea of each sentence to the preceding or succeeding sentence so that everything makes sense or connects. Talk to yourself and analyze. Follow steps 1–3 in every sentence.
4. Organize in your mind the ideas that you got from reading. Doing well in college requires that you consistently engage in the process of developing and strengthening good learning habits while eliminating poor habits that prevent you from doing well. Think about the good habits that you need to continue and strengthen and bad habits that you need to change.
5. Respond by reciting or writing what you understand. State the main idea and details. Doing this enables you to find out if you understand and remember what you read. This information will later be a part of your prior knowledge that can help you in reading, writing, and other tasks in the future.

The diagram shows that the main idea is found at the end of the paragraph. Six sentences include the good habits that need to be strengthened and the bad habits that need to be changed and replaced. The last sentence, the main idea, states that to achieve academic excellence you consistently need to engage in the process of developing and strengthening good learning habits while eliminating poor habits that interfere with your academic performance.

Specific Detail
Specific Detail
Specific Detail
Specific Detail
Specific Detail
Specific Detail
Main Idea

1Coming to class prepared, taking good lecture notes, paying attention in class, developing a stronger vocabulary, and reviewing notes are often good habits that can help you to survive academically in college. 2Slouching in your chair in the back of the class, procrastinating, and not completing the assigned readings before coming to class are bad habits that interfere with academic performance. 3Take an inventory of your academic habits, and differentiate between habits that can contribute to your academic success and ones that create barriers to success. 4Habits have a profound influence on the way we approach academia and future learning situations beyond college. 5Making a conscious decision to replace ineffective learning habits with more effective ones can have a powerful effect on your potential and capacity to process and retain vital information. 6Begin to change your behavior by initiating small changes to avoid overwhelming yourself. 7<u>Achieving academic excellence requires that you consistently engage in the process of developing and strengthening good learning habits while eliminating poor habits that interfere with your academic performance.</u>

Topic: <u>Ways to achieve academic success</u>

Main idea: <u>Achieving academic excellence requires that you consistently engage in the process of developing and strengthening good learning habits while eliminating poor habits that interfere with your academic performance.</u>

Reasons for the main idea: <u>Sentence 1 tells about the good habits that can help you survive in college. Sentence 2 tells you about the bad habits that need to change. Sentence 3 tells about differentiating the good from the bad habits. Sentence 4 tells about the effects of habit. Sentences 5 and 6 tell about replacing and changing bad habits.</u>

Practice

Identify the topic, the main idea, and the reasons for the main idea in each group. Write your answers in the spaces provided.

Group 1

₁Imagine that you own a company that manufactures and markets high-quality fishing equipment. ₂What would you want to know about consumers and your target market? ₃You might want to know how often consumers in your target market go fishing, why they go fishing, their satisfaction with current fishing equipment sold in retail stores and online, their desire for need for higher-quality fishing equipment, how much they currently spend on fishing equipment, and how much they would be willing to spend on higher-quality fishing equipment. ₄Marketers and business managers need information to make decisions and to compete in the marketplace.

Graeff, Marketing Research for Managerial Decision Making, E5 Kendall Hunt Publishing Company 2013.

Topic: _____

Main idea: _____

Reasons for the main idea: _____

_____

Group 2

₁Individuals in one religion may feel their faith is best, while people in another religion may feel just as strongly that they are on the correct path. ₂People active in one political party may feel their ideas are superior to that of a different group. ₃They also believe that their candidate should win in the election. ₄When a couple goes through a divorce, family and friends may take sides, supporting one spouse over the other. ₅Our judgment depends on whose side we belong.

Topic: _____

Main idea: _____

Reasons for the main idea: _____

_____

Stated Main Idea at the Beginning and End of the Paragraph

Sometimes, you find the main idea at the beginning and end of a paragraph in a textbook. Pay attention to the first sentence and make sure that you understand what it tells you. Determine what it is about—the subject of the sentence and what is being said about it—the predicate. If it is a long sentence, break it down or apply the strategies that were discussed in Chapter 1 to make sure that you understand it because succeeding sentences flow from it or connect to it.

This general sentence may give a definition of a word that is used in a discipline such as sociology, psychology, and other content courses. It may also state a list of items. In addition, it may state information that shows comparison, contrast, narration, or cause and effect. Sometimes, the idea that is stated at the beginning of the paragraph is also the same as the idea in the last paragraph but stated in different words.

Let us examine the example below.

₁By providing marketing managers with information obtained from marketing research, managers can hopefully make fewer risky and intuitive decisions that are often based on nothing more than gut feelings and hunches. ₂Marketing research provides a means by which marketing managers can make decisions based on information in a systematic, objective, and unbiased manner. ₃Marketing research also provides managers with a means for quantifying their decisions. ₄For example, you might choose to first enter the southeastern U.S. market with your high-quality fishing equipment because the quantitative data you received from marketing research indicates that this part of the country has the highest concentration of potential customers. ₅Marketing research provides information to managers in making objective decisions instead of using feelings or beliefs that may be bad for business.

Source: Graeff, Marketing Research for Managerial Decision Making.
Kendall Hunt Publishing Company, 2013.

To help you fully understand this paragraph, use the steps in ACTOR. Following the steps may take time and patience at the beginning. However, continuous practice will enable you to use these naturally and automatically, better understand, and remember what you read.

Using ACTOR

1. Read the first sentence. By providing marketing managers with information obtained from marketing research, managers can hopefully make fewer risky and intuitive decisions that are often based on nothing more than gut feelings and hunches. What or who is being talked about? (Providing information obtained from marketing research to managers) What is being said about it? (This information helps managers avoid risky decisions.) **Activate** prior knowledge of the content or vocabulary. Without the information and just using their feelings and hunches, managers make bad business decisions. Marketing information research is needed.
2. **Connect** this knowledge to the new information, so you can relate to what you are reading.
3. **Trigger strategies**: Break down the sentence, ask questions, or visualize. Do these and other strategies to be sure that you understand every sentence. Connect the idea of each sentence to the preceding or succeeding sentence so that everything makes sense or connects. Talk to yourself and analyze the sentences by asking what is it about and is said about it. Follow steps 1–3 in every sentence.

4. **Organize** in your mind the ideas that you get from reading. Marketing research information that will help them make a wise decision. Why do we say this? Marketing research provides a means by which marketing managers can make decisions based on information in a systematic, objective, and unbiased manner. The main idea is repeated in the last sentence using different words.
5. **Respond** by reciting or writing what you understand. State the main idea and details using mostly your own words. Doing this enables you to find out if you understand and remember what you read. This information will later be a part of your prior knowledge that can help you in reading, writing, and other tasks in the future.

The diagram shows that the main idea is found at the beginning and at the end of the paragraph. These sentences mean the same but use different words. The three sentences show the details that answer why the first and last sentences are the main idea. Why do we say that by providing marketing managers with information obtained from marketing research, managers can hopefully make fewer risky and intuitive decisions that are often based on nothing more than gut feelings and hunches?

| Main Idea |
| Specific Detail |
| Specific Detail |
| Specific Detail |
| Main Idea |

1By providing marketing managers with information obtained from marketing research, managers can hopefully make fewer risky and intuitive decisions that are often based on nothing more than gut feelings and hunches. 2Marketing research provides a means by which marketing managers can make decisions based on information in a systematic, objective, and unbiased manner. 3Marketing research also provides managers with a means for quantifying their decisions. 4For example, you might choose to first enter the southeastern U.S. market with your high-quality fishing equipment because the quantitative data you received from marketing research indicates that this part of the country has the highest concentration of potential customers. 5Marketing research provides information to managers in making objective decisions instead of using feelings or beliefs that may be bad for business.

Topic: Use of marketing research information that will prevent risky business decisions.
Reasons for the main idea: Sentences 2, 3, and 4 answer why we say that the first and last sentences state the main idea.

Practice

Identify the topic and the reasons for the main idea in each group. Write your answers in the spaces provided.

Group 1

1Much of development occurs due to a natural, biological unfolding of growth over the course of time. 2Pioneering child development psychologist Arnold Gesell coined the term maturation to describe this natural course of development that is similar for all children. ₃According to maturation theory, children have an inner timetable for development. ₄It is exemplified by the study of physical development, which is mostly determined by genetics. ₅Genes are inherited from parents and to varying degrees determine characteristics like height, strength, speed, and coordination. ₆Physical development includes the biological changes evident during puberty and is also concerned with variables related to health and illness. ₇We understand physical development by studying similarities and averages between children as well as differences like those exhibited by preterm infants, malnourished children, and anorexic teens. ₈Children usually show stages of development that happen naturally during a period of time.

From *Child and Adolescent Development*, by Ronald Mossler.
Copyright © 2013 by Bridgepoint Education, Inc. Reprinted by permission.

Topic: _____

Reasons for the main idea that is found at the beginning and end of the paragraph:

_____

_____

Group 2

₁The information collected by marketing research is used to connect consumers and other publics to the marketer. ₂This information is used to identify marketing problems and opportunities. ₃It is also used to help marketing managers make and evaluate marketing decisions. ₄And, it is also used to monitor marketing performance. ₅More formally, the American Marketing Association defines marketing research as the function that links the consumer, customer, and public to the marketer through information used to identify and define marketing opportunities and problems; generate, refine, and evaluate marketing actions; monitor marketing performance; and improve understanding of marketing as a process. ₆Marketing research specifies the information required to address these issues, designs the method for collecting information, manages and implements the data collection process. ₇Marketing research information enable the marketer to know the consumers and the public.

Source: Graeff, *Marketing Research for Managerial Decision Making*.
Kendall Hunt Publishing Company, 2013.

Topic: _____

Reasons for the main idea that is found at the beginning and end of the paragraph:

_____

_____

Mastery Test 1

The following paragraphs are based on a chapter in *Introduction to Sociology, pp. 2–4*. Choose the main idea for each group. Write the letter of your answer in the space provided.

What is Sociology?

BRAINSTORMING
Creative idea

littleWhale/Shutterstock.com

_____ Group 1

₁Consider this example—when you have money troubles, is it just an economic problem? ₂It influences the way you feel about yourself (perhaps you feel panicky, angry, or frustrated). ₃You might be irritable and yell at someone you live with when they make a mistake that normally wouldn't bother you. ₄They may get upset and move out, so then you've got to figure out how to make ends meet on your own. ₅You go to the bank for a loan and they think you're not a good credit risk and won't give it to you. ₆This may put you into a tailspin as you have no idea what to do or where to go for help. ₇Sociology assumes that all aspects of human relationships and institutions are related to each other.

    A. Sentence 1   B. Sentence 2   C. Sentence 6   D. Sentence 7

_____ Group 2

₁Sociology is the study of group behavior through the use of scientific investigation and research. ₂It includes ideas about how society affects individuals and social interaction. ₃The field also examines how people's life chances are influenced by social forces. ₄Sociologists, as scientists, do not rely on "common sense" assumptions or tradition. ₅Instead they use the scientific method to figure out what is happening and why.

    A. Sentence 1   B. Sentence 2   C. Sentence 3   D. Sentence 5

_____ Group 3

₁Everyone has self-interests and experiences that influence what they think and why. ₂So the way we view things may be quite different from how other people view things. ₃Who is right? ₄We all like to think that our way of viewing things is the best. 5But other people think the way they see things is correct also. 6You cannot assume that your experience reflects that of others. 7You cannot assume you're right and your explanations are necessarily valid.

A. Sentence 1　　　　B. Sentence 2　　　　C. Sentence 6　　　　D. Sentence 7

_____ Group 4

1Looking at social phenomena from different points of views is an important part of the sociological perspective. 2Sociologists view the causes and consequences of reality as products of social construction. 3What we think of as real is merely one possible outcome; many competing versions of reality could also exist. 4This way of thinking is an important component of sociology.

A. Sentence 1　　　B. Sentences 2 and 4　　　C. Sentence 4　　　D. Sentences 1 and 4

_____ Group 5

1How we view the world creates real and tangible outcomes in how we feel and what we do. 2W. I. Thomas (1863–1947) (1966) stated that whatever we believe to be real will become real in its consequences. 3So if we believe one religious or political group is right, we will act in a way that supports that view, and we may disagree with those who view things differently. 4We may try to convince them that our view is right. In a divorce, when we pick sides it could influence how the couple feels about each other and how children view their parents. 5The way we think about things has real ramifications.

A. Sentences 1 and 5　　B. Sentences 2 and 4　　　C. Sentence 2　　　D. Sentences 4

_____ Group 6

1People didn't look the same, act the same, or believe the same things. 2Conflicts, crime, health problems, ownership issues, and competition resulted from many diverse peoples being thrown together in a small space over a short period of time. 3All the social systems that previously guided people's lives, such as the agrarian and feudal systems, were being challenged. 4Society was in flux. 5New systems of economic production, government, and lifestyles were being created. 6The Industrial Revolution was just beginning, and a whole host of social problems emerged as people with different backgrounds, cultures, races, religions, and nationalities merged together in newly developing cities to find work. 7The early sociologists wanted to understand these changes.

A. Sentence 1　　　　B. Sentence 2　　　　C. Sentence 6　　　　D. Sentence 7

Adapted from Vissing, An Introduction to Sociology, Kendall Hunt Publishing Company, 2013.

Mastery Test 2

The following paragraphs are based on college textbook texts. Choose the main idea for each group. Write the number of the sentence that states the main idea in the space provided.

_____ **Group 1**

1In the West, the definition of art has changed significantly over the centuries, even more so in recent decades as new technologies emerge. 2In fact, due to developments like digital photography and the Internet, people today have virtual access to more artworks than in any previous generation. 3As a result, our concept of art continues to expand. 4Art is defined differently by varying cultures—there is no single definition of art, it is an ever-evolving term that is constantly being revised.

Adapted from Comeau, Architecture of the World: The Story of All of Us,
Kendall Hunt Publishing Company, 2014.

A. Sentence 1   B. Sentence 2   C. Sentence 3   D. Sentence 4

_____ **Group 2**

1Often, we use sight and perception interchangeably for some reasons. 2However, simple ocular sensations (vision) are the result of passively collecting and streaming outside graphic information into our bodies and brains. 3Perception, on the other hand, deals with actively selecting, assembling and *interpreting* that visual information. 4It's easy to confuse the two terms because we make assumptions about sight. 5We tend to *think* that what we're seeing or experiencing is a universal reality. 6In fact, that is often not the case. 7A litany of things affects our perception, including our moral, psychological, cultural, causal, aesthetic, experiential, social, emotional, and intellectual references and views. 8Even gender may color our perspective.

A. Sentence 1   B. Sentence 4   C. Sentence 5   D. Sentence 7

_____ **Group 3**

1Artistic standards and visual traditions may be linked to a society's religious belief system or governmental structure. 2For example, in the Ife region of Nigeria, beginning around 1100, artists produced an array of metal and terracotta figures, which are likely depictions of kings and other important members of the community. 3These sculptures are not considered to be portraits, as such, but representations of the divinity that resides within every living thing. 4According to Ife tradition, Obatala, the god of creativity, formed the first human being from divine clay. 5This archetypal figure was further refined by Ogun, the god associated with iron tools and weaponry, and then given life by the breath of Oludumare, the Supreme Being.

A. Sentence 1   B. Sentence 4   C. Sentence 5   D. Sentence 7

_____ Group 4

1The Medieval period, 500–1450, is by far the longest. 2It is a time dominated by the influence of the Catholic Church. 3During this time, sacred, religious music evolves from monophonic Gregorian Chant to polyphonic sacred works such as motets and masses. 4Secular, non-religious music such as dances and songs, are represented by the music of the Troubadours. 5The Renaissance, 1450–1600, is a time when the polyphonic style became more refined, with an emphasis on using the simultaneously sounding melodic lines in a more harmonically conceived manner. 6Imitative polyphony, where each melodic line imitates a previously heard melody, was the predominant style in both instrumental and vocal works. 7The Baroque period, 1600–1750, saw the harmonic basis of Western art music firmly established. 8Western art music is usually discussed in terms of historical periods, spans of time during which similar characteristics are evident across many types of music.

A. Sentence 1   B. Sentence 5   C. Sentence 7   D. Sentence 8

_____ Group 5

1Water is essential for life and development, and fortunately, it is plentiful. 2On earth, 97% of the surface is covered by water and only 3% by land. 3However, most of the life that exists on land needs freshwater, which represents only a small portion of the earth's total water supply. 4Less than 2.5% of the earth's water is freshwater, and over half of this freshwater is for now locked in ice caps, glaciers, and permanent snow mass. 5Less than 1% of the earth's total water is freshwater available for use by life on the earth's landmasses. 6Even this 1% is not evenly distributed across the earth's landmasses; some areas such as the northern and tropical forests have more, and desert areas of the southwest United States and northern Africa have less.

A. Sentence 1   B. Sentence 2   C. Sentence 3   D. Sentence 6

Mastery Test 3

Write the number of the main idea in the space provided.

_____ Group 1

1Information appearing in periodicals constitutes the bulk of published information; there are thousands of periodicals published regularly, each containing an abundance of articles on different topics. 2The material found in newspapers, magazines, and journals is the most recent printed information you can find outside of the Internet. 3nformation in periodicals, particularly newspapers, reflects contemporary opinion. 3Articles written shortly after an event occurred, whether it was in the nineteenth century, the 1930s, or the 1990s, convey what people thought of the event at the time it occurred. 4Periodical literature reflects the constantly evolving nature of information. 5No matter when an event occurred, the facts surrounding it and the event's significance are constantly being reinterpreted. 6Periodical literature provides comparative information for different periods. 7Compare, for example, the role of women in the workplace in the 1920s with those of the 1990s. 8There are many reasons that show the value of information found in periodicals in research.

_____ Group 2

1Some people consider graffiti as vandalism. In fact, it is a crime to deface public property. 2The "artist" would be no more than a common criminal. 3Graffiti has emerged as a new urban art form. 4It is an acceptable activity in some metropolitan centers worldwide. 5Some regard its practitioners as progressive artists who are challenging the meaning of art. 6As evidence of this, in April 2011, the Museum of Contemporary Art in Los Angeles organized Art in the Streets, the first major museum exhibition focusing on graffiti and street art. 7Therefore, this form of painting becomes a legitimate art as opposed to mere spray painted images defacing city walls.

_____ Group 3

1Thermoelectric power production was the largest use of freshwater in 2005. 2With 37% of the total, irrigation was the next largest use of freshwater. 3Public systems represented 13% of the freshwater withdrawn. 4One of the goals of sustainability is to assure long-term safe drinking water supplies for every person in the world. 5Unfortunately, this goal has not been reached. 6Most people in the United States get their water from a public system. 7Freshwater was used for different purposes.

_____ Group 4

1Water is essential for life and development, and fortunately, it is plentiful. 2On earth, 97% of the surface is covered by water and only 3% by land. 3However, most of the life that exists on land needs freshwater, which represents only a small portion of the earth's total water supply. 4Less than 2.5% of the earth's water is freshwater, and over half of this freshwater is for now locked in ice caps, glaciers, and permanent snow mass. 5Less than 1% of the earth's total water is freshwater available for use by life on the earth's landmasses. 6Even this 1% is not evenly distributed across the earth's landmasses; some areas such as the northern and tropical forests have more, and desert areas of the southwest United States and northern Africa have less.

_____ Group 5

1Sources of freshwater vary from one region to another. 2In some regions, groundwater from shallow aquifers is widely available, while other regions must use modern pumps to access aquifers that exist thousands of feet below the surface. 3Some regions have access to surface water from lakes and rivers, while in other regions, water supplies are scarce and the lack of surface or groundwater limits human activities. 4Many major urban areas, such as Boston, New York, San

Francisco, Los Angeles, and Phoenix, move water from watersheds hundreds of miles away to meet the water demand of their region.

Source: Pijawka, Sustainability for the 21st Century, Kendall Hunt Publishing Company, 2015

Implied Main Idea

Sometimes, the main idea is not stated; it is implied. Pay attention to the first sentence and make sure that you understand what it is telling you. Determine what it is about—the subject of the sentence and what is being said about it—the predicate. If it is a long sentence, break it down or apply the strategies that were discussed in Chapter 1 to make sure that you understand it because succeeding sentences flow from it or connect to it. Do these for every sentence to be sure that you understand, connect ideas in sentences, and make sense. Ask yourself what the paragraph is about. Construct your own sentence that gives the general idea of the paragraph since there is no sentence that states the main idea.

Let us examine the example below.

To help you fully understand this paragraph, use the steps in ACTOR. Following the steps may take time and patience at the beginning. However, continuous practice will enable you to use these naturally and automatically, better understand, and remember what you read.

1Listening attentively to the class discussions may help you fully grasp the subject matter. 2Reviewing your assignments before coming to class may enable you to connect and understand the new lesson. 3Asking questions may help you clarify matters. 4Participating in classroom discussions may allow you to show your interest in the lesson.

Using ACTOR

1. Read the first sentence. Listening attentively to the class discussions may help you fully grasp the subject matter. **Activate** prior knowledge of the content or vocabulary. What/who are we talking about? (Listening attentively to class discussion). What is being said about it? (May help you fully grasp the subject matter). What do you know about this topic? (A good practice of students).
2. **Connect** this knowledge to the new information, so you can relate to what you are reading.
3. **Trigger strategies**: Break down the sentence, ask questions, or visualize. Do these and other strategies to be sure that you understand every sentence. Connect the idea of each sentence to the preceding or succeeding sentence, so that everything makes sense or connects. Talk to yourself and analyze the sentences by asking "What is it about and what is said about it?" Follow steps 1–3 in every sentence.

4. **Organize** in your mind the ideas that you got from reading. The four sentences tell you about the good practices of college students that can help them understand and show interest in the lesson. Therefore, the main idea is <u>there are practices that can help them understand and show interest in the lesson</u>. List the practices. Here, you were able to give the unstated or implied main idea by asking yourself this question. What do all of the sentences tell you? You make your own sentence based on your answer.

5. **Respond** by reciting or writing what you understand. State the main idea and details using mostly your own words. Doing this enables you to find out if you understand and remember what you read. This information will be a part of your prior knowledge that can help you in reading, writing, and other tasks in the future.

The diagram shows that the paragraph includes four details. Since the main idea is unstated or implied, you have to state a main idea. What do these specific details tell about?

Specific Detail
Specific Detail
Specific Detail
Specific Detail

₁Listening attentively to the class discussions may help you fully grasp the subject matter. ₂Reviewing your assignments before coming to class may enable you to connect and understand the new lesson. ₃Asking questions to the professor may help you clarify matters. ₄Participating in classroom discussions may allow you to show your interest in the lesson.

Topic: <u>Good practices of college students</u>

Main idea: <u>There are practices that students can follow to help them understand and show interest in the lesson.</u>

Reason for the main idea: <u>Sentences 1–4 tell about the good practices of college students that may help understand and show interest in the lesson.</u>

Practice

Identify the topic, the main idea, and the reasons for the main idea in each group. Write your answers in the spaces provided.

Group 1

₁Securing a parking space is usually a problem if you come late. ₂Attending to a sick relative while in college may lead to unwanted absences. ₃Tardiness and absences can cause poor performance in tests and assignments. ₄Insufficient funding can prevent you from buying the required college textbooks. ₅Students are faced with possible problems in college.

Topic: _____

Main idea: _____

Reasons for the main idea: _____

_____

Group 2

1Each day in the United States, approximately 3,600 young people between the ages of 12 and 17 years start cigarette smoking. 2In 2009, 19% of high schools students reported current cigarette use and 14% reported current cigar use. 3In addition, 9% of high school students and 20% of white male high school students reported current smokeless tobacco use.

Topic: _____

Main idea: _____

Reasons for the main idea: _____

_____

_____

5

Supporting Details

In writing a paragraph, a writer usually includes a main idea that tells what the paragraph is about. This is supported by details. Since the reader reads what has been written by a writer, recognizing the major and minor details will help a reader to understand what is being read. This chapter will show you the strategies and activities that will enable you to identify the major and minor details. Most of the reading materials that are used for reading applications are found in college textbooks because this chapter intends to help you better understand textbooks in other courses. Specifically, the objectives of this chapter are the following:

1. Recognize the major details that support the main idea of a paragraph
2. Identify the minor details that support the major details
3. Outline given information
4. Summarize passages

Topics

Major Details

Major and Minor Details

Major Details   CHAPTER 5

The things that you learned about ACTOR, vocabulary enhancement, transitions in sentence rela-tionships, and main ideas in previous chapters will help you understand what you read. In addi-tion, supporting details will also enable you to become a better reader. Supporting details may be major or minor. The major details support the main idea while the minor details tell about the major details. Sometimes there are details that elaborate the introduction.

Let us review the words below. What do you notice about the words? How are the words related to each other? Complete the outline that follows.

| Food | Fruits | Fish | Cabbage | Grapes | Salmon |
| Broccoli | Vegetables | Kiwi | Apple | Tilapia | Mangoes |

Food

    1. Fruits

        a. _____

        b. _____

        c. _____

        d. _____

    2. Vegetables

        a. _____

        b. _____

    3. _____

        a. _____

        b. _____

Notice that the most general word is food because all the rest are food. The three words that directly tell about the food are vegetables, fruits, and fish. Cabbage and broccoli are minor details because these are vegetables. Grapes, kiwi, mangoes, and apples are fruits while tilapia and salmon are fish. Recognizing relationships between and among ideas and organizing these will help you better understand what you read because a paragraph may consist of major and minor details.

Supporting details include examples, reasons, steps, explanations, and other details to support or clarify a topic sentence or a given statement. The information about ACTOR, vocabulary enhance-ment strategies, transitions, and main ideas that were discussed in previous chapters will sharpen your skill of identifying supporting details and relationships between the main idea and details.

Major Details

Let us analyze the sentences below. What does each sentence tell you?

1Researchers follow basic steps to acquire information. 2First, identify your research topic. 3Next, determine the information requirements for your assignment 4Third, locate and retrieve relevant information resources. 5Fourth, evaluate information resources. 6Finally, cite your sources.

> To help you fully understand this paragraph, use the steps in **ACTOR.** Following the steps may take time and patience at the beginning. However, continuous practice will enable you to use these naturally and automatically, better understand, and remember what you read.

Using ACTOR

1. Read the first sentence. Researchers follow basic steps to acquire information. What or who is being talked about? (Researchers). What is being said about researchers? (Follow basic steps to acquire information). **Activate** prior knowledge of the content or vocabulary. Researchers are looking for information. They follow basic steps. Steps are the things that they do to get information.
2. **Connect** this knowledge to the new information, so you can relate to what you are reading.
3. **Trigger strategies**: Break down the sentence, ask questions, or visualize. Do these and other strategies to be sure that you understand every sentence. Connect the idea of each sentence to the preceding or succeeding sentence, so that everything makes sense or connects. Talk to yourself and analyze. The second sentence starts with the word first. It means it is the first step in information research. The third sentence starts with the word next. It shows the second step. The fourth sentence starts with third. It shows the third step. The fifth sentence starts with fourth. It means it is the fourth step. The last sentence starts with the word finally. It means it is the last step. So, how many steps are there? There are five. Therefore, there are five major details.
4. **Organize** in your mind the ideas that you got from reading. Researchers follow basic steps to acquire information. Think about the four steps.
5. **Respond** by reciting or writing what you understand. State the main idea and the major details. Doing this enables you to find out if you understand and remember what you read. This information will be a part of your prior knowledge that can help you in reading, writing, and other tasks in the future.

Being able to create an outline in your mind or on paper and recite it helps you to monitor if you understand what you read. The information that you recite may be similar to the one below.

Steps in Information Research

1. Identify research topic
2. Determine information requirements

3. Locate and retrieve relevant information
4. Evaluate information resources
5. Cite your sources.

Usually in textbooks, authors define a special word in the discipline. The definition is followed by examples. Sometimes, a list of items is given. Pay attention to these signal words because these may give you clues to the major details especially if transitions are not used.

Signal Words

different kinds	several types	some steps
few reminders	five ways	series of events
various results	many ways	a number of reasons
as follows	following	among the similarities

Practice

Read the following paragraphs. Identify the main idea and the major supporting details. Fill out the missing details in the outline.

Group 1

1A primary source provides information that has not been published anywhere else, or put into a context, or interpreted, or translated by anyone else. 2Examples of primary sources include the following. 3The professor tells you about what happened in the class you missed because you were ill. 4Reporters write accounts of events on the scene, such as the Web site and newspaper articles about the Iditarod sled-dog race in Alaska. 5A researcher reported a scientific study on a virus that causes AIDS. 6An artist displays an original artwork or photograph. 7A principal writes a letter to a parent.

Topic: _____

Main idea: _____

_____

_____

_____

Examples of Primary Sources

1. _____

_____

_____

_____

2. Reporters write accounts of events

_____

3. _____

_____

4. _____

_____

5. A principal writes a letter to a parent.

Group 2

1Secondary information is a restatement, examination, or interpretation of information from one or more primary sources. 2It has been removed in some way from its original (primary) source and repackaged. 3Examples of secondary sources include the following materials. 4A friend provides her notes to you from the class you missed (she interpreted what the professor said and passed that interpretation on to you). 5A newspaper article summarizes a journal article on the AIDS virus. 6A student submits a research paper that shows a review to a critique to a painting or a novel.

Topic _____

Main Idea _____

Major Details _____

1. _____

2. _____

3. _____

Major and Minor Details

Some paragraphs show both major and minor details. Remember the major details tell about the main idea while the minor details tell about the major details. Let us examine this example.

1Research points to some human tendencies as key factors involved in the development of preju-dice. 2One factor is feeling comfortable with the familiar and uncomfortable with the unknown or unfamiliar. 3Psychological research indicates that familiarity has a powerful effect on human judgment and decision making. 4Simply stated, the more exposure humans have to somebody or something, the more familiar it becomes and the more likely it will be perceived positively and judged favorably. 5Another factor is using selective perception and selective memory to support prejudicial beliefs. 6Once prejudice has been formed, it can often remain intact and resistant to change through the psychological process of *selective perception*—the tendency for biased (preju-diced) people to see what they *expect* to see and fail to see what contradicts their bias.

Using ACTOR

1. Read the first sentence. Research points to some human tendencies as key factors involved in the development of prejudice. What or who is being talked about? (Research) What is being said about research? (States some human tendencies as key factors to the development of prejudice.) **Activate** prior knowledge of the content or vocabulary. (Prejudice is a bias and is not good. People do something that shows prejudice.)
2. **Connect** this knowledge to the new information, so you can relate to what you are reading.
3. **Trigger strategies**: Break down the sentence, ask questions, or visualize. Do these and other strategies to be sure that you understand every sentence. Connect the idea of each sentence to the preceding or succeeding sentence, so that everything makes sense or connects. Talk to yourself and analyze. The second sentence starts with one factor—familiarity and unfamiliarity. It means that this can lead to prejudice. The third sentence states that familiarity can affect judgment. This is not a factor, but a detail that tells about the first factor. So, this is a minor detail. Keep on analyzing each sentence to fully understand and connect to other ideas. Follow steps 1–3.
4. Organize in your mind the ideas that you got from reading. According to research, people have some tendencies that lead to the development of prejudice. How many factors are mentioned? What is being said about each factor?
5. Respond by reciting or writing what you understand. State the main idea and the major details. Doing this enables you to find out if you understand and remember what you read. This information will be a part of your prior knowledge that can help you in reading, writing, and other tasks in the future.

Topic _____

Main idea _____

_____

Reason for choosing the main idea _____

Major Detail 1-Sentence _____

Minor Details-Sentences _____

Major Detail 2-Sentence _____

Minor Detail 1-Sentence _____

Practice 1

Read the following paragraphs and answer the questions that follow. Write your answer in the space provided.

Group 1

1According to the U.S. Census Bureau, there are five races. 2White has origins in any of the original peoples of Europe, the Middle East, or North Africa. 3The Black or African American is a person or has origins in any of the Black racial groups of Africa. 4An American Indian or Alaska Native is a person having origins in any of the original peoples of North and South America (including Central America) and who maintains tribal affiliation or community attachment. 5An Asian is a person having origins in any of the original peoples of the Far East, Southeast Asia, or the Indian subcontinent including, for example, Cambodia, China, India, Japan, Korea, Malaysia, Pakistan, the Philippine Islands, Thailand, and Vietnam. 6A Native Hawaiian or Other Pacific Islander is a person having origins in any of the original peoples of Hawaii, Guam, Samoa, or other Pacific Islands.

Cuseo, Humanity, Diversity, & The Liberal Arts, 2E Kendall Hunt Publishing Company, 2010.

_____1. The main idea is stated in the _____ sentence.
    a. first   b. second   c. last

_____2. There are _____ major details.
    a. four   b. five   c. six

_____3. Cambodia is a detail for the _____ major detail.
    a. third   b. fourth   c. fifth

_____4. The topic of the paragraph is _____.
    a. People in America   b. Races in America   c. Races

_____5. North Africa is a detail for the _____ major detail.
    a. first   b. second   c. third

Group 2

1You just received news that a family member just suddenly passed away due to a car accident. 2You just saw him this morning. 3When the store was about to close, your boss told you that you could not come back to work anymore. 4Where would you get money for your tuition? 5On your way, your engine failed and had to wait for a tow truck. 6When you reached home, you found out that your house has been burglarized. 7You lost your laptop and favorite watch. 8These were stressors that really changed your life.

_____1. The main idea is stated in the _____ sentence.
    a. first   b. second   c. last

_____2. There are _____ major details.
    a. four   b. five   c. six

_____3. Losing your laptop is a/an _____ detail.
    a. major   b. minor   c. introductory

_____4. The topic of the paragraph is _____.
    a. bad luck   b. stressors   c. unwanted incidents

_____5. Sentence 6 is a/an _____ detail.
    a. major   b. minor   c. introductory

Practice 2

Read the following paragraphs and answer the questions that follow. Write your answer in the space provided.

1To further illustrate the differences between surveys and focus groups, consider a researcher interested in the purchase process for digital televisions. 2A survey will allow the researcher to measure factors such as where consumers purchase a television, the factors that are important in the purchase process, and even past purchase history. 3However, little will be learned except for the particular item that is checked on the survey. 4The survey researcher will not know why a consumer checked a particular box on the survey, or the consumer's motivations for responding as he or she did. 5In contrast, a researcher conducting a focus group might spend an hour probing the nuances of the actual purchase process itself, including the feelings associated with the purchase decision, the thoughts associated with deciding where to make the purchase, the emotions associated with the actual purchase, and even the social and emotional components of the interaction between the consumer and the salesperson. 6As such, focus groups allow researchers to better understand the beliefs, perceptions, feelings, and motivations behind responses to questions.

_____1. The main idea is stated in the _____ sentence.
    a. first   b. second   c. last

_____2. There are _____ major details.
    a. four   b. two   c. six

_____3. Finding out where an item is bought is a detail for the _____ major detail.
    a. third   b. first   c. second

_____4. The topic of the paragraph is _____.
    a. surveys   b. focus groups   c. surveys and focus groups

_____5. Understanding the feelings of a customer is a detail for the _____ major detail.
    a. first   b. second   c. third

Group 2

1Western art music is usually discussed in terms of historical periods, spans of time during which similar characteristics are evident across many types of music. 2The Medieval period, 500–1450, is by far the longest. 3It is a time dominated by the influence of the Catholic Church. 4During this time sacred, religious music evolves from monophonic Gregorian Chant to polyphonic sacred works such as motets and masses. 5Secular, non-religious music such as dances and songs, are represented by the music of the Troubadours. 6The Renaissance, 1450–1600, is a time when the polyphonic style became more refined, with an emphasis on using the simultaneously sounding melodic lines in a more harmonically conceived manner. 7Imitative polyphony, where each melodic line imitates a previously heard melody, was the predominant style in both instrumental and vocal works. 8The Baroque period, 1600–1750, saw the harmonic basis of Western art music firmly established. 9Many of the characteristics of modern music were developed during this time. 10The basso continuo provided a bass line, the harmony, and a rhythmic regularity that we have come to expect in today's music. 11The Classical period, 1750–1825, is a time when concepts such as reason, symmetry, balance, and elegance are in evidence. 12A clearly defined form in all musical compositions is highly valued during this time.

_____1. The main idea is stated in the _____ sentence.
    a. first   b. second   c. last

_____2. There are _____ major details.
    a. two   b. four   c. five

_____3. Sentence 5 is a detail for the _____ major detail.
    a. third   b. first   c. second

_____4. The topic of the paragraph is _____.
    a. historical periods in art music
    b. music history
    c. historical periods in western art music

_____5. Evidence of concepts and reasons is a detail for the _____ major detail.
    a. first   b. fourth   c. third

Mastery Test

Read the selection below and choose the word from the list that completes the map.

Psychoanalytic Perspective

Sigmund Freud (1856–1939) constructed his psychoanalytic theory in the early part of the 1900s. He developed his ideas mostly from his therapeutic sessions with adults, many of whom complained of various *psychosomatic disorders*. Freud theorized that his patients exhibited physical symptoms due to unconscious processes related to childhood conflicts. He believed that our most basic instinct is to derive pleasure by giving in to our innate aggressive and sexual impulses.

Personality Structure

Based on his patient's reports, Freud came to believe that personality developed around three essential components: the id, the ego, and the superego. He theorized that infants are governed by basic unconscious instincts of pleasure, and their energy is directed to primitive, biological desires. Freud viewed infants as basically selfish creatures who are only interested in reducing tension that builds up when their selfish needs are not met. Freud called this pleasure-seeking part of the personality, the **id,** which is completely unconscious. Although the id dominates an infant's life, according to Freud, humans spend their lives trying to overcome the aggressive and sexual impulses of the id. Freud might have described *Tiger Woods*, who subjected himself to private and public scrutiny by admitting to multiple affairs, as "mostly id." When we engage in pleasure-seeking behaviors without thought of the consequences, it is the unconscious id that is seeking immediate gratification.

In Freud's view, in the second and third years, conscious awareness begins to develop. It becomes the job of the **ego** to satisfy the demands of the id and to have realistic plans for obtaining what the id wants. The ego is rational as it tries to rein in the instincts of the id. It therefore operates on the **reality principle** as it tries to balance instinctual needs with societal expectations. For instance, instead of forcefully taking a toy that another child is using, a 3-year-old can learn to ask an adult if there are any more toys. This behavior would be the result of the *reality principle* of the ego.

Yuri Turkov/Shutterstock.com

Sigmund Freud believed that personality developed largely as a result of unconscious processes.

As the child's personality matures between the ages of 3 and 6, it develops a sense of morality, which Freud called the **superego**. This part of the personality has two parts. The first part is the **conscience**, which makes distinctions between right and wrong according to parental and societal standards. When decisions are made, the ego has the difficult task of balancing the demands of the id while maintaining rules that the superego dictates. A 6-year-old must balance the demands of wanting a cookie *now* (id) to satisfy a hunger urge, with the admonishment not to eat sweets before dinner (superego). It is up to the ego to find a compromise—perhaps asking for a piece of fruit. The second part of the superego is the **ego ideal**. It is the part of the personality that strives for perfection—the ideal to which the ego should aspire. It is concerned with things that make us feel accomplished and proud.

Write each of the following in the appropriate space.

1. ego ideal
2. personality components
3. id
4. superego
5. looks at reality

6. conscience
7. satisfies the demand of the id
8. selfish behavior
9. unreasonable

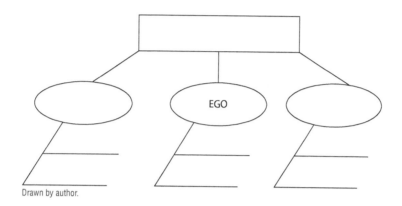

EGO

Drawn by author.

GLOBAL CLIMATE CHANGE AND OZONE DEPLETION

PSD photography/Shutterstock.com

The Basics of Climate Change—Frequently Asked Questions

1. *What factors determine the Earth's climate?*

   Our climate system is powered by solar radiation from the sun and is determined by the energy balance of incoming and outgoing energy About one-third of incoming, short-wave solar radiation is reflected by clouds or light surfaces on the Earth (like ice and snow) and bounced back to space. Much more of this shortwave radiation is absorbed by the Earth's surface and then given off or reradiated as heat energy. If you've ever stood barefoot on a dark surface on a sunny summer day, you've experienced this first-hand. Greenhouse gases such as water vapor and carbon dioxide are present naturally in the atmosphere, and they absorb and trap some of this outgoing radiation and help keep the Earth's surface relatively warm.

Learn more about this here:
https://www.ipcc.unibe.ch/publications/wg1-ar4/faq/wg1_faq-1.1.html

The sun emits shortwave solar radiation onto the Earth's surface. Some of this radiation is reflected back into space by clouds and light surfaces such as snow or ice on mountains. Most of the shortwave radiation is absorbed by the Earth's surface and then reradiated or released back as infrared or heat energy. Some of this heat energy is then absorbed and reradiated back toward the Earth's surface by greenhouse gases like carbon dioxide and water vapor.

2. *What is the greenhouse effect?*
The two most abundant gases in the atmosphere are nitrogen and oxygen, together accounting for roughly 99% of the total. These gases play almost no role in trapping or absorbing the outgoing heat energy coming from the Earth's surface. Instead, other gases present in extremely small quantities in the Earth's atmosphere absorb and reradiate outgoing heat or longwave radiation. These gases—including water vapor, carbon dioxide, methane, and nitrous oxide—act like a blanket helping to hold heat energy close to the Earth's surface. These gases could also be thought of as windows in a greenhouse or car, allowing sunlight to pass through the atmosphere but trapping the heat that tries to escape. Although they only make up a fraction of a percent of the composition of the atmosphere, these greenhouse gases are responsible for the greenhouse effect and essentially for life as we know it. It's estimated that without greenhouse gases, the average temperature on Earth would be about 0 degrees Fahrenheit (F). Instead, the average surface temperature globally is 59 degrees F.

Learn more about this here:
• https://www.ipcc.unibe.ch/publications/wg1-ar4/faq/wg1_faq-1.3.html
• http://www2.sunysuffolk.edu/mandias/global_warming/greenhouse_gases.html

3. *How are the greenhouse effect, global warming, and global climate change different?*
The greenhouse effect is a natural phenomenon without which we might not be here. When we talk of global warming we are really referring to an *enhanced* greenhouse effect caused by human emissions of greenhouse gases like carbon dioxide. These human emissions, for example from burning fossil fuels, are increasing the concentration of greenhouse gases in the atmosphere and contributing to global warming. While essentially the same thing, most scientists prefer to use the term global climate change since warming of the Earth is also altering precipitation patterns and other factors related to climate.

Learn more about this here:
• http://www.bis.gov.uk/go-science/climatescience

4. *What is the difference or the relationship between climate and weather?*

The old saying is that "climate is what you expect, weather is what you get." Climate can thus be explained as the average weather in a particular place over many years. Global warming or global climate change does not mean that we will no longer have cold weather. Instead, it means that on average, we should expect to see less cold weather and an increase in warmer temperatures in most parts of the world, a prediction that is borne out definitively by the data.

Learn more about this here:
- https://www.ipcc.unibe.ch/publications/wg1-ar4/faq/wg1_faq-1.2.html
- http://www.eo.ucar.edu/basics/

5. *How do human activities contribute to climate change, and are they more or less important than natural factors?*

While we know that we are currently experiencing a period of warming, how can we be certain that this is a result mainly of human activities? Scientists call this a question of *attribution*; to what can we attribute the observed warming? Scientists start by looking at all of the different possible causes of warming and then examine whether any of them provide a plausible explanation for what we are seeing. For example, throughout the history of the planet, factors like tectonic activity, volcanic eruptions, variations in the Earth's orbit, changes in solar radiation, and internal variation in the Earth's climate system (e.g., the El Niño phenomenon) have contributed to climate change. However, when scientists examine all of these factors, none of them alone or in combination comes close to explaining the actual warming we are currently seeing. In contrast, the steady increase in greenhouse gas concentrations in the atmosphere due to human activities like fossil fuel burning does explain the observed warming. Therefore, climate scientists are confident in attributing current climate change largely to human factors.

Learn more about this here:
- https://www.ipcc.unibe.ch/publications/wg1-ar4/faq/wg1_faq-2.1.html
- http://www2.sunysuffolk.edu/mandias/global_warming/natural_causes_climate_change.html
- http://www.c2es.org/science-impacts/basics/faqs/climate-science#Causes

6. *How are temperatures changing, and is it true that global warming has stopped or paused?*

Measurements of surface temperatures from around the planet going back to about 1850 show a clear trend of increasing temperature over time. Furthermore, average temperatures have generally been rising at an increasing rate. However, recent claims have been made that global warming has paused and that the planet has stopped warming since the late-1990s. Such claims are a good example of how scientific data can be misrepresented to make misleading and false claims. In reality, a number of factors are currently at work. First, persistent La Niña conditions and an increase in volcanic activity (which puts particles into the atmosphere that block incoming sunlight) have *slowed the rate* of temperature increases in recent years, but 20 of the warmest years on record have occurred in the last 25 years. Second, the oceans have been warming far faster than land areas, suggesting that they are, at least temporarily, storing much of the increased heat caused by higher levels of greenhouse gases in the atmosphere. Third, some climate skeptics have been using graphs showing trends in global temperatures since 1998, suggesting that temperatures have flattened out. However, 1998 was tied for the second-warmest year on record, so using that year as your starting date paints a misleading picture of the long-term trend.

Learn more about this here:
- http://www.youtube.com/watch?v=r_qdETSYcDM
- http://www2.sunysuffolk.edu/mandias/global_warming/global_cooling.html
- http://www2.sunysuffolk.edu/mandias/global_warming/modern_day_climate_change.html
- https://www.ipcc.unibe.ch/publications/wg1-ar4/faq/wg1_faq-3.1.html
- http://svs.gsfc.nasa.gov/vis/a000000/a004000/a004030/

Greenhouse effect

The greenhouse effect derives its name from the fact that the atmosphere acts something like a greenhouse. The sun's rays can pass through the atmosphere, which acts like glass in a greenhouse, and strike the Earth's surface where they are converted to infrared or heat energy. However, just like the glass in a greenhouse, the various greenhouse gases help to trap some of that heat inside the structure. Adding more greenhouse gases to the atmosphere is like thickening the glass in a greenhouse, trapping more heat in and increasing the temperature.

7. *Is global climate change an ethical issue? Won't "solving" the global warming problem ruin our economy?*

    While the debate over climate change might appear to be mainly a scientific one, it is also one of the most important ethical issues of our time. Because climate change can lead to rising sea levels, changes in precipitation patterns, and disruptions in water supply, it could have serious impacts on our ability to grow enough food to feed ourselves. While relatively wealthier countries like the United States have the resources and technology to adapt to some of these changes, poorer countries are far more vulnerable and less able to adapt. Since the vast majority of the greenhouse gas emissions that are causing climate change have come from wealthy countries like the United States, there is a clear ethical problem in this situation. Likewise, today's population changing the climate for future generations poses an enormous ethical dilemma. In terms of economic impact, many of the most immediate approaches to reducing greenhouse gas emissions actually involve reducing energy use and saving money. Also, renewable energy sources like wind and the sun are domestic forms of energy whose development could help spur economic activity in the United States. Much of the opposition to addressing climate change has come from fossil fuel industries (especially coal and oil) that stand to see their profits reduced dramatically if any serious efforts are made to address global climate change.

    Learn more about this here:
    - http://www.ucsusa.org/global_warming/solutions/reduce-emissions/climate-2030-blueprint.html

8. *What are the major impacts of global climate change? What does the future hold and what chance do we have to adapt to changing conditions?*

    While not all of the impacts of global climate change will be entirely negative, we are already witnessing some of the consequences of a warming world. Scientists studying the impacts of climate change typically categorize these into water supply and quality, ecosystem changes, food production, coastal flooding and erosion, and human health impacts. For example, climate change is contributing to shifts in precipitation patterns and thus in water availability. While some areas get more water, others get less, and shifting human settlements and food production systems to where water is available is not really feasible on any sort of large scale. Ecosystem impacts include shifting ranges for wildlife and plants and the possible extinction of as many as one-third of all species on the planet. More erratic weather and shifting precipitation patterns could disrupt food production in many areas, especially for some of the poorest and most vulnerable people on the planet. Sea level rise from warmer oceans and melting ice is already resulting in increased floods and coastal erosion in low-lying areas home to tens of millions of people around the world. Finally, negative impacts on human health include increased heat stress, increased malnutrition from crop failures, and the spread of diseases into new areas. While adaptation is possible in some cases, the ability to adapt is often a function of wealth and technological capacity. It is the poorest and most vulnerable populations on the planet who are least responsible for global climate change but who will feel the worst consequences of this phenomenon.

Learn more about this here:
• http://www2.sunysuffolk.edu/mandias/global_warming/impact_climate_change.html
• http://changingclimates.colostate.edu/docs/BellCurveAveragesExtremes.pdf
• http://www.climatehotmap.org
• http://extremeicesurvey.org

Vocabulary Check up

The italicized words below are found in the article on *Global Climate Change and Ozone Depletion*. Use clues to get the meaning of each word. Write the letter of the word in the space provided.

_____1. Much more of this sun's shortwave *radiation* is absorbed by the Earth's surface and then given off or reradiated as heat energy.
   a. effect   c. transfer
   b. circulation   d. emission

_____2. These gases could also be thought of as windows in a *greenhouse* or car, allowing sunlight to pass through the atmosphere but trapping the heat that tries to escape.
   a. room chiefly of glass with certain temperature
   b. house that is colored green
   c. house of plants
   d. room that is hot

_____3. When we talk of global warming, we are really referring to an *enhanced* greenhouse effect caused by human emissions of greenhouse gases like carbon dioxide.
   a. uncertain earth's temperature
   b. increased earth's temperature
   c. very cold and very hot temperature
   d. hot temperature

_____4. Scientists *attribute* the absence of rainfall to warming of the atmosphere.
   a. answer   c. point to
   b. consider   d. question

_____5. Scientists start by looking at all of the different possible causes of warming and then examine whether any of them provide a *plausible* explanation for what we are seeing.
   a. correct   c. smooth
   b. very likely   d. different

_____6. It is the poorest and most *vulnerable* populations on the planet who are least responsible for global climate change but who will feel the worst consequences of this phenomenon.
   a. developed   c. defenseless
   b. underdeveloped   d. wealthy

_____7. Today's population changing the climate for future generations poses an *enormous* problem that has to be solved immediately.
   a. important   c. current
   b. huge   d. indirect

_____8. While not all of the *impacts* of global climate change will be entirely negative, we are already witnessing some of the consequences of a warming world.
   a. direct cause   c. strong effects
   b. problems   d. questions

Comprehension

Use your own words to answer the following questions.

1. What is a greenhouse effect? _____
   _____

2. How are the greenhouse effect, global warming, and global climate change different?
   _____
   _____
   _____
   _____

3. How do human activities contribute to climate change, and are they more or less important than natural factors?
   _____
   _____
   _____
   _____

4. Do you believe in climate change? Why or why not?

_____

_____

_____

_____

_____

_____

Paragraph Patterns

A paragraph usually shows a topic, a main idea, and supporting details. Sentences in a paragraph connect and make sense through transitions or logical ideas that are presented in a pattern. The things that you learned in previous chapters will help you recognize how the ideas in a paragraph are presented or organized. Identifying the organizational pattern of a paragraph will help you better understand what you read.

Topics

List

Time

Definition and Example

Comparison

Contrast

Comparison and Contrast

Description

Spatial

Classification

Cause and Effect

In writing a paragraph, a writer usually considers a topic, a main idea, and supporting details. Sentences in a paragraph are organized or presented in a pattern. Since you read what a writer has written, it is important that you are able to recognize the different organizational patterns or how paragraphs are presented and organized.

A paragraph pattern may show a list of ideas, events, processes or steps, a definition of a word and examples, similarities between things or ideas, differences between given information, description of a thing or a place, location of a place, classifications or groups, and outcomes with reasons. A pattern repeatedly shows the same way of presenting ideas. For example, a comparison pattern includes sentences that show how given things are similar.

List

The organizational pattern of a paragraph is a list if it includes a number of major details that support or tell about the main idea. Rearranging the order of the major details does not affect the main idea and the sense of the paragraph. Paying attention to the signal words that help you recognize the major details in Chapter 4 and the transitions on additions in Chapter 3 will help you identify the list that is given and the number of major details or items in the list. It is important to pay attention to the signal words because these help you to comprehend what you read.

Example

There are many ways to become a successful student in college. It is telling you about many ways to become a successful student. Due to the word many, you may expect to hear the different ways to become a successful student or a list of sentences that follow tell you the different ways. If you see sentences that state the different ways, then the pattern is a list. A list of signal words that show a list pattern is shown below.

Signal Words		
different kinds	several types	some steps
few reminders	five ways	series of events
various results	many ways	a number of reasons
as follows	following	among the similarities

In a list pattern, you may see words that show addition. The purpose of these words is to show that the writer is including two or more ideas in the list. Recall that you learned these words when we discussed about the relationships between ideas in sentences. A list of addition words is shown below. In case a paragraph does not show any transition, you will recognize a list pattern if the major details support the main idea or show why the sentence is a main idea.

Rearranging the order of given major details will not affect the sense of the paragraph.

Addition Words

one	to begin with	for one thing	first (of all)
second(ly)	in addition	next	further
third(ly)	other	another	also
last (of all)	moreover	finally	furthermore

Example

₁Students can follow some good habits that may help them to become successful in college. ₂To begin with, attend your class regularly, so you will not miss any discussion notes. ₃Second, listen attentively to the class discussion. ₄In addition, follow the guidelines for submitting assignments. ₅Finally, do well on tests.

Using ACTOR

1. Read the first sentence. <u>Students can follow some good habits that may help them to become successful in college.</u> What or who are we talking about in this sentence? (Students). What is being said about them? (Can follow some strategies to become successful in college). **Activate** prior knowledge of the content or vocabulary.
2. **Connect** this knowledge to the new information, so you can relate to what you are reading.
3. **Trigger strategies**: Break down the sentence, ask questions, or visualize. Do these and other strategies to be sure that you understand every sentence. Connect the idea of each sentence to the preceding or succeeding sentence, so that everything makes sense or connects. Talk to yourself and analyze. The second sentence says <u>to begin with, attend your class regularly, so you will not miss any discussion notes</u> (this is one way to do well in college). The third sentence is about <u>listening attentively to the class discussion</u> (this is another way that may help you do well because you pay attention). The fourth sentence is about <u>following the guidelines for submitting assignments</u> (this may help students do well because all assignment requirements are met). The last sentence tells you <u>to do well on tests</u> (this may help to succeed in college).
4. **Organize** in your mind the ideas that you got from reading. The first sentence, the main idea states that students can follow some good habits that may help them to become successful in college. The rest of the sentences list these habits. Therefore, the pattern is a list.
5. **Respond** by reciting or writing what you understand. State the main idea and details. Doing this enables you to find out if you understand and remember what you read.

₁Students can follow some good habits that may help them to become successful in college. ₂To begin with, attend your class regularly, so you will not miss any discussion notes. ₃Second, listen attentively to the class discussion. ₄In addition, follow the guidelines for submitting assignments. ₅Finally, do well on tests.

Topic: Ways to become a successful student

Main idea: Students can follow some good habits that may help them to become successful in college.

Major details: Four ways to become a successful student—Sentences 2, 3, 4, and 5

Reason for the list pattern: The details show a list of ways to become a successful student.

Practice 1

Identify the topic, main idea, and reasons for the list pattern of the paragraph. Write your answers in the spaces provided.

1Environmental health professionals are well known for their efforts to ensure the safety of what we eat, breathe, touch, and drink. 2They monitor air quality, water and noise pollution, toxic substances, and pesticides. 3They also conduct restaurant inspections. 4In addition, they carry out vector control. 5Fourth, they promote healthy land use and housing.

Source: Beck, Environmental Health, Kendall Hunt Publishing Company, 2013.

Topic: _____

Main idea: _____

Major details: Sentences: _____

Reason for the list pattern: _____

Practice 2

Complete the list below.

1. A cell phone is a necessity in life for the following reasons.

   a. _____

   b. _____

2. Some of the benefits of space research and launching to mankind are as follows:

   a. _____

   b. _____

3. There are various positive developments in the treatment of serious diseases.

   a. _____

   b. _____

   c. _____

4. Regular exercises are good for the body for a number of reasons.

   a. _____

   b. _____

   c. _____

5. It may benefit someone who experiences hopelessness to do the following:

   a. _____

   b. _____

   c. _____

Time

The organizational pattern of a paragraph is time if it includes a number of major details that support or tell about the main idea in a certain order. Rearranging the order of the major details affects the smooth flow of ideas or the sense of the paragraph. Paying attention to the signal words that help you recognize the major details in Chapter 4 and the transitions on time in Chapter 3 will help you identify this pattern and the number of major details or items. If you do not see any time transition, you can still recognize if the paragraph follows a time pattern. Ask what is the paragraph telling you? Does it show a sequence of events, steps, or processes that should be in order?

Time Words

before	previously	first (of all)	until
immediately	next	second(ly)	then
following	eventually	final(ly)	later
whenever	while	when	last (of all)
third(ly)	during	often	by
frequently	now	after	currently

Example

1In the 1950s, a very successful research mathematician named George Polya began writing a series of insightful articles and books on problem solving. 2The four steps that Polya used to describe the mathematical problem-solving process follow. 3Understand the problem. 4Devise a plan. 5Carry out the plan. 6Look back.

Using ACTOR

1. Read the first sentence. In the 1950s, a very successful research mathematician named George Polya began writing a series of insightful articles and books on problem solving. What or who are we talking about in this sentence? (George Polya). What is being said about him? (Began writing a series of insightful articles and books on problem solving). **Activate** prior knowledge of the content or vocabulary.
2. **Connect** this knowledge to the new information, so you can relate to what you are reading.
3. **Trigger strategies**: Break down the sentence, ask questions, or visualize. Do these and other strategies to be sure that you understand every sentence. Connect the idea of each sentence to the preceding or succeeding sentence, so that everything makes sense or connects. Talk to yourself and analyze. The first sentence is an introduction while the second sentence is the main idea. The second sentence says that the four steps Polya used to describe the mathematical problem-solving process follow. The third sentence is about understanding the problem. To solve it, there is a need to devise a plan as shown in the fourth sentence. (It is the next step because there is a problem.) The fifth sentence is about carrying the plan. (This is the next step because if there is a plan, there is a need to carry it.) The last sentence is look back. (This is the last step in the problem-solving process. This means to review the result of the plan.) Sentences 3–6 are the steps. Therefore, the paragraph follows a time order because the sentences must be in order to complete the problem-solving process. Notice that transitions are not used.
4. **Organize** in your mind the ideas that you got from reading. What is the paragraph about?
5. **Respond** by reciting or writing what you understand. State the main idea and details. Doing this enables you to find out if you understand and remember what you read. This information will be a part of your prior knowledge that can help you in reading, writing, and other tasks in the future.

1In the 1950s, a very successful research mathematician named George Polya began writing a series of insightful articles and books on problem solving. 2The four steps that Polya used to describe the mathematical problem-solving process follow. 3Understand the problem. 4Devise a plan. 5Carry out the plan. 6Look back.

Topic: _____ Steps in a mathematical problem _____

Main idea: The four steps that Polya used to describe the mathematical problem-solving process.

Major details: Fours steps that are found in sentences 3, 4, 5, and 6

Reason for the time pattern: ___ The list of steps are in order to complete the problem-solving process. Rearranging the sentences does not make sense. _____

Practice 1

Identify the topic, main idea, major details, and reason for the time pattern. Write your answers in the spaces provided.

₁A man jumped out of his car when he saw an elderly woman who was trying to cross the tracks in front of an oncoming train. ₂Then he quickly sprinted on to the tracks, pulled her out of the way according to witnesses. ₃He guided the woman away from the tracks. ₄Onlookers gave the driver a big round of applause. ₅The police officers took the woman to a nearby hospital for evaluation while the man went to work. ₆To his surprise, he was greeted by cheering co-employees.

Topic: _____

Main idea: _____

Major details: Sentences: _____

Reason for the time pattern: _____

Practice 2

Fill in the blanks with words that will complete the sense of each item.

1. Last year, I _____ in _____ school.
   This year, _____ graduate.
   Later, I will _____ company.

2. In 2017, _____ was elected _____.
   In 2008, Barack Obama _____.
   After four years, _____ was reelected.

3. Decades ago, computers were _____ and heavy. Later, these became small.
   Now, these are even _____.

Definition and Example

The organizational pattern of a paragraph is a definition and an example if a word is being defined and examples are given to clarify the meaning. The clues that you learned in Chapter 2 will help you determine if a word is being defined. These clues include is defined as, are, means, refers to, and punctuation marks like a comma, parenthesis, and a dash. The words that signal examples will also help you recognize the definition and example pattern. Review the example words that follow.

Example Words

for example	specifically	including
for instance	to illustrate	includes
to be specific	like	such as

Example

1Norms are the established standards of behavior that is understood and observed by the members of a society. 2For example, in movie theaters in a certain country, it is typically expected that people will be quiet while a serious artistic film is shown. 3Another example is children respect their elders.

Using ACTOR

1. Read the first sentence. Norms are the established standards of behavior that is understood and observed by the members of a society. What are we talking about in this sentence? (Norms). What is being said about it? (Established behavior that is understood and shown by the people in a community). **Activate** prior knowledge of the content or vocabulary.
2. **Connect** this knowledge to the new information, so you can relate to what you are reading.
3. **Trigger strategies**: Break down the sentence, ask questions, or visualize. Do these and other strategies to be sure that you understand every sentence. Connect the idea of each sentence to the preceding or succeeding sentence, so that everything makes sense or connects. Talk to yourself and analyze. The second sentence begins with an example in a movie theater where everyone is expected to be quietly watching a movie. (This is an accepted behavior that everyone is expected to show.) The third gives an additional example of an observed practice (respecting the elderly).
4. **Organize** in your mind the ideas that you got from reading. The first sentence, the main idea, states the meaning of norms. The rest of the sentences provide examples of norms. Therefore, the paragraph pattern is a definition and an example because the word <u>norms</u> is defined and followed by two examples.
5. **Respond** by reciting or writing what you understand. State the main idea and details. Doing this enables you to find out if you understand and remember what you read. This information will be a part of your prior knowledge that can help you in reading, writing, and other doing other tasks in the future.

1Norms are the established standards of behavior that is understood and followed by the members of a society. 2For example, in movie theaters in a certain country, it is typically expected that people will be quiet while a serious artistic film is shown. 3Another example is children respect their elders.

Word that is defined: _____Norms_____

Meaning: Norms are the established standards of behavior that is understood and observed by the members of a society.

Examples: ___Sentences 2 and 3 give examples of norms._____
_____

Reason for the definition and example pattern: ___The first sentence gives the definition while the second and third sentences give examples of norm._____

Practice 1

You use indicators, the things, situations or knowledge that help you make decisions based on the current state, what might change that state, and why. For example, a blue sky and 85°F temperatures when you wake up on a July morning *indicate* that you should wear a T-shirt, shorts, or other light clothing that day (current state of the weather). If you are familiar with the climate system in which you live, then you can also anticipate what might cause the weather to change that day and why. If you live in the southwestern and much of the western United States, you know that typical weather patterns in July and August cause the weather to change from clear blue skies in the morning to rainy thunderheads by the afternoon. Based on this information, you might choose to bring along an umbrella because climate records *indicate* what might cause the current state to change.

Source: Beck, Environmental Health, Kendall Hunt Publishing Company, 2013.

Word that is defined: _____

Main idea: _____
_____

Major details: _____
_____

Reason for the definition and example pattern: _____
_____
_____

Practice 2

Each of the words below is defined. Write an example in the space provided.

Example:

Import means goods or services are brought into a country from abroad for sale. Example—Cars and car spare parts from Japan are sold in the United States.

1. Export—send goods or services to another country for sale

   Example _____

   _____

2. Trade deficit—an economic condition that occurs when a country is importing more goods than it is exporting.

   Example_____

   _____

Comparison

The organizational pattern of a paragraph is a comparison if the paragraph shows similarities between or among things, places, persons, or items. Paying attention to the comparison words that you learned in Chapter 3 will help you recognize given similarities in a paragraph or in given information. Review the list below.

Comparison Words

just as	both	in like manner	in a similar fashion	same
just like	common	in the same way	in a similar manner	because similarity
similarly	alike	equally resemble	in like fashion	likewise

Example

1The computer is similar to fire because they both have dual natures. 2Fire provides warmth on a cold night. 3Sometimes, it destroys property or kills people. 4Likewise, the computer provides access to knowledge. 5It can also be used to steal our identities.

Using ACTOR

1. Read the first sentence. The computer is similar to fire because they both have dual natures. What or who are we talking about in this sentence? (Computer and fire). What is being said about them? (Have dual natures). **Activate** prior knowledge of the content or vocabulary.
2. **Connect** this knowledge to the new information, so you can relate to what you are reading.

3. **Trigger strategies**: Break down the sentence, ask questions, or visualize. Do these and other strategies to be sure that you understand every sentence. Connect the idea of each sentence to the preceding or succeeding sentence, so that everything makes sense or connects. Talk to yourself and analyze. The second sentence says <u>fire provides warmth on a cold night</u>. (This is a nature or characteristic of fire—something good.) The third sentence tells us that sometimes, <u>fire destroys property or kills</u>. (This is true about fire—something negative.) The fourth sentence starts with likewise, a signal word that signals similarity. <u>The computer provides knowledge</u>—something good. The fifth sentence states that the computer <u>can be used for stealing information</u>—something bad.

4. **Organize** in your mind the ideas that you got from reading. The first sentence, the main idea, states that <u>fire and computer have dual natures</u>. Sentences 2 and 3 tell about the good and bad natures of fire. Like fire, a computer also has good and bad qualities as shown in Sentences 4 and 5. Therefore, the pattern is comparison because the fire and computer are compared and both have bad and good characteristics.

5. **Respond** by reciting or writing what you understand. State the main idea and details. How is fire similar to a computer? Doing this enables you to find out if you understand and remember what you read. This information will be a part of your prior knowledge that can help you in reading, writing, and doing other tasks in the future.

1The computer is similar to fire because both have dual natures. 2Fire provides warmth on a cold night. 3Sometimes, it destroys property or kills people. 4Likewise, the computer provides access to knowledge. 5It can also be used to steal our identities.

Topic: _____ Dual natures of fire and computer _____

Main idea: _____ Fire and computer have dual natures or characteristics _____

Reason for the comparison pattern: ___ Computer and fire can be both good and bad. ____

Practice

Read the paragraph and identify the topic, main idea, and reason for the comparison pattern.

1A Trojan horse is an attack used along with viruses and worms in a computer. 2The term comes from a story in ancient Greek mythology about a beautiful wooden horse that was left outside the gates of Troy. 3The horse looked like a gift, but when the citizens of Troy brought it inside the city's gates and opened it up, Greek soldiers jumped out and managed to capture the city. 4Similarly, in computer terminology, a Trojan horse is a program that hides its true intent and looks like it is performing important functions. 5In reality, it is hiding a malicious intent, which is usually to allow someone to gain unauthorized access to a computer or network.

Topic: _____

Main idea: _____

_____

_____

Reason for the comparison pattern: _____

_____

Contrast

The organizational pattern of a paragraph is a contrast if the paragraph shows differences between or among things, places, persons, or items. Paying attention to the contrast words that you learned in Chapter 3 will help you recognize given differences in a paragraph. A list of contrast words is shown below.

Contrast Words				
however	instead	yet	in spite of	rather than
but	in contrast	as opposed to	even though	despite
while	on the contrary	unlike	although	
conversely	different	on the other hand	nevertheless	

Example

Let us study the example below using ACTOR, What are being contrasted in this paragraph? What is the main idea? What are the details that show differences?

1In high school, you are required to attend classes at 8:00 a.m. to 3:00 p.m. every day. 2You take the same subjects for the academic year. 3On the other hand, you can choose the days and time that you want to attend classes every term in college. 4In high school, tests are announced during the year. 5In college, test schedules are written in the syllabus that is distributed at the beginning of the term.

Topic: _____ Differences between high school and college

Main idea: _____ There are differences between high school and college.

Differences: _____ Start and end of classes and test schedules

Practice

What are being contrasted in this paragraph? What is the main idea? What are the details that show differences?

Industrial health professionals are usually the heroes behind the scenes. They keep companies in compliance with a variety of regulations, and consequently help save a significant amount of money in the process. So, what exactly is the difference between public and industrial environmental health careers? Well, public health officials are typically the enforcers of regulations set forth by the state and/or federal government. They protect the public from environmental influences such as lead, radiation, insect vectors, and disease or illness caused by food, pools, sewage, and the like. Industrial professionals protect the environment from the byproducts of manufacturing, assembling, and packaging of commodities we all depend on.

Source: Beck, Environmental Health, Kendall Hunt Publishing Company, 2013.

Topic: _____

Main idea: _____

Differences: _____

_____

Comparison and Contrast

The organizational pattern of a paragraph is a comparison and contrast if the paragraph shows both similarities and differences between or among things, places, persons, or items. Paying attention to comparison and contrast words and given similarities and differences will help you recognize this pattern.

Example:

1Both electric and gas ranges are used for cooking. 2These are also available in different models. 3Like the electric range, the gas range features four burners. 4The electric range uses electricity while the gas range uses gas. 5When there is power failure, the electric range does not work. 6However, the gas range functions during a power outage.

Topic: Similarities and differences between an electric range and a gas range

Main idea: There are similarities and differences between an electric range and a gas range.

Major details: Similarities—Sentences 2 and 3 and Differences—Sentences 4 and 5

Reason for the comparison and contrast pattern: The paragraph shows both similarities and differences between an electric range and a gas range.

Description

The organizational pattern of a paragraph is a description if all or most of the sentences state the characteristics or features of an object, a person, a place, or a thing. Ask, what is being described? What are the characteristics of this?

Example

When you go to New Jersey or New York, you may try to visit the New York Harbor, Liberty Island. There, you will see the Statue of Liberty. It is a female figure standing upright. It is dressed in a robe and a seven point spiked rays representing a nimbus (halo), holding a stone tablet close to her body in her left hand and a flaming torch high in her right hand. The tablet bears the words "JULY IV MDCCLXXVI" (July 4, 1776), commemorating the date of the United States Declaration of Independence. The statue is made of a sheeting of pure copper, hung on a framework of with the exception of the flame of the torch, which is coated in gold leaf. The height of the copper statue to torch is 151 feet 1 inch (46 meters).

Source: https://www.nps.gov/npnh/learn/news/fact-sheet-stli.htm.

What is described? _____

Descriptions: _____

_____

Practice

Describe the following:

1. Twenty-dollar bill _____

   _____

   _____

   _____

   _____

   _____

2. Your dream house _____

   _____

   _____

   _____

   _____

   _____

Spatial

The organizational pattern of a paragraph is spatial if it tells about a location of a thing, a place, or an object. Words that signal locations include west, south, north, east, on top, next to, adjacent to, behind, to the left, at the bottom, and other words that show whereabouts.

Example

Florida is a state of the United States of America. It is located in the southeastern region of the United States. It is bordered to the west by the Gulf of Mexico, to the north by Alabama and Georgia, to the east by the Atlantic Ocean, and to the south by the Straits of Florida and Cuba.

Topic: Florida

Reason for the spatial pattern: The paragraph tells about the location of Florida.

Classification

The pattern of a paragraph is classification if it shows different categories, sections, parts, divisions, or groups.

Example

The Constitution of the United States divides the federal government into three branches to ensure a central government in which no individual or group gains too much control, the legislative, executive, and judicial. The legislative makes laws (Congress). The executive carries out laws (president, vice president and cabinet). The judicial branch evaluates laws (Supreme Court and other courts).

Topic _____ Branches of US government _____

Branch 1 _____

Function _____

Branch 2 _____

Function _____

Branch 3 _____

Function _____

Practice

Write the missing information.

1. Academic structure

   a. Superintendent

   b. _____

   c. Teachers

2. Family structure

   a. _____

   b. Parents

   c. _____

3. Types of loans

   a. Business

   b. _____

Cause and Effect

The paragraph pattern is cause and effect if it presents a cause or reason and effect or outcome of a situation or an event. Paying attention to the cause and effect words that you learned in Chapter 3 and reasons and outcomes or results will help you recognize a cause and effect paragraph organizational pattern. A list of words that signal this pattern is shown below.

Cause and Effect Words

due to	so	therefore	accordingly
because	as a result	effect	reason
as a consequence	results in	cause	thus
consequently	leads to	if . . . then	since

Example

1Sudden bleeding in the brain can cause a hemorrhagic stroke. 2The bleeding causes swelling of the brain and increased pressure in the skull. 3The swelling and pressure damage brain cells and tissues.

Cause (Due to)	Effect (Result to)
Sudden bleeding in the brain	hemorrhaging stroke
Bleeding	swelling in the brain
Swelling	damage brain cells

Practice

Fill in the blanks with the missing cause or effect.

1. I am inspired because _____.

2. Some people did not survive from the wrath of the storm, so _____
_____.

3. Due to the severe snowstorm, _____
_____

   and _____.

4. All the players worked extremely well as a team. As a result, _____
_____.

5. The new job opportunity came as a surprise because _____
_____.

6. Since more people buy online, some retail stores that used to be profitable _____
_____.

7. The drought devastated the farmers because _____
_____.

8. The government helped the farmers in order to _____
_____.

9. I would like to graduate with honors, so I _____
_____,_____
_____, _____
_____,

   and _____.

10. To protect your computer from viruses, _____
_____
_____.

Summary of Patterns of Paragraph Organizations

Paragraph Patterns	Purpose	Sample Signal Words
List	presents major details in any order	several, some, few, series, many, various, types, following, and as follows
Time	shows events that follow an order	first, next, during, now, finally, last, later, then, before, as soon as, while, and until
Definition and Example	defines a term and gives examples	means, is, is defined as, for example, to illustrate, for instance, such as, and includes
Comparison	shows similarities	in a similar way, in like manner, also, and likewise
Contrast	presents differences	however, yet, although, but, nevertheless, conversely, and on the other hand
Description	lists characteristics	is, are, can be described as, makes, and will be
Spatial	states location	adjacent to, near, around, below, at the right side, and to the left
Classification	gives categories or groups	categories, groups, sections, levels, and parts
Cause and Effect	states the reason and outcomes or results	because, due to, for this reason, therefore, as a result, thus, and consequently

Mastery Test 1

Each of the items shows a paragraph pattern. Write the letter of the pattern in the space provided.

_____1. A computer is a storage of a vast amount of information on people all over the world. Data such as books checked out at the library, food purchased at the grocery store, clothing bought online, phone calls made and the duration, medical histories, and tax and educational records are all stored in a computer.
    a. definition and example   c. time
    b. description   d. classification

_____2. The story of the computer is both positive and negative. You can buy something without leaving your house. You can also conduct research without going to the library. However, it can also be used to steal money online. There are some murder cases that involve victims who communicated through online chats.
    a. comparison   c. contrast
    b. comparison and contrast   d. list

_____3. In 1960, the US Navy put into service its Transit satellite to help ships to go to different locations. In 1973, the US military began to plan for a comprehensive worldwide navigational system, which eventually became known as the GPS (global positioning system). In 1983, President Reagan announced that the navigation capabilities of the GPS would be available to civilian use. Currently, new cars have built-in GPS that guides drivers to previously unknown destinations.

  a. list   b. spatial   c. time   d. contrast

_____4. Computers can often be at risk from a program called a virus. A virus is a series of computer instructions or code that can replicate itself and infect other computers. Viruses include Storm, Sasser, and Melissa.

  a. description   c. list

  b. time   d. definition and example

_____5. People contract viruses by opening e-mail attachments. Another way of infecting your computer is from downloading files and programs from the Internet. Your computer may also get a virus by opening suspicious greeting cards and screen savers. Lastly, browsing through a bad website may affect your computer.

  a. list   c. definition and example

  b. classification   d. comparison

_____6. The sculptor's formula for achieving ideal symmetry and balance in representations of the human form rests in his belief in the existence of underlying harmonic proportions that could be expressed in mathematical terms. In its practical application, Polykleitos's canon resulted in a figure that measured seven and one-half heads tall, with the distance from the top of the head to the chest one-fourth of the total height. Thus, each part of the body of Doryphoros is harmoniously related to all of the other parts, beginning with an appendage as small as a finger joint. In fact, the pinkie finger of the figure's left hand is extended to emphasize this point.

  a. list   c. definition and example

  b. cause and effect   d. comparison

_____7. Delving more deeply into the climate science behind these patterns can explain why monsoon season weather causes the system to change throughout the day. There is moisture in the air during the monsoon. The air temperature rises from 85°F in the morning to 110°F in the afternoon. The moist hot air rises and, as it rises, it cools. Cold air holds less moisture than hot air so, at some high altitude in the atmosphere, the maximum capacity for the cooler air to hold moisture will eventually be exceeded, and it will rain.

  a. list   c. definition and example

  b. cause and effect   d. comparison

_____8. Once a person chooses a career, there are many different options they may be explored such as public health. One can work for the federal, state, or local government. One may practice as a generalist or specialize in one of the many different areas within the purview of public health. One may also become an epidemiologist, work in the preparedness arena, and prepare state and local employees for all hazards and disasters.

  a. time   c. cause and effect

  b. time and cause and effect   d. list

Mastery Test 2

Each of the items shows a paragraph pattern. Write the letter of the pattern in the space provided.

_____1. Basic research is the term used to describe research that is conducted to increase our general understanding of a topic, phenomenon, or area of study. Its purpose is to increase our basic level of knowledge. Examples of this include basic medical research, archeological research, and basic physics or chemistry research. Basic research is often conducted by academic researchers who hope to increase our understanding of the world around us.

    Source: Graeff, Marketing Research for Managerial Decision Making. Kendall Hunt Publishing Company, 2013.

  a. definition and example   c. description

  b. time   d. cause and effect

_____2. The entire system by which marketing research data and information is collected, analyzed, stored, and transformed into reports that can be used for making managerial decisions is referred to as a marketing information system. The marketing information system for an organization can be as simple as a single paper and pencil survey that is manually administered and analyzed, or as complex as a computerized customer loyalty program for automatically capturing customer purchase behavior by using scanner data.

    Source: Graeff, Marketing Research for Managerial Decision Making. Kendall Hunt Publishing Company, 2013.

  a. definition and example   c. definition and description

  b. description   d. cause and effect

_____3. Sometimes, respondents will even answer questions when they know nothing about the topic of the question. People do not want to appear ignorant, so they will sometimes give uninformed opinions about products or brands. If this happens, marketing managers will make decisions based on meaningless answers that respondents gave merely because they felt obligated to respond. This is called uninformed response bias. To illustrate how often this occurs and how easy it is for someone to provide such uninformed opinions, look at the exercise survey shown in the box titled "Take This Survey." If you completed this survey and you circled a number on the attitude scale for Pontrey athletic shoes, then you just gave an uninformed opinion. Pontrey is a fictitious brand—it does not exist!

    Source: Graeff, Marketing Research for Managerial Decision Making. Kendall Hunt Publishing Company, 2013.

  a. definition and example

  b. cause and effect and definition

  c. cause and effect, definition, and example

  d. cause and effect and example

_____4. Let's go through some scenarios that might be encountered by an industrial environmental, safety, and health professional on any given day: A new waste is discovered and needs to be disposed of properly. A sample must be sent to a lab to determine whether it is a hazardous waste or not. You must obtain the sample and ensure it gets to the lab promptly. Once the results are received, you must then create a profile based on the contents (metals, volatile organic compounds, etc.), ignitability, corrosivity, reactivity, and toxicity. Using what you've learned from training, you profile this waste and determine the best, most economical way to dispose of it.

a. list of items
b. cause and effect
c. time
d. list and cause and effect

_____ 5. Someone announces over the intercom that there's been a spill in the facility. You drop what you're doing and respond to the area immediately. Since you manage the company's hazard communication program, you are very familiar with the chemicals that are used. After running to the spill area, you learn that the spill is hydrochloric acid. After you clear the area of employees, you and the facility's emergency responders put on proper personal protective equipment and work to clean up the spill, then ensure that it's disposed of properly.

a. time
b. time and cause and effect
c. cause and effect
d. list

_____ 6. A wastewater-treatment operator informs you that an excess of chromium was released to the sanitary sewer, which flows to the city's wastewater-treatment plant. This is a problem because the facility has a permit from the city utility and cannot exceed the limits set forth by the permit. You must notify the utility immediately of the release and determine the root cause for it. Within seven days you must send a report to the utility explaining what you found and what countermeasure you have implemented to fix the problem so that it doesn't happen again.

a. time
b. time and cause and effect
c. cause and effect
d. list

_____ 7. Oil was initially used in the United States to produce kerosene for illumination. It was discovered in large quantities first in Pennsylvania in the 1850s, though it would not be until the 1890s when demand for it rose because internal combustion engines were becoming more commonplace in industry and transportation. Oil was discovered in California and Texas around 1900, during which time a single company dominated the system for distributing and refining it—Rockefeller's Standard Oil Company. After 1900, the demand for oil products exploded—and so did Standard's wealth, along with threats from new competitors and government displeasure with Rockefeller's ruthless anti-competitive behavior. In 1911, Standard was broken up into more than a dozen independent companies, many of which still exist today, such as Chevron, Exxon, Mobil, Amoco, ARCO, and Conoco, among others.

a. time
b. time and cause and effect
c. cause and effect
d. list

_____ 8. A list of the traits and characteristics of environmental health practitioners has been developed by a group of experts (www.cdc.gov). Some of them include the following: Always try to keep a positive attitude, even though you are stressed. Negativity is like a virus that spreads to others and is not productive or becoming of anyone. Remember that everything won't always happen the way you want it to, but you have to work together in order to accomplish a common goal. Don't overthink situations. Use your common sense! You must uphold the highest ethics and resist the temptation to do something the easy way.

From *Contemporary Environmental Issues*, Second Edition, by Jon Turk and Terrence Bensel.
Copyright © 2014 by Bridgepoint Education, Inc. Reprinted by permission.

a. time
b. time and cause and effect
c. cause and effect
d. list

Mastery Test 3

Each of the items shows a paragraph pattern. Write the letter of the pattern in the space provided.

_____1. Environmental health specialists are expected to possess certain qualifications. They specialize in any area of environmental health, particularly milk and dairy production, food protection, sewage disposal, pesticide management, air and water pollution, hazardous waste disposal, occupational health, and wildlife health/management. They have to be comfortable with computers and other high-tech devices because they may be called upon to prepare and calibrate the equipment used to collect and analyze the samples. These professionals need to possess good social skills, as well as oral and written communication skills, because they may have to conduct, analyze, and dispense epidemiologic data regarding disease outbreaks within a community.

Contemporary Environment Issues p.29

a. list
b. list and cause and effect
c. cause and effect
d. description

_____2. The automobile has several [computers], including the GPS (global positioning system), a dashboard computer to control the digital gauges, an embedded computer in the DVD player, and a computer that runs the engine. As a result, a typical car now has more computers than many thought would exist in the entire United States.

From *Introduction to Digital Literacy*, Second Edition, by Mark D. Bowles.
Copyright © 2013 by Bridgepoint Education, Inc. Reprinted by permission.

a. list
b. list and cause and effect
c. cause and effect
d. description

_____3. It is important to understand the distinction between computers and information. The computer is the boxlike device that is connected to components like a monitor, mouse, and keyboard. It is the tablet-shaped device you are holding in your hand and interfacing with by swiping your fingers over the surface. The information is the data that can be stored, processed, and output from the computer.

From *Introduction to Digital Literacy*, Second Edition, by Mark D. Bowles.
Copyright © 2013 by Bridgepoint Education, Inc. Reprinted by permission.

a. list
b. contrast
c. comparison
d. definition and example

_____4. Digitizing information, which means turning books, music, and videos into a string of ones and zeros that computers can understand, would be useless without the corresponding advancements in computer technology. Likewise, the fastest

computers in the world would have very little significance if they had no information to process.
   a. comparison and list   c. comparison and cause and effect
   b. comparison and example   d. definition and example

_____5. Although it would be impossible to list all the places that people encounter computers today, a representative sample includes the following. Besides the standard desktop computer you can purchase at Best Buy® or Staples®, computers are also found in automobiles, jet airplanes, grocery store cash registers, ATM machines, cell phones, cameras, PDAs, e-book readers, televisions, video games, toys—and the list goes on. Small computers are even found in the printers used to print words and images from computers!
   a. list   c. description
   b. contrast   d. definition and example

_____6. Computers are used in the workplace for writing letters, compiling financial data in spreadsheets, tracking inventory and for other purposes. Law enforcement uses computers to track criminals. Scientists use computers to perform experimental simulations and map the human genome. Medical students can practice the art of surgery on a virtual computer-generated patient instead of a living one or a cadaver. Physicians use computers to create 3-D diagnostic images of the human body and to share patient data with other specialists throughout the world
   a. list   c. description
   b. cause and effect   d. definition and example

_____7. If your computer is hacked, important information such as your Social Security number may be stolen. This can pose a problem because the hacker can use your number to apply for a credit card. Using this credit card may put you in huge debt. If you get a bill for a debt that you did not incur, notify your creditor immediately to avoid paying it.
   a. list   c. description
   b. cause and effect   d. definition and example

_____8. Stop thinking that you will fail in this class because you are not a good test taker. Do something to improve your grades. If you do not do well on tests, search for effective test-taking strategies. Inquire from your professor if there is a provision for extra credits. Study with your classmates before the taking tests. Seek help from your professor or a tutor.
   a. time   c. cause and effect
   b. time and cause and effect   d. list

DEVELOPING GOOD CLASSROOM SURVIVAL TACTICS

1Remember when you were in elementary school and received a grade on your report card for classroom behavior? Even though you may not be given a conduct grade now, professors do have expectations related to your behavior in their class. Certain behaviors tend to differentiate the more successful academic students from other students.

Stockbyte, Learning, Curve, 162344RKERGB75, Kendall Hunt Publishing Company Resources

2 **Attend class regularly and arrive on time.** Students who attend class on a regular basis do better than other students. Attend class every day, *including the first day*. Professors generally give out the class syllabus and begin to lecture on the first day of class. A professor who is requesting a lot of assignments or presenting a fairly complex syllabus may choose to spend the entire period going over the syllabus and addressing other expectations related to the course. We have had many students in our classes over the years who seem confused about an assignment, paper, or project two weeks into the semester. Often, it's because they were not in class the first day. On the first day, we thoroughly review the syllabus and advice students on not only how to survive our classes, but how to excel.

3 **Know your class syllabus.** Your class syllabus is a "contract" between the students in the class and the professor teaching the class. Take notice of assignments, readings, tests, the grading procedure, and when and how to get in touch with your professor. As you read through the syllabus, take the time to transfer all deadlines to a master calendar. Know what is expected of you and when it is expected. What if you lose your syllabus? Replace it as soon as possible. See if your professor has a copy online or ask directly for a replacement. You could always borrow one from a classmate to copy. Do not try to navigate the class without a syllabus.

4 **Get a good seat.** (No, not in the back as far away from the professor as possible.) Sit up front, focus your attention on your professor, and remember to make eye contact. Your professor will notice you and will also notice if you appear interested. Sitting close to the professor will help you (or force you) to concentrate better. During class, avoid unnecessary communication with students seated around you. Also, avoid reading a newspaper, eating, texting, and other activities that show your disinterest.

5 **Prepare for class.** Read assignments and work problems, be familiar with terminology, and come with questions. Bring all needed supplies such as a calculator, paper, pencils, pens, a blue book, or other books.

6 **Get to know your professors.** What are your professors' office hours? E-mail addresses? Your professors are part of an educational system that can be difficult to maneuver in. When searching for answers to questions related to your college experience and career, remember to use your

professors as resources. Professors are also often more willing to write a letter of recommendation for a student who has taken the time and interest to get to know them.

7**Get to know some of your classmates.** Identify a responsible student in each class whom you can call or e-mail to get notes if needed. You might also want to identify students in class who may want to form a study group. When forming a study group, be sure to set up guidelines that spell out expectations for group members (e.g., commitment, regularly scheduled meeting times, and collaborative teaching within the group).

8**Know each professor's policy about absences.** Does your professor want you to call or e-mail? Is it okay to go by the professor's office to obtain handouts that you may have missed? You are responsible for all assignments and notes.

9**Participate in class.** Ask questions and share comments, appropriately. When you have a question to ask or a comment to make, think about it first and then ask yourself, "Will my question reveal the fact that I have not completed the assigned readings?" If so, do not take up class time with your question. Also, consider the timing of your comments or questions, avoid monopolizing class discussions, and respect different points of view.

Recall

Answer the following questions based on the given article, *Developing Good Classroom Survival Tactics.* Choose the word from the list that completes the sentence.

_____1. The contrast transition in the first paragraph is _____
    a. although   c. even though
    b. however   d. yet

_____2. The time transition in the third paragraph is _____.
    a. time   c. during
    b. as soon as   d. always

_____3. A time transition in paragraph six is _____.
    a. time   c. everyday
    b. often   d. sometimes

_____4. An addition transition in paragraph six is _____.
    a. too   c. resources
    b. also   d. in addition

_____5. The pattern of organization of the article is _____.
    a. time   c. cause and effect
    b. list   d. addition

Fill in the blanks

1. Students need to attend classes regularly due to the following reasons.

   a. _____

   _____

   b. _____

   _____

2. Your class syllabus is a "contract" between the students in the class and the professor teaching the class means that _____

   _____

3. Paragraph 4 states that you need to avoid the following:

   a. _____

   _____

   b. _____

   _____

4. The title is appropriate because it _____

   _____

   _____

5. Following the given tips for academic success will help students to become _____

   _____

   because of the following reasons.

   a. _____
   b. _____
   c. _____

6. Will you recommend to your friend to read this article? Explain your answer.

   _____

   _____

   _____

   _____

   _____

   _____

Reading Journal Guide (Informational Text)

Name _____ Date Submitted _____ Date Due _____

Title of Article _____ Date of Publication _____

Source of Publication _____

Choose any article from *Times, Newsweek,* or any informative magazine. The article must be related to Psychology, Sociology, Philosophy, Economics, Health, and other college courses. The article must have two pages or more. Attach a copy of the article. **(5 points)**

I. **Summary**—Write a summary using ten sentences or more. Be sure your summary is based on the entire article. It must have a thesis statement and relevant supporting details. **(10 points)**

II. **Comments**—Discuss your feelings, reactions, or beliefs about the article. Answer five questions from the list. Write your answer and details for each question in a paragraph form. Your answer in your point (1 sentence) and supports (at least four sentences) are major details. **(20 points)**

1. What did you feel while reading the article? Describe your feelings.

2. What were you reminded of while reading it? Discuss it.

3. Why did you choose this for your journal?

4. What did you learn from this article? Is it important to you? Explain.

5. What questions do you want to ask the author of the article? Why?

6. What is the importance of this article to you or to others? Discuss it.

7. What part of the article strikes you? Discuss it.

8. Have you read something similar to this? In what way is it the same or somehow related to the article?

9. Have you seen or heard something related to the article? Discuss it.

10. After reading this, is there a change in your established beliefs? Explain.

11. Do you think other people should read this? Why or why not?

12. Is it good that you read this article? Why or why not?

III. **Vocabulary**—Choose five words in the article. You may include unfamiliar words. Using the dictionary, write the meaning of each word. Be sure the meaning is similar to the way it is used in the article. Underline these words on the copy of the article that you are required to attach. **(5 points)**

IV. **Sentences**—Write your own sentence for each word. The sentence is satisfactory if it makes sense, gives clues to the meaning, and the meaning is the same as that of the given vocabulary word in the article. **(5 points)**

Grammar and Spelling (5 points)

Total Points _____/50 = _____   Letter Grade _____

7

Inference

Reading comprehension involves understanding what is clearly stated in every sentence. It also involves reading what is suggested in a sentence or groups of sentences. This comprehension skill is important in making interpretations and conclusions. In this chapter, you will learn to improve these skills.

Topics

Making Decisions

Figures of Speech

Inference in Fiction

Inference in Sayings or Quotes

Inference in Informational Texts

Perhaps, it may rain. What is the basis of your answer? Your answer is an inference. Making an inference is figuring out the unknown or giving a conclusion that is based on the given information, prior knowledge, and a logical explanation for the conclusion or the unknown that makes sense.

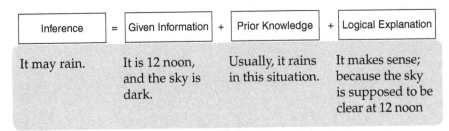

Inference	=	Given Information	+	Prior Knowledge	+	Logical Explanation
It may rain.		It is 12 noon, and the sky is dark.		Usually, it rains in this situation.		It makes sense; because the sky is supposed to be clear at 12 noon

Inference guides us in making decisions, reading fiction, proverbs or sayings, and informational texts, answering test questions and working on assignments and projects. For example, you bring an umbrella when there is a forecast that it will rain. When you read fiction—make-believe stories—you interpret what the author suggests. In poetry, the writer sometimes uses figures of speech such as simile, metaphor, hyperbole, idioms, euphemism, and other indirect statements. These words do not literally mean what you read. In reading informational texts, answering test questions, completing your projects and working on other tasks, you need to make interpretations based on common sense or logic.

Making Decisions

Every day, we are faced with a manageable routine or difficult situation that needs attention and actions. In a manageable situation, it is easy to handle because it does need a careful study. For some people, the attire to wear is not a problem. Determining the food to eat for lunch and dinner is simple. For some people, however, it may be a problem because they do not have the money to buy food. There are some difficult situations that need careful study. How do we deal with these situations? Inference can help you by studying the situation (the given information), prior knowledge, and a logical explanation for your action.

Example

You just lost your job. What will you do? _____
What is the reason for your action? _____

Practice

Study the situations below. Write your action and the reason for this action in the spaces provided.

1. You have a final examination today, and the professor does not allow for a makeup test. However, the accident on your way to school does not allow you to come on time.
    What will you do? _____
    _____
    Reason _____

2. You have an appointment for a job interview at 1 p.m. A woman rides with you in the elevator, and she tells you that she is scared and requests you to take her to the fifth floor.
   However, it is already 12:57 p.m.
   What will you do? _____

   Reason_____

3. It is the middle of the semester and your test scores are very low. In addition, you have many absences.
   What will you do? _____

   Reason _____

4. Your mother won five million dollars in the lottery. She is dying and tells you to take care of the money. You have five siblings.
   What will you do? _____

   Reason _____

5. Your father is very ill from a serious heart attack. He has so many tubes and kept alive by a machine. He has been staying in the hospital for one week.
   What will you do? _____

   Reason _____

Figures of Speech

Sometimes, writers use figures of speech in writing a story or poetry. These words do not have literal meanings. These words will stimulate your thinking because these do not convey the literal meanings—those that are found in the dictionary. Recognizing these figures of speech will help you better understand what you are reading. You may have learned how to recognize and interpret the meanings of words using figures of speech when you were in grammar and secondary schools.

Simile and Metaphor

Let us review the examples below.
   1. Your skin is silk.
   2. Your skin is as smooth as silk.

Let us analyze the sentences.
   1. What are we talking about in the first sentence? What is being said about it?
   2. What are we talking about in the second sentence? What is being said about it?
   3. How are the two sentences similar? How are the two sentences different?

The first sentence is a metaphor while the second sentence is a simile. What is a simile? What is a metaphor?

Hyperbole

A speaker uses hyperbole, an exaggeration of ideas to emphasize something.
Example
      I told you a million times, complete your reading lab requirement.
      What does a million times mean? _____
      Why does the speaker say it? _____

Personification

Personification is a figure of speech in which a thing, an idea, or an animal is given human qualities. The non-human objects are portrayed in such a way that we feel they have the ability to act and think like human beings.

Example: This desk is crying due to so many unnecessary writings on it.
What is the human quality of the desk? _____
Why is the desk crying? _____

You carry something in class, and you use it when you need it. It cries when you use it? What is it?
Answer _____Reason _____

Euphemism

A euphemism is a generally harmless word or expression that is used in place of one that may sound unpleasant.

Example: My aunt passed away.
What does it mean? _____
What is another word that is used to tell children that someone passed away?_____
Reason for using it _____

Practice

Identify the figure of speech in each sentence. Write the letter of the correct answer in the space provided.

_____1. The leaves were smiling to see a new sibling.
      a. simile   c. personification
      b. metaphor   d. hyperbole

_____2. I know that I will win the race because I fly like Superman.
      a. simile   c. euphemism
      b. metaphor   d. hyperbole

_____3. My heart melts when I hear the cry of a baby coming from the garbage can.
   a. hyperbole   c. euphemism
   b. metaphor   d. simile

_____4. I have been waiting for one year. Isn't our appointment at 9:00 a.m.? It is already 10 a.m.
   a. simile   c. euphemism
   b. metaphor   d. hyperbole

_____5. My love for you is as sweet as your favorite chocolate.
   a. hyperbole   c. euphemism
   b. metaphor   d. simile

_____6. You have to inspect the correctional facility to be sure that the prisoners will not escape.
   a. simile   c. euphemism
   b. metaphor   d. hyperbole

_____7. My computer is listening to the discussion in the classroom and ready to respond.
   a. euphemism   c. hyperbole
   b. personification   d. simile

_____8. The well will always have water, just like my heart will always have a room for you.
   a. hyperbole   c. euphemism
   b. metaphor   d. simile

_____9. She roars like a lion when she is very angry.
   a. euphemism   c. hyperbole
   b. simile   d. personification

_____10. When she is in a good mood, she is very lovely as a very cute little girl.
   a. hyperbole   c. euphemism
   b. metaphor   d. simile

Inference in Fiction

Writers use vivid descriptions of persons, places, or things. From these descriptions, readers can infer the characteristics and feelings of the character, the location where the story happens, the time when the story happens, the things that happen from the beginning to the end, and the person who is narrating the story.

Example:

"I have enjoyed so many things in life," whispered a man with so many tubes in his body. "With my days numbered, I cannot bring these things to where I will go."

   1. Who is speaking in the story? _____
   2. What is your basis for the answer? _____
   3. What did the man mean by my days are numbered?_____
   4. Where will he go? _____
   5. What is the basis for your answer for Question 4? _____

"The place where I worship, my college alma mater, my employees who helped me grow my company, the shelter where I grew up, and to you who has been with me through the years, I evenly leave $ 134 million. Then he pulled his last breath.

1. What is the meaning of last breath? _____
2. How much will the college receive? _____
3. What is the basis of your answer for Question 2? _____

Practice

Read the paragraph below. Use **ACTOR**—Activate prior knowledge, connect to new information, trigger strategies to understand every sentence and connect all ideas, organize, and respond. Apply the things that you have learned about vocabulary enhancement, transitions, main idea, supporting details, and paragraph patterns. Answer the questions that follow.

1In my country, I directly supervised 56 teachers and took care of about 2,000 students. 2Toward the end of the year, it gave me great joy to hand deserving students the fruits of their accomplishments as their parents, friends, and relatives joyfully watched. 3This time, I have to incessantly make all tables spotless. 4The traffic is so heavy with people who love to eat this circular-shaped ground meat between two slices of bread and sometimes leave the reddish sauce. 5I want to go back to my country to hug my children who I dearly love. 6Thanks to technology, I have been regularly talking and seeing them for 36 months. 7I have to endure the extreme cold at times, so I can help my son who needs a costly surgery and treatment. 8I can't wait to touch them in two years.

Choose the best word that completes the idea of each sentence. Write the letter of this word in the space provided. Write the logical explanation or the basis for your answer.

_____1. The speaker is a former _____ .
     a. store helper   c. principal
     b. teacher   d. superintendent
     Basis for the answer _____

_____2. The fruits of accomplishment means _____
     a. diploma   c. certificates
     b. awards   d. gifts
     Basis for the answer _____

_____3. The narrator is currently working in a _____
     a. deli store   c. hamburger restaurant
     b. supermarket   d. school cafeteria
     Basis for the answer _____

_____4. The narrator is working in a _____ country.
    a. tropical   c. poor
    b. rural area   d. Western
    Basis for the answer _____

_____5. The word endure in the last sentence means _____ .
    a. allow   c. withstand
    b. take   d. fight
    Basis for the answer _____

_____6. The main pattern of organization is _____.
    a. spatial   c. time
    b. list   d. description
    Basis for the answer _____

_____7. It takes _____ years for the narrator to go back to her country of origin.
    a. three   c. five
    b. two   d. one
    Basis for the answer _____

_____8. In sentence 4, people love to eat _____ .
    a. ham   c. tuna fish
    b. hamburger   d. mustard
    Basis for the answer _____

_____9. The word incessantly in sentence 3 means _____ .
    a. tirelessly
    b. carefully
    c. regularly
    d. sometimes
    Basis for the answer _____

____10. The cause and effect transition in sentence 7 is _____ .
    a. because
    b. due to
    c. so
    d. at times
    Basis for the answer _____

Inference in Sayings or Quotes

Some people say things that make you think and analyze your actions or situations, give you advice, or guide you to do better. These are called proverbs, quotes, or sayings. People from different cultures and places have unique proverbs. However, there are some that sound universal, and are commonly accepted and relatable. According to Mahatma Gandhi, "Live as if you were to die tomorrow. Learn as if you were to live forever." What does it mean? What are the benefits of remembering this quote?

Examine each saying below, write the meaning and an example. Write your answers in the space provided. You may share your answers with your classmates.

1. Happiness is when what you think, what you say, and what you do are in harmony. *(Mahatma Gandhi)*

   Meaning _____

   _____

   Example _____

   _____

   _____

2. It takes courage to grow up and become who you really are. *(E. E. Cummings)*

   Meaning _____

   _____

   Example _____

   _____

3. Great minds have great purposes, others have wishes. Little minds are tamed and sub-dued by misfortune; but great minds rise above them. *(Washington Irving)*

   Meaning _____

   _____

   Example _____

   _____

4. Anger is the enemy of non-violence and pride is a monster that swallows it up. *(Mahatma Gandhi)*

   Meaning _____

   _____

   Example _____

   _____

Read more at: https://www.brainyquote.com/quotes/authors/m/mahatma_gandhi.html
https://www.brainyquote.com/quotes/quotes/m/mahatmagan133995.html

Inference in Informational Texts

Information in textbooks is presented in paragraphs, pictures, charts, maps, graphs, and tables. You have to look at all details, so you can give a reasonable inference. You have to pay attention to the given information, prior knowledge, and a reasonable basis for your inference or conclusion. Use ACTOR and the things that you have learned in previous chapters.

Examine the picture and the paragraph that follows. What do these mean to you?

Pressmaster/Shutterstock.com

1Primary groups are small, intimate group of individuals whose opinions are very important to us. 2We try to please them and don't like it when they're mad at us. 3Primary group members are usually family and close friends. 4Secondary groups contain more people who are of less emotional importance to us. 5We associate with them in order to accomplish a particular social purpose. 6They may include our colleagues at work or school, our favorite waitresses at the diner, or members of our bowling league. 7Secondary group members may influence our behavior and attitudes (think of how youth are influenced by peer pressure), but in the big picture, it's what our family and close friends think that matters the most to us.

Source: Vissing, An Introduction to Sociology, Kendall Hunt Publishing Company, 2013.

The following statements are based on the paragraph. What does each sentence mean? Write an example to illustrate the meaning. The number in parentheses is the location of the sentence.

1. We try to please them and don't like it when they're mad at us. (2)
   Meaning _____
   Example _____

2. We associate with them in order to accomplish a particular social purpose. (5)
   Meaning _____
   Example _____

3. Secondary group members may influence our behavior and attitudes but in the big picture, it's what our family and close friends think that matters the most to us. (7)
   Meaning _____
   Example _____

Practice

Study the picture and answer each question.

CHANGING PARENTAL ROLES

Irinia/Shutterstock.com

1. What does the title suggest? _____
   _____

2. What is the basis of your answer?
   _____
   _____

3. Why is the father changing the baby's diaper? Write three possible reasons.

   a. _____
      _____

   b. _____
      _____

   c. _____
      _____

Study the information in the chart below. What does it mean?

States Ranked by Per Capita Income

All data is from the 2010–2014 American Community Survey 1-Year Estimates

Rank	State	Per capita income	Median household income	Median family income	Population	Number of households	Number of families
	District of Columbia	$45,877	$71,648	$84,094	658,893	277,378	117,864
1.	Connecticut	$39,373	$70,048	$88,819	3,596,677	1,355,817	887,263
2.	New Jersey	$37,288	$69,160	$87,951	8,938,175	2,549,336	1,610,581
3.	Massachusetts	$36,593	$71,919	$88,419	6,938,608	3,194,844	2,203,675
4.	Maryland	$36,338	$73,971	$89,678	5,976,407	2,165,438	1,445,972
5.	New Hampshire	$34,691	$66,532	$80,581	1,326,813	519,756	345,901
6.	Virginia	$34,052	$64,902	$78,290	8,326,289	3,083,820	2,058,820
7.	New York	$33,095	$58,878	$71,115	19,746,227	7,282,398	4,621,954
8.	North Dakota	$33,071	$59,029	$75,221	739,482	305,431	187,800
9.	Alaska	$33,062	$71,583	$82,307	736,732	249,659	165,015
10.	Minnesota	$32,638	$61,481	$77,941	5,457,173	2,129,195	1,369,594
11.	Colorado	$32,357	$61,303	$75,405	5,355,866	2,039,592	1,315,283
12.	Washington	$31,841	$61,366	$74,193	7,061,530	2,679,601	1,725,099
13.	Rhode Island	$30,830	$54,891	$71,212	1,055,173	409,654	257,165
14.	Delaware	$30,488	$59,716	$72,594	935,614	349,743	233,000
15.	California	$30,441	$61,933	$71,015	38,802,500	12,758,648	8,762,059
16.	Illinois	$30,417	$57,444	$71,796	12,880,580	4,772,421	3,099,184
17.	Hawaii	$29,736	$69,592	$79,187	1,419,561	450,769	314,151
18.	Wyoming	$29,698	$57,055	$72,460	584,153	232,594	149,032
19.	Pennsylvania	$29,220	$53,234	$67,876	12,787,209	4,945,972	3,185,054
20.	Vermont	$29,178	$54,166	$67,154	626,562	257,229	162,017

https://en.wikipedia.org/wiki/List_of_U.S._states_by_income

Practice

Choose six statements that the chart shows. Put a check (/) before these statements. Write the logical explanation for each answer.

_____1. California is the most populated state.

_____2. New Jersey is the second most populated state.

_____3. Massachusetts has the second highest number of household.

_____4. The number of households is higher than the number of families in every state.

_____5. Members in some households do not work.

_____6. The median family income is higher than the household income in all fifty states.

_____7. New York has the second highest number of households and second highest number of families.

_____8. The District of Columbia is not considered a state.

_____9. The difference between the state that has the highest capita income and the state with the lowest capita income is $23,000 plus.

Logical Explanations for the Answers

1. Sentence _____ is correct because _____

   _____

2. Sentence _____ is correct because _____

   _____

3. Sentence _____ is correct because _____

   _____

4. Sentence _____ is correct because _____

   _____

5. Sentence _____ is correct because _____

   _____

6. Sentence _____ is correct because _____

   _____

Mastery Test 1

Put a check (/) by the five sentences that are supported by the information in the paragraph. Indicate the reasons for your answer and the number of the sentence in the passage that supports your answer.

1For every group we belong to, there are groups we do not. 2Have you ever gone to a party and found that people naturally segregate themselves into clusters, sometimes by age, by gender, or by race? 3People gravitate to others that they have something in common, and until people know more about their interests, they sometimes seek out people who have a similar set of physical characteristics. 4This does not mean that we will actually have much in common with them, but it is a natural process for people to feel a sense of belongingness with others. 5When we are **in-group** members, we share information and support. 6When we are **out-group** members, we are not given access to privileged information and we may feel excluded, or even made to seem like the enemy. 7Most of the time, people accept that there are some groups they are in and some they aren't, but not feeling included may be uncomfortable. 8At work, as new employees, we may feel like an outsider and try very hard to become a member of the in-group, since that's where the information and perks occur.

Source: Vissing, An Introduction to Sociology, Kendall Hunt, 2013.

_____ 1. It is usually normal for any person who does not feel to belong to a group even though that person works in that group.

_____ 2. It is good to know someone in the group when you go to a party or gathering.

_____ 3. It is normal that some people accept you right away and others do not.

_____ 4. All ethnic groups go together when there are gatherings.

_____ 5. Some people who have the same religion, political affiliation, or country of origin are likely to talk to each other than others who do not have.

_____ 6. People tend to share personal information even though they are not in the in-group.

_____ 7. People in the out-group will later join the in-group.

Reasons for Answers

1. Sentence _____ is correct because _____

_____

2. Sentence _____ is correct because _____

_____

3. Sentence _____ is correct because _____

_____

4. Sentence _____ is correct because _____

_____

5. Sentence _____ is correct because _____

_____

Mastery Test 2

Read the paragraphs and choose the best word from the lists that completes each statement that follows. Write the letter of your answer in the space provided.

DIVERSITY

The word "race" did not even exist until Americans introduced the term in the 18th and 19th centuries. Prior to that point in history, the term was not used anywhere else in the world. English settlers created the phrase "white race" to distinguish themselves from Native Americans and African Americans whom they deemed to be "uncivilized" and "savages." At that time, the cotton industry was booming, which created demand for more land and a larger labor force. To meet these needs, white Anglo-Protestant elite devised and disseminated the idea of a privileged "white race" to justify their taking land occupied by Native Americans and using African Americans as slaves to build a larger labor force (Berlin, 2004; Fogel, 1989). This was also seen as a means of providing privileges to incoming British and European immigrants who did not own property. Immigrants who initially defined themselves as German, Irish, or Italian slowly began to refer to themselves as "white" as they began to move up to higher levels of socioeconomic and political status (Feagin & Feagin, 2003). Thus, white privilege was gained at the expense of oppressing groups deemed to be "non-white."

Source: Thompson/Cuseo, Diversity and the College Experience, 2E. Kendall Hunt Publishing Company, 2014.

_____1. The word race was introduced by _____ .
   a. Africans
   b. Anglo-Protestant elite
   c. English settlers
   d. Americans

_____2. Groups of people except _____ had the privilege to acquire land that belonged to others.
   a. Germans
   b. Italians
   c. Irish
   d. Native Americans

While humans may display diversity in the color or tone of their outer layer of skin, the reality is that all members of the human species are remarkably similar at an underlying biological level. More than 98% of the genes of humans from all racial groups are exactly the same (Bridgeman, 2003; Molnar, 1991). This large amount of genetic overlap among humans accounts for the many similarities that exist among members of the human species, us, regardless of the differences in color that appear at the outer surface of their skin. All humans have internal organs that are similar in structure and function, and whatever the color of our outer layer of skin, when it's cut, we all bleed in the same color.

Source: Thompson/Cuseo, Diversity and the College Experience, 2E. Kendall Hunt Publishing Company, 2014.

_____1. It is possible for a person who has a dark skin to receive a liver transplant from a person with a light skin to live. The answer is _____ .
   a. no   b. yes   c. cannot tell

_____2. The information from the paragraph is likely to appear in a _____ textbook.
   a. sociology
   b. medical
   c. psychology
   d. education

Mastery Test 3

Read the paragraphs and choose the best word from the lists that completes each statement that follows. Write the letter of your answer in the space provided.

WHAT IS CRIMINAL JUSTICE?

The criminal justice system, which comprises the police, courts, and correctional facilities, is how the government enforces social norms, laws, and justice. Criminal justice is also an academic discipline. It is important to understand and study the criminal justice system in a reasoned and scientifically accurate manner because this knowledge helps explain why the police, judicial, and correctional systems interact as a part of the larger justice system. Ideally, this knowledge will then lead to intelligent and effective policy choices.

_____1. When a criminal is given a sentence, the person who is least involved is the _____ .
   a. police officer   c. doctor
   b. warden   d. judge

_____2. After a verdict is announced, the first person who approaches a criminal is a _____ .
   a. jail warden   c. judge
   b. police officer   d. juror

Criminal justice incorporates the study of other social sciences such as sociology, psychology, political sciences, and law. While interdisciplinary, the study of criminal justice is closely related to and intertwined with the study of sociology. Sociologists are individuals who study society and apply their findings for the benefit of society. Criminologists use sociological skills to study crime and criminals, often with the goal of advancing theoretical knowledge. Criminal justice scholars have similar goals, often focusing on the benefits and consequences of policy choices.

3. A criminologist needs to study _____ in order to infer from facial expressions if a person is telling a lie.
   a. sociology   c. science
   b. psychology   d. political science

Criminal justice researchers look at how the decisions of one part of the justice system, widely defined, affect the other parts. These researchers seek to understand how the system adapts to new trends and how the system can handle any problems that arise. Like sociologists and other social scientists, criminal justice researchers pull from many different disciplines to analyze and understand why a problem is occurring.

*Source: Mentor, **Criminal Justice**. Kendall Hunt Publishing Company, 2013.*

_____4. Criminal justice researchers and sociologists have similar goals in understanding problems. This statement is _____ .
   a. true   b. false   c. not true or false—no basis for the answer

Mastery Test 4

Read the passage and choose the best word from the lists that completes each statement that follows. Write the letter of your answer in the space provided.

THE ART OF DANCE

In the absence of a common verbal language, people used their bodies to express thoughts and feelings. Movements and gestures became an essential part of all facets of people's lives. Life's daily rhythms, to which these people had a strong connection (internal rhythms, such as breathing, walking and the beat of one's heart, and external rhythms, such as the cycle of day and night and the change of the seasons), were a natural precursor to dancing and singing.

One of the most important aspects of their lives—where dance was used as the ultimate means of expression—was during dance rituals. People used rituals to worship and appease the gods and believed that these rituals held magical and spiritual powers. The occasion of a birth, marriage, or death required that a dance ritual be performed in conjunction with the event. These rituals held great meaning for the participants and the viewers. For example, in some societies, a dance ritual held at birth would ensure a long, healthy life for the infant. A marriage ritual would celebrate the transition from single to married life (much like our own traditional wedding ceremony). A ritual at someone's death would ensure that the deceased's spirit would rest peacefully. Probably the most important rituals that occurred in these societies were those that revolved around fertility (for food and children). Many fertility rituals were done to ask the gods for rain, sunshine, an abundant harvest, and healthy children.

It is sometimes hard for contemporary society to understand the magnitude of dance rituals and to see how much early humans' lives revolved around them. It is also difficult to visualize what these dances looked like. Many writers, such as Margaret H'Doubler, state that the movements were very basic; such as running, hopping, swaying, stomping and clapping. The movements were also imitative, devoted to the mimicry of animals, forces of nature and of the gods. The length of the rituals varied, depending on their function. Some lasted only hours, whereas others were conducted over a period of several days.

_____1. The passage suggests that the time of performing dance movements is _____ .
   a. at present   c. decades ago
   b. centuries ago   d. months ago

_____2. The people believed that their gods listened and saw them. This statement is _____ .
   a. true   b. false   c. not true or false—no basis for the answer

_____3. The people mentioned in the passage probably lived in the _____ .
   a. mountain   c. urban area
   b. open fields   d. near a city

_____4. Dance rituals would least likely be performed to ask for _____ .
   a. healthy children   c. healthy animals
   b. good harvest   d. spouses

STRETCH YOUR DOLLAR

1You earned it. You set goals, created a budget, stashed away savings, and now you are ready to spend. Spending wisely is as important as saving. The best way to spend wisely is to comparison shop. Before you shop, clearly identify what you want, what you need, and what you can afford. Once you clearly identify those three parameters, you are ready to shop. As you shop, compare purchases against each other and against your list. Expensive purchase like automobiles, appliances, and dream vacations take more time to research and compare than smaller daily purchases. Don't think the small purchases don't matter though: If you watch the pennies, the dollars will take care of themselves. It won't take as long to choose which package of corn to buy as it does to decide which vehicle to purchase, but consistently spending wisely is as good as saving.

In the Grocery Store

2Wise spending involves comparing like products for price, value, and features while filtering your choices through your wants, needs, and budget. In the grocery store, compare unit price, nutritional information, and quality, but filter your food selections by your personal tastes and your budget.

BRANDS

3**Brands** indicate the manufacturer and the intended consumer of the product. **National brands** are the common household name brands. They are well advertised and typically are more expensive. Keebler®, Folgers®, and Frito Lay® are examples of national brands. Store brands are items manufactured for a specific grocery store. Dillon's grocery stores have Kroger and private selections store brands. Price Chopper sells products under a Price Chopper brand. Generics are those items that either are not sold under a store or private label brand and are not a national brand. They may be labeled generic or carry a label like always save or Best Choice. It always helps to remember that generics and store brands are often manufactured by the national brand companies, only under store or generic labels. For this reason, there also is not a lot of difference between items in some cases.

4Cost of advertising plays the largest role in the additional cost of the product. National brands are often perceived to be higher quality because they cost more—this is not always the case. Each consumer has personal preferences. For example, an Oreo cookie may be the only chocolate sandwich cookie you want. In that case, you may not want to compare other cookies if you know only an Oreo will do. However, there are some generic or store products that surpass their name brand counterparts. Compare the unit cost of items and try the lowest cost product. If you like the flavor and quality of the product, continue to buy it; if you don't, move up to the next expensive brand. You may be surprised how many items you will find that you prefer over their national brand counterparts.

PRICE

5Price is easiest to compare on a unit cost basis. Which is more economical, a 12 oz. package for $2.99 or a 14 oz. package for $3.19. The **unit price** is the price per ounce (oz.), pound (lb.), or some other measurement (such as per 100 in tissues). To calculate the unit price, divide the price by the weight or volume.

$2.99/12 oz. = 24.9 cents per oz.
$3.19/14 oz. = 22.7 cents per oz.

In this case, the 14 oz. package for $3.19 is a more economical buy because it costs only 22.7 cents an ounce compared to 24.9 cents an ounce for a 12 oz. package.

Label Information

Product

6The label must clearly state the common name of the product, for example, cereal or coffee. Most labels are easy to read and understand. Cheese is a good example of labeling that isn't always clear to the consumer. Cheese is cheese, right? What is the difference between Cheddar and Muenster? Cheese comes in many varieties, but all cheeses share some commonalities. To be labeled cheese, the product must be a dairy product, made basically from milk. Cheese is classified by its moisture content and its milk fat content. Typically, as the milk fat content increases, so does its calcium content. Harder cheeses tend to be higher in milk fat content, lower in moisture, and higher in calcium. What is the difference between cheese, pasteurized process cheese, and pasteurized process cheese food? Cheese is the basic dairy product, made from milk, and is classified by its moisture content and milk fat content.

Cheese	Milk Fat Content	Moisture Content
Cheddar	50%	39% or less
Munster	50%	46%
Mozzarella	45%	52–60%

7Pasteurized process cheese is a mixture of one or more cheeses and emulsifiers. The cheese is heated and ingredients are added to soften the cheese. The product is still predominantly cheese. Pasteurized process cheese food is a mixture that is only part cheese—the FDA requires products with this label be at least 51 percent cheese. You may also see products labeled imitation cheese. These products are not made from milk or cheese; they are made from oil. Most product labels are obvious, but not all product names are clearly understood by the consumer. If you are not sure of the difference between butter and margarine, check the nutritional information and the ingredients list.

Net Weight

8The **net weight** tells you the amount of product in the package, computed as the total weight minus the weight of the package. In a can of tomatoes, the net weight would include the weight of both the tomatoes and the liquid they are packaged in but not the weight of the can. The net weight is listed by either a dry ingredient measure or a liquid ingredient measure in both U.S. and metric units.

- Dry product: Net wt. 12 oz. (340 g)
- Liquid product: Net wt. 32 f l. oz. (1qt.) 946 ml

Nutritional Information

9The Federal Food and Drug Administration (FDA) requires all food products be labeled with the same basic nutritional information. The FDA suggests you minimize your intake of the items shown in yellow and maximize your intake of the items shown in blue. When comparing products, your personal dietary needs and lifestyle are also an important part of comparison shopping.

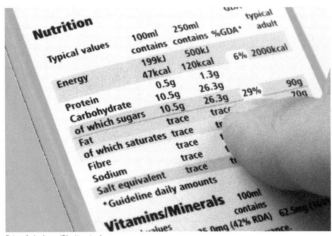

Brian A Jackson/Shutterstock.com

Ingredients

10Ingredients are listed in the order of quantity, from highest to lowest. If a product contains 4 ounces of sugar, 2 ounces of flour, and 1 ounce of butter, the ingredients would be listed as sugar, flour, and butter. A typical package of cheddar cheese lists the ingredients as: pasteurized milk, cheese culture, salt, enzymes, and vegetable coloring.

11It takes time to compare labels, unit prices, and nutritional information, but the time you spend comparing products in the grocery store is an investment for future savings. Once you determine which brand and package size of a product is best for you needs, you can repeat the purchase and the savings without continually repeating the process.

From *Personal Finance: An Interactive Applications Approach*, Second Edition.
Copyright © by Kendall Hunt Publishing Company. Reprinted by permission.

Comprehension

Choose the best answer from the list that completes each sentence. Write the letter of your answer on the space provided.

_____1. The author most likely agrees that buying something is based on _____
    a. budget   c. brand
    b. need   d. personal taste, needs and budget

_____2. A national brand tends to be more expensive than the generic brand. The national brand usually spends money on _____ in addition to the cost of producing the product.
    a. good quality   c. advertising
    b. product samples   d. transportation

_____3. The list of ingredients include milk, flour, butter, and sugar. The ingredient that contains the least number of ounces is _____ .
   a. milk   c. sugar
   b. butter   d. flour

_____4. The FDA suggests that you minimize your intake of _____ .
   a. sodium   c. salt equivalent
   b. sugar   d. sugar

_____5. The cheese which has the least amount of calcium is _____ .
   a. Cheddar   c. Mozzarella
   b. Munster   d. cannot tell

_____6. To explain the meaning of net weight in the eighth paragraph, a/an _____ is given.
   a. comparison   c. contrast
   b. example   d. narration

_____7. The example in the fifth paragraph shows that it is more economical to buy a package that contains a higher number of ounces than one that has less.
   a. true   b. false   c. cannot tell

_____8. An imitation cheese is made from _____ .
   a. milk   c. cheese
   b. oil   d. cannot tell

_____9. The sentence that follows suggests that the meaning of parameters is _____ .
   a. instructions   c. tools
   b. lessons   d. guidelines

Before you shop, clearly identify what you want, what you need, and what you can afford. Once you clearly identify those three parameters, you are ready to shop.

____10. The sentence that follows shows a/an _____ .
   a. comparison   c. time
   b. example   d. contrast

It takes time to compare labels, unit prices, and nutritional information, but the time you spend comparing products in the grocery store is an investment for future savings.

8

Fact and Opinion

Writers include factual information and opinions in different forms of printed materials. Since you read what they write, it is important that you are able to recognize the difference between a fact and opinion. This skill will help you better understand what you are reading and apply this in listening, speaking, writing, and performing academic and personal tasks.

Topics

Fact

Opinion

Fact and Opinion

Recognizing a fact and an opinion is important in evaluating a given information in printed and digital materials. A fact is something that you can prove to be true. To prove it, look at actual evidence such as experiences, observations, statistics, and records. The information is subject to verification. An opinion is a belief, point of view, or feeling of a writer. It is subject to agreement or disagreement. Sometimes, writers combine facts and opinions.

Fact

Example
An apartment building in Houston, Texas has a rooftop pool.
What are we talking about in this sentence?
Can you prove it? How do we know if the apartment building has a rooftop pool?
If the answer is yes, and you can prove it, then it is a fact.
You can find it from records or google it.

Practice

The following sentences are facts. Why are these facts? Write the reason for every sentence in the space provided.

1. Washington D. C. is the capital of United States.

   Reason _____

2. According to estimates released today by the Bureau of Economic Analysis, the personal income increased $57.7 billion (0.4%) in February 2017.

   Reason _____

3. The current population of the United States of America is 325,944,738 as of Tuesday, April 11, 2017, based on the latest United Nations estimates.

   Reason _____

4. Earth is the place where human beings, animals, plants, and other organisms live.

   Reason _____

5. The Bureau of Labor Statistics has published a new report showing that the top three most common professions in the United States are salespeople, cashiers, and fast-food workers.

   Reason _____

Opinion

An opinion is a sentence that shows a writer's judgment or value that includes beliefs, feelings, or points of view on something, person, place, or idea.

Sample Opinion Words

best	most	good	better	well	worse
graceful	less	bad	beautiful	must	should
can	important	maybe	perhaps	could	probably

Example

The apartment building is luxurious.
What are we talking about in this sentence? (apartment building)
What word gives a judgment? (luxurious)

Practice

The following sentences are opinions. Why are these opinions? Identify the word in each sentence that makes it an opinion. Write this word in the space provided.

1. She is the most wonderful mother in the world.
   Opinion word/s _____

2. He can make you fall for him when he smiles at you.
   Opinion word/s _____

3. You have to trust your doctor, so you can get well.
   Opinion word/s _____

4. This project looks very interesting and appealing to our investors.
   Opinion word/s_____

5. The most valuable basketball player is very inspiring to the kids.
   Opinion word/s_____

To be able to correctly recognize if a sentence is a fact, opinion, or fact and opinion, say the sentence to yourself and imagine that you are the speaker or writer. Ask if you are you telling someone, factual information, feeling, belief, point of view, or a combination of fact and opinion.

Fact and Opinion

Sometimes, writers combine facts and opinions by including information that you can verify to be true or false and points of view, feelings, or beliefs.

Example
A middle-aged beautiful woman who wears a red scarf is in the lunchroom.
The highlighted part, <u>middle-age beautiful woman</u>, is an opinion because it shows a belief or what the writer thinks about the woman. The part in the box, <u>who wears a red scarf is in the lunchroom</u>, is a fact because you can prove it to be true or false by looking for her in the lunchroom and find out if she wears a red scarf.

Practice

Each of the following sentences shows a fact and an opinion. Underline the part that shows an opinion.

1. An ad for a brand of cigarette shows a handsome man on a dazzling car.
2. Five outstanding researchers conducted an experiment to determine the difference between the numbers of hours that two given species of mice sleep during a 24-hour period.
3. Life refers to an existence, and many appear to show this very clearly in their actions.
4. An annoying passenger said unpleasant words to the stewardess, however, the passenger later apologized for his behavior.
5. The persuasive and intelligent woman was able to sell 50 pairs of shoes in her first week of work in the store.
6. In some states, heroin is legal, but this situation is unacceptable.
7. The world population is 7.5 billion, so people have to consider family planning.
8. Although everybody has a certain blood type, some people are not educated enough to ask for their blood types.
9. The research shows that elephants can communicate by making sounds, a report that is music to my ear.
10. Although there is a job opening for a cashier in that store, I am not interested in that position.

Mastery Test 1

Decide if each statement is a fact, opinion, or a fact and opinion. Write F (fact), O (opinion) or FO (fact and opinion) in the space provided. Underline all words that show opinions. Two sentences include facts and opinions.

_____1. After preliminary hearings regarding admissibility of evidence, the trial began after nine months.

_____2. The jury found Simpson not guilty of both murders.

_____3. Simpson's sizable team of defense attorneys, referred to as the "Dream Team," included lovely, and very intelligent lawyers and DNA experts.

_____4. Simpson's acquittal shocked the nation according to several interviews.

_____5. The criminal justice system is ineffective.

_____6. On December 23, 1991, Willingham's home caught fire and Willingham was able to escape with minor burns.

_____7. His three young daughters were killed and Willingham was charged in their deaths.

_____8. Prosecutors sought the death penalty for Willingham.

_____9. Eight months after the deaths of his daughters, Willingham was convicted of capital murder and sentenced to death.

____10. At trial, an expert witness testified that an accelerant had been used to purposely light the house on fire.

____11. I think the prosecutor did a good job of presenting a jailhouse informant who testified that Willingham described squirting lighter fluid around the house and lighting it on fire.

____12. Willingham's two attorneys, who were appointed to represent him, failed to find a fire expert to counter the prosecution's claims and only presented one witness, a babysitter who did not believe Willingham could have killed his daughters.

____13. Lack of sufficient and reliable witness is a very sad situation.

____14. If Willington had the money to hire great lawyers and experts, he could have been acquitted.

____15. Willingham appealed his conviction, but the Court of Criminal Appeals of Texas affirmed the judgment and sentence of the trial court.

Adapted from Source: Mentor, **Criminal Justice**. *Kendall Hunt Publishing Company, 2013.*

Mastery Test 2

Decide if each statement is a fact or an opinion. Write F (fact) or O (opinion). In the space provided. Underline all words that show opinions.

_____1. Culture is not only expressed by food preferences but also by the way we eat according to anthropologists.

_____2. In America, some people hold a fork in the right hand.

_____3. Eating with the fork on the right hand is a good table manner.

_____4. In Australia, an article reports that eating with a fork is considered too casual and lazy except when eating salad, dessert, or cake.

_____5. According to records, the utensils used in cannibalism were kept separate from utensils used for daily meals in an ancient Polynesian society.

_____6. Several TV series that have explored viewers' culinary boundaries between what is edible and what is disgusting is fine.

_____7. The job of the cultural anthropologist is to understand the larger context within which the "yuk" factor and the "delicious" factor make sense.

_____8. To make sense of what we do is important.

_____9. I find some ethnic desserts very intriguing.

_____10. Jews and Muslims do not eat pork, and Hindus do not eat beef.

Source: Nowak and Laird, Cultural Anthropology. Bridgepoint, 2010.

Mastery Test 3

Write two sentences, one is a fact and another is an opinion for the given topic.

Example: money
Fact: The $100 bill shows the face of Benjamin Franklin.
Opinion: Money is very important to survive.

1. Body parts

    Fact _____

    Opinion _____

2. Behavior

    Fact _____

    Opinion _____

3. Environment

    Fact _____

    Opinion _____

OBESITY AND WEIGHT MANAGEMENT

1As Americans, we hear a lot about being "overweight" and "obese." In fact, for the first time in several decades, obesity is the **second** leading cause of preventable death in the United States and is close to trading places with tobacco use, which is the *first* leading cause of preventable death in the United States. Despite efforts to deal with increasingly sedentary lifestyles, Americans are, for the most part, getting fatter. Today, 65 percent of American adults over age 20 are overweight or obese, which is a pretty scary statistic. A cost of $250 billion a year is estimated for medical treatment and lost productivity from obesity and increased risk for heart disease, stroke, high blood pressure, and some forms of cancer. Obesity in our children and teens is of special concern, because an estimated one of every three kids in America today is overweight. Time spent watching television, playing video games, or sitting at the computer contributes to the problem, as do the cutbacks in physical education at many schools.

2How Did so Many People Get so Heavy?

Most of us are eating more calories than we are burning. The problem of an overweight population comes from a combination of factors:

- Increasing portion sizes,
- More processed foods with fewer nutrients, and
- A more sedentary lifestyle.

Africa Studio/Shutterstock.com

3*We are eating more food.* Portions have increased dramatically in the last 20 years. Bigger portions mean that we have to work a lot harder to burn the extra calories that those larger portions add. We are eating a lot of foods that do not provide many nutrients. We are also consuming more added sugars, which is found in carbonated drinks, fruit drinks, sports beverages, and processed foods. Evidence suggests that drinking calorie-containing beverages may not make you feel full, which can lead you to eat and drink more than you need, adding even more calories to your diet. We are eating out more often than ever before. The danger in eating out is that many types of food eaten away from home, including fast-food and prepared meals you buy at the grocery store, are high in saturated fat, trans fat, cholesterol, added sugars, and sodium. They also can be low in fiber and vitamins and minerals. In addition, people tend to eat larger portions when eating out.

4*We are less active.* Current estimates indicate that more than half of the adults in the United States do not engage in any regular physical activity at all. As we spend more of our free time in front of televisions, computers, and video games, we are more likely to put on pounds. Our increasingly sedentary lifestyles are putting us at risk for serious health problems, including cardiovascular disease, type 2 diabetes, osteoporosis, depression, and breast and colon cancer.

- More than 50 million Americans are currently on a diet, with roughly 5 percent losing weight over the long term.
- Obesity among adults has more than doubled since 1980.
- Less than one-third of Americans meet the federal recommendations to engage in at least 30 minutes of moderate physical activity most days of the week, and 40 percent of adults engage in no physical activity at all.

Measuring Overweight and Obesity

5There are a few different ways to assess whether or not a person is overweight or obese. Many people rely on a traditional scale at home or at the doctor's office, but in some cases, these numbers can be misleading.

Height and Weight Charts

6Height and weight tables were originally developed and heavily used by life insurance actuaries. An actuary determines a person's eligibility for insurance based on different health factors, weight being one of them. You can imagine the slight conflict of interest. In other words, when a huge insurance company creates a height–weight table, it is in its best financial interest to establish the weight ranges on the low end. Why is this? It means because you do not meet the strict weight requirements, you must pay more money to be insured.

Waist Circumference

7Waist circumference is defined as the perimeter around your natural waist, where your belly button falls, not your hips. Assessing this number provides clues about a person's health that charts and tables cannot. Most importantly, it indicates where you are carrying any excess weight. People tend to fall into one of two categories: pears and apples. In general, men tend to be apples, whereas women tend to be pears. Once a woman hits menopause, however, she may start to accumulate body fat through the abdominal region and have more of an apple appearance instead of a pear. This is due in large part to the decrease in estrogen, which dictates where fat is stored.

What Does It Mean to Be an Apple or a Pear?

8Pears tend to accumulate any excess body fat in the hip, buttock, and thigh region whereas apples tend to accumulate it through the abdominal area. As it relates to health, it is always preferable to store excess body fat in the hip, buttock, and thigh region rather than the abdominal area. Why is this? By the time your tailor's tape says your waistline is larger than 39 inches, you may already be on the road to diabetes or heart disease. This holds true for both men and women (Wahrenberg, 2005). Excessive abdominal fat is serious because it places you at greater risk for developing obesity-related conditions, such as type 2 diabetes, high blood cholesterol, high triglycerides, high blood pressure, and coronary artery disease. More specifically, it is recommended that men maintain a stricter waist circumference of 35" or less and women maintain a waist circumference of 32.5" or less (Roizen & Oz, 2006). Why? Wahrenberg's research found that half of all men and women with waistlines of one meter or more—that's 39.37" or more in the United States—already have insulin resistance, where the body's cells are less responsive to the hormone insulin. On the other hand, very few people with smaller waists have developed this dangerous condition.

How to Measure Your Waist Size and Waist-to-Hip Ratio

9To measure your waist size (circumference), place a tape measure around your bare abdomen above your hip bones around your belly button. Be sure that the tape is snug, but does not compress your skin, and is parallel to the floor. Relax, exhale, and measure your waist.

Remember, where you carry body fat is just as important as how much you carry. People who tend to accumulate fat around the waist (apple shape) have a higher risk of heart disease, diabetes, and high blood pressure than those who carry excess weight on the hips and thighs (pear shape). In addition to measuring your waist circumference, you can calculate your waist-to-hip ratio (WHR). This is another way to determine if the weight in your abdomen exceeds that of your thighs. WHR is the measurement of your waist divided by the measurement of your hips. Measure your waist at the level of your belly button as instructed above. A WHR greater than 1 for men and 0.8 for women is considered unfavorable.

Body Mass Index (BMI)

10Today, most physicians and other health professionals rely on a type of measurement called body mass index (BMI). Body mass index is a method of measuring a person's *degree* of overweight or obesity. It is thought to be a more sensitive indicator than traditional height–weight charts (Drummond & Brefere, 2004). To determine your BMI, you must know your weight in pounds and your height in inches. For example, a person who is 5'6" (66") and weighs 136 lbs. has a BMI of 22 (see the following chart).

BMI	19	20	21	22	23	24	25	26	27	28	29	30	31	32	33	34	35
Height (Inches)							**Body Weight (pounds)**										
58	91	96	100	105	110	115	119	124	129	134	138	143	148	153	158	162	167
59	94	99	104	109	114	119	124	128	133	138	143	148	153	158	163	168	173
60	97	102	107	112	118	123	128	131	138	143	148	153	158	163	168	174	179
61	100	106	111	116	122	127	132	137	143	148	153	158	164	169	174	180	185
62	104	109	115	120	126	131	136	142	147	153	158	164	169	175	180	186	191
63	107	113	118	124	130	135	141	146	152	158	163	169	174	180	186	191	197
64	110	116	122	128	134	140	145	151	157	163	169	174	180	186	192	197	204
65	114	120	126	132	138	144	150	156	162	168	174	180	186	192	198	204	210
66	118	124	130	136	142	148	155	161	167	173	179	186	192	198	204	210	216
67	121	127	134	140	146	153	159	166	172	178	185	191	198	204	211	217	223
68	125	131	138	144	151	158	164	171	177	184	190	197	203	210	216	223	230
69	128	135	142	149	155	162	169	176	182	189	196	203	209	216	223	230	236
70	132	139	146	153	160	167	174	181	188	195	202	209	216	222	229	236	243
71	136	143	150	157	165	172	179	186	193	200	208	215	222	229	236	243	250
72	140	147	154	162	169	177	184	191	199	206	213	221	228	235	242	250	258
73	144	151	159	166	174	182	189	197	204	212	219	227	235	242	250	257	265
74	148	155	163	171	179	186	194	202	210	218	225	233	241	249	256	264	272
75	152	160	168	176	184	192	200	208	216	224	232	240	248	256	264	272	279
76	156	164	172	180	189	197	205	213	221	230	238	246	254	263	271	279	287

Source: National Heart, Lung, and Blood Institute (NHBLI) of the U.S. Department of Health and Human Services.

Understanding Your BMI

There are four main BMI categories:

1. **Underweight** = <18.5
2. **Normal weight** = 18.5–24.9
3. **Overweight** = 25–29.9
4. **Obesity** = BMI of 30 or greater

Overweight Versus Obese

11What is the difference between being overweight and being obese? Overweight and obesity are both labels for ranges of weight that are greater than what is generally considered healthy for a given height. The terms also identify ranges of weight that have been shown to increase the likelihood of certain diseases and other health problems (Centers for Disease Control and Prevention, 2007). For adults, overweight and obesity ranges are determined by using weight and height to calculate body mass index. An adult who has a BMI between 25 and 29.9 is considered overweight whereas an adult who has a BMI of 30 or higher is considered obese. If you have been thinking about your current weight, it may be because you've noticed a change in how your clothes fit. Or maybe you have been told by a health care professional that you have high blood pressure or high cholesterol and that your weight could be a contributing factor. The first step is to determine whether or not your current weight is healthy. BMI is just one way to determine whether your weight is a healthy one.

Body Fat Percentage

12One of the best ways to really determine your "fatness" is to have your body composition assessed. The human body is made up of water (roughly 60 percent), bone mineral, organs and other tissue/viscera, muscle, and fat. When a person steps on a scale, the number he or she sees is greatly influenced by factors such as water retention, hormone fluctuation, and the weight of the fecal matter in the intestines. If you are going to weigh yourself, do so no more than one time per week (unless your doctor instructs otherwise), after a bowel movement, and before eating or drinking anything. Have you ever noticed how two people whose heights and weights are the same can look so different? For example, let's say that in front of you stand two women who have the exact same statistics:

- Both are 5'8"
- Both are 35 years old
- Both weigh 145 lbs.
- Both have a medium bone frame

13When you look at both of these women, even though they share all of the above statistics, they look very different. One of the women looks much smaller than the other. What's going on? The answer is that they have different body composition. At this point, it is important to recognize that muscle and adipose (fat) are two different types of tissue. Adipose tissue is like marshmallow, oozy, and fluffy. It takes up a lot of space. Muscle tissue, on the other hand, is dense and tight. It takes up very little space. Muscle, however, does not weigh more than adipose. What differs though is their density. Because muscle tissue is so dense, it takes up less space than adipose tissue making a person's appearance smaller or leaner.

The "Skinny-Fat Person"

14Some obesity researchers now believe that the internal fat surrounding vital organs like the heart, liver, or pancreas, invisible to the naked eye, could be as dangerous as the more obvious external fat that bulges underneath the skin. In other words, being "thin" does not necessarily mean you are lean. A skinny-fat person, sometimes referred to as "thin outside, fat inside" (TOFI), typically has very little lean muscle mass and a lot of adipose tissue, which makes their total body weight appear normal. In fact, fat, active people, sometimes called "fit and fat," can be healthier than their skinny, sedentary counterparts. Normal weight people who are sedentary and unfit are at much higher risk for developing disease than obese persons who are active and fit. How can this be? Obesity researchers believe that people who are not overweight but still have a high percentage of body fat may have more inflammation in their bodies. These people are often referred to as "normal-weight obese" because of their high body fat percentage.

15When researchers took blood samples from research subjects, they found those who were overweight or obese had the highest levels of inflammatory chemicals, LDL (bad) cholesterol, and triglycerides (a type of blood fat). However, the "normal-weight obese" women also had higher levels of inflammatory chemicals than those with both a normal BMI and lower body fat. These findings indicate that the normal-weight women with high body fat "were in an early inflammatory state," because body fat is thought to release inflammatory chemicals, according to the researchers (De Lorenzo et al., 2007). Chronically, high levels of inflammation have been associated with a host of health problems, including heart disease and arthritis. Research also shows that people who maintain their weight through diet rather than exercise are likely to have major deposits of internal fat, even if they are otherwise slim. Typically, thin people may falsely assume that because they are not overweight, they are healthy. In reality, a skinny fat person may have a "normal" weight, but this does not make them immune to diabetes or other risk factors for heart disease. Skinny-fat people, who are fat on the inside, are essentially on the threshold of being obese. They eat too many fatty, sugary foods, and exercise too little to work it off, but they are not eating enough to actually be overweight. Most experts believe that being of normal weight is an indicator of good health, and that BMI is a reliable measurement. BMI won't give you the exact indication of where fat is, but it can be a useful clinical tool. Still, getting a body composition assessment would be a better indicator of body fat percentage.

Comprehension

Choose the best word that completes the idea of each sentence. Write the letter of this word in the space provided. Write the logical explanation or the basis for your answer.

_____1. It takes about _____ billion for three years for treatment of diseases and unpro-
      ductivity due to obesity.
      a. 250   b. 50   c. 500   d. 750

_____2. The first leading cause of preventable death is _____.
      a. obesity   c. tobacco
      b. useheart disease   d. physical inactivity

_____3. The word <u>sedentary</u> is the first paragraph most likely means _____.
      a. active   b. sad   c. inactive   d. playful

_____4. A person who has a BMI of 23 is considered _____.
      a. underweight   b. normal weight   c. overweight   d. obese

_____5. The following factors contribute to obesity except _____.
      a. sugar   b. saturated fat   c. salt   d. minerals

_____6. An estimated _____% of adults engage in daily physical activity.
      a. 5   b. 40   c. 60   d. 30

_____7. A/an _____ person will likely pay the lowest insurance premium.
      a. obese   b. smoker   c. non-smoker   d. ill

_____8. A_____ who is obese tend to be apples due to excess fat.
      a. teen ager   b. man   c. woman   d. baby

_____9. Excessive abdominal fat places you at greater risk for developing obesity-related condi-
      tions except _____.
      a. type 2 diabetes   c. high blood pressure
      b. normal blood cholesterol   d. coronary artery disease

____10. Body mass index is a method of measuring a person's _____.
      a. weight   c. condition of overweight or obesity
      b. blood pressure   d. cholesterol

Fact, Opinion, and Fact and Opinion

Decide if each statement is a fact, opinion, or a fact and opinion. Write F (fact), O (opinion), or FO
(fact and opinion). Underline all words that show opinions in each item.

_____1. People who tend to accumulate fat around the waist (apple shape) have a higher risk of
      heart disease, diabetes, and high blood pressure than those who carry excess weight on
      the hips and thighs (pear shape).

_____2. WHR is the measurement of your waist divided by the measurement of your hips.

_____3. My body mass index is 30, and it is fine with me.

_____4. An obese person has a BMI of 35.

_____5. Eating big portions of food is one of the causes of obesity, yet we eat as long as we want.

_____6. The human body is made up of water (roughly 60%), bone mineral, organs and other tissue/viscera, muscle, and fat.

_____7. When a person steps on a scale, the number he or she sees is greatly influenced by factors such as water retention, hormone fluctuation, and the weight of the fecal matter in the intestines.

_____8. Although my girlfriend is obese, I still love her.

_____9. My baby who weighs 10 pounds is very cute.

____10. Most experts believe that being of normal weight is an indicator of good health, and that BMI is a reliable measurement according to a survey.

9

© Charlie Edwards/Photodisc/Getty Images

Purpose

Writers write with a purpose. Recognizing the purpose of the writer will help you better understand what you read. Although the purpose is not explicitly stated, you will be able to infer it by using some strategies. In this chapter, you will be able to identify the author's purpose and use it to comprehend what you read.

Topics

General Purposes

    Inform

    Persuade

    Entertain

Specific Purposes

    Instruct

    Describe

    Compare

    Contrast

    Explain

    Narrate

Authors have a reason or purpose in creating print and digital materials that include stories, informational texts, poetry, pictures, charts, maps, and other visual materials. Since the purpose is not usually stated in these materials, you will apply the things that you have previously learned in this book such as ACTOR, vocabulary enhancement, transitions, main idea, supporting details, paragraph patterns, inference, and fact and opinion to figure out the intent of the author. Purposes maybe categorized into general, specific, and mixed. Recognizing the author's purpose will help you better understand what you read.

General Purposes

The three general or common purposes are to inform, to persuade, and to entertain.

Inform

Newspapers, magazines, reference books, biographies, textbooks, and other informative materials present information that tells about something without including the writer's opinions; the purpose is to inform.

Example

According to research, the leading cause of death at present is tobacco use.

This sentence provides you the information about tobacco as the leading cause of death. You can find out if it is true or false. It is a fact. The purpose is to inform.

Practice

State the reason why the purpose of each sentence is to inform.

1. Several schools in the northeastern part of the United States were closed during the snowstorm last week.

   Reason _____

2. Electric power was restored in all parts of New Jersey and New York two days after the snowstorm.

   Reason _____

Persuade

Advertisements, political speeches, editorials, and other opinionated materials usually persuade readers because these materials include a position or point of view for or against something. These can move you into positive or negative actions. The writer's purpose of these materials is to persuade.

Example

You should stop smoking cigarette because tobacco use is the leading cause of death according to reports.

> This sentence persuades you to stop smoking. It provides an opinion because it states the writer's belief or point of view—you should stop smoking. The second part is a fact because it is based on reports—tobacco use is the leading cause of death. Usually, writers include an opinion and support it by facts in order to convince readers to take an action on something. The purpose is to persuade.

Practice

State the reason why the purpose of each sentence is to persuade.

1. You must examine the characteristics of modern and ancient art forms in order to understand the differences between the two.

    Reason _____

2. There is a limited number of scholarships that are provided to students during the year. You have to apply right away and be sure you are qualified.

    Reason _____

Entertain

Usually, jokes, stories, poetry, and other forms of writing stimulate you to imagine things, use your senses, teach you a moral lesson or convey a meaningful message, and appeal to your emotions. The purpose of these materials is to entertain.

Example

An alien, six-foot high with three big eyes, blue hair, and shining skin who appeared to come from outer space came to earth and disguised as a tall and handsome man. After befriending a woman, he fell in love with her.

> This example describes a character and states what this character did. It appeals to imagination, emotions, and senses. It does not give a factual information. It does not convince you take an action. The purpose is to entertain.

Practice

State the reason why the purpose of each item is to entertain.

1. The moaning sound became louder as I approached the end of the hallway. I embraced him tightly until I noticed the loss of movement in his chest. Then he moved, opened his eyes, and smiled at me.

    Reason _____

2. As he stood up, he heard a thunderous applause. He waved to the crowd, and the applause and stomping grew louder.

   Reason _____

Mastery Test 1

Identify if the main purpose of each item is to inform (I), persuade (P), or entertain (E). Write the letter and the reason for your answer in the spaces provided. Writing the reason helps you to fully understand purposes and check the accuracy of your answers.

Example

_P_ You should consider taking law because you are so good in making arguments and convincing people to believe what you say.

Reason <u>The speaker gives an opinion and tries to convince someone to take law because</u> that person is good in giving arguments.

_____1. Students need to have a purpose in life to attain academic success.

   Reason _____

_____2. One way to achieve your long-term goal is to complete all short-term goals.

   Reason _____

_____3. I have already a goal in life—basketball goal.

   Reason _____

_____4. A goal in life is not a basketball goal. It is something that you want to be or have that gives you a sense of direction.

   Reason _____

_____5. You must evaluate the things that you are doing to be sure that these help you to achieve your goal.

   Reason _____

_____6. According to reports, the chance of being hit by lightning is greater than winning a lottery.

   Reason _____

_____7. The man who was hit by lightning had discovered that he was able to make an electric range work when there was a power outage.

   Reason _____

_____8. Since lightning casualties usually happen in the field, be sure to take shelter to be safe.

Reason _____

_____9. People need to be educated on the dangers of lightning that include burns, death, and other possible risks.

Reason _____

____10. A report just came in about a telephone that exploded during a thunderstorm.

Reason _____

Mastery Test 2

Identify if the main purpose of each item is to inform (I), persuade (P), or entertain (E). Write the letter of your answer in the space provided.

1. Eustress, although it makes you uncomfortable, gives you the opportunity to try your best in performing a task.
2. It will be helpful to get educated in changing a stressful condition to a learning experience because the focus is not on the feelings of being stressed but on the ways to deal with stress.
3. One example of addiction is continuously taking a controlled substance in spite of its negative consequences to the body.
4. Many people who want to lose weight try many things. Continuous research on how to lose weight should be conducted.
5. He looked for his eyeglasses a hundred times only to find out that these were on his head.
6. Gallstones are hard substances that form in your gallbladder. The gallbladder is located on the right side of your abdomen, near your liver.
7. A doctor told Mr. Stone that he found two pieces of diamonds in his gallbladder. When he looked at the diamonds, these turned into salt.
8. Nearly 30 million Americans—three times more women than men—suffer from migraine, a type of headache that often has severe symptoms.
9. The researchers reported that the happier study participants finished their projects ahead of those who reported not to be happy.
10. More field trips to the zoo should be encouraged because children are happy to see several cute animals.

Specific Purposes

Authors have a reason or purpose in creating print and digital materials that include stories, informational texts, poetry, pictures, charts, maps, and other visuals. When you read, you may acquire useful information, move into action, or feel relaxed. You may also infer that a reading material is giving you instructions or directions to follow, describing, comparing, contrasting or explaining something, or narrating what happened. Your knowledge of transitions and paragraph patterns will greatly help you to recognize these purposes.

Instruct

Self-help books, textbooks, and other reading materials sometimes give instructions on the steps to follow in order to complete a task.

Example

1. Prepare ingredients. (ground pork, soy sauce, garlic onion, and shredded carrots and cabbage. These are the fillings of the roll.
2. Mix all ingredients.
3. Place the mixed ingredients onto the rolls. Take the bottom point of your wrap and fold it on top of the filling.
4. Seal the egg wrap with water or egg.
5. Preheat your deep fryer or frying pan.
6. Pour cooking oil in the pan.
7. Cook your egg rolls.

This example presents directions or instructions to follow in order to cook egg rolls. The purpose is to instruct.

Describe

Informational texts, poetry, and stories sometimes include a description of things, persons, animals, feelings, or situations. The purpose is to describe.

Example

My brother has a commercial passenger tricycle. It is composed of a bicycle or a motorcycle that is attached to a sidecar, a one wheeled covered passenger seat, thus producing a three wheeled vehicle. The sidecar can accommodate two or more persons. His sidecar is painted sky blue.

This example presents a description of a commercial tricycle passenger. Through this description, you can imagine how a tricycle looks like. The purpose is to describe.

Compare

In both informational texts and literature, writers sometime show a comparison of characters, places, things, or events. Signal words that show similarities and the comparison pattern of organization are helpful in recognizing if the purpose is to compare.

Example

Cats and dogs are similar in some ways. Both give birth to their babies. They can be domesticated and become good pets. If they sense your care, love, and affection to them, they also show their affection to you by doing lovely things that can make you smile. They also look at your eyes when you talk to them.

> This example presents similarities between cats and dogs. The author's purpose is to compare.

Contrast

A writer's purpose for writing an informational text, story, or poetry is to contrast if differences between two persons, things, places, or events are presented.

Example

Annual plants live for only one year. They come in different colors usually in spring through fall. You need to plant these again in the following year. On the other hand, perennial plants live for two to five years.

> This example presents the differences between annual and perennial plants. The purpose is to contrast.

Explain

In both informational texts and literature, writers sometimes show an explanation of the causes and effects of situations that involve persons, places, things, or animals.

Example

Why do we need to become digitally literate? One reason is that computers have very quickly come to play a central role in society. Prior to World War II, some experts predicted that the United States would never need more than four or five digital computers. Today, although it is impossible to determine the exact number, billions of computers are in use. More and more are produced each minute of the day, and computers are now being embedded in almost every electronic device. The automobile has several, including the GPS (global positioning system), a dashboard computer to control the digital gauges, an embedded computer in the DVD player, and a computer that runs the engine. As a result, a typical car now has more computers than many thought would exist in the entire United States. Today, very few (if any) professions exist that do not use computers.

> This example explains the reasons for the need to become literate. There are many uses of computers. The purpose is to explain.

Narrate

Writers, reporters, witnesses to incidents, and persons who experience something give detailed information that happen from the beginning to the end. Their purpose is to narrate. Words and the paragraph organization pattern that signals time will help you recognize the author's pattern to narrate in both informational texts and literature.

Example

Abraham Lincoln won the election in 1860 as the first Republican president. On September 22, 1862, following the dramatic Union victory at Antietam, he presented the Preliminary Emancipation Proclamation.

This example presents what happened in 1860 and 1862. The purpose is to narrate.

Authors have a reason or purpose in creating print and digital materials that include literature and informational texts. Since the purpose is not usually stated in these materials, you will need to apply the things that you have previously learned in this book such as ACTOR, vocabulary enhancement, transitions, main idea, supporting details, paragraph patterns, inference, and fact and opinion to figure out the intent of the author. Purposes include general, specific, or a combination of general and specific purposes.

Mastery Test 1

Choose from the list the purpose that each paragraph mostly presents. Write the letter of your answer in the space provided.

_____1. Margaret catches her breath as she nervously opens the envelope that bears a familiar address.
   a. inform   c. narrate
   b. describe   d. explain

_____2. J. Willard Marriott started his career as a restaurateur in Washington, D. C., during the late 1920s. At the urging of his son, J. W. (Bill) Marriott, Jr., he opened his first hotel in 1957, and eventually decided to focus exclusively on lodging.
   a. entertain   c. explain
   b. narrate   d. describe

_____3. Inexpensive lodging was common throughout the United States, but quality levels were inconsistent and often poor.
   a. entertain   c. explain
   b. narrate   d. describe

_____4. A generation ago, almost every hotel brand was owned and operated separately. Now, major hotel companies have collections of hotel brands.
   a. give information about hotel brands
   b. explain the changes in hotel business
   c. contrast the state of hotel ownership before and at present
   d. persuade major companies to buy small hotels

_____5. Fred Harvey opened a restaurant in the railroad station at Topeka, Kansas, in 1876. The company succeeded based on his formula for excellent food, good service, and reasonable prices.
   a. entertain on the story of Fred Harvey
   b. give information about Fred's restaurant success
   c. describe Fred's restaurant
   d. narrate the beginning and later development of the restaurant

_____6. White Castle established a system involving counter service, mass production of a Limited menu, strict sanitation procedures, and a chain of identical units.
   a. entertain on the story about White Castle
   b. give information about White Castle's success
   c. describe White Castle's system operation
   d. persuade us to buy White Castle burger

_____7. After eating six White Castle hamburgers, I become sleepy. In my dreams, I still see White Castle's small burgers.
   a. persuade us to buy White Castle burgers   c. entertain us
   b. inform us of the tasty burgers   d. describes the burger

_____8. Do not eat too much burgers because these are greasy and fatty.
   a. inform   c. describe
   b. narrate   d. persuade

_____9. At the aftermath of the super typhoon that directly hit the province of Leyte in the Philippines, the devastation that it brought became clear. About 11,000 people died, streets flooded for several days, thousands of families were dislocated and properties were destroyed. Peoples across the world promptly extended their help to the country.
   a. inform us about the problems brought by the super typhoon to Leyte
   b. narrate the things that happened after a typhoon had hit Leyte
   c. highlight the generosity of people to those who are in need
   d. persuade us to be ready when a typhoon is announced

_____10. Military and police officers knocked at every door in the town that was projected to get hit by a powerful hurricane. Many did not want to leave their homes. After one day, the same people were seen on rooftops of their houses asking for help. They should have listened to warnings.
   a. inform us on the things that the military and police officers did to save the people from the flood
   b. persuade us to decide wisely
   c. teach us a lesson to survive flooding by going to the house rooftop
   d. persuade us to act accordingly to authoritative warnings

Mastery Test 2

Choose from the list the purpose that each paragraph mostly presents. Write the letter of your answer in the space provided.

_____1. Babies cry because they communicate something, but they cannot talk. They cry to communicate pain, discomfort, hunger, boredom, or loneliness.
    a. persuade you to find out why babies cry
    b. inform you about the reasons why babies cry
    c. explain the things to do when babies cry
    d. compare the reasons why babies cry

_____2. Sometimes when babies cry, parents and caregivers become frustrated, they shake the babies in order to stop them from crying. Unfortunately, some babies die due to intense shaking. Parents and caregivers must take childrearing education to foster good communication with babies.
    a. persuade you to find out why babies cry
    b. inform you about the reasons why babies cry
    c. persuade parents and caregivers to study how to take care of children
    d. explain the effects of shaking babies

_____3. The relationship between humanity and diversity is analogous to the relationship between sunlight and the variety of colors that make up the visual spectrum. Similar to how sunlight passing through a prism disperses into the variety of colors that comprise the visual spectrum, the human species inhabiting planet earth is dispersed into a variety of different groups that comprise the human spectrum.

Source: Cuseo, Humanity, Diversity, and the Liberal Arts, 2E. Kendall Hunt Publishing Company, 2015.

    a. inform you about humanity and diversity
    b. persuade you to respect diversity
    c. compare diversity with the sunlight
    d. entertain

_____4. In a national survey of American voters, the vast majority of respondents agreed that diversity is more than just "political correctness" Diversity is also an *educational* issue— an integral element of a liberal arts education that enhances learning, personal development, and career preparation of *all* students. It magnifies the quality of the college experience by bringing multiple perspectives and alternative approaches to *what* is being learned and *how* it's being learned.

Source: Cuseo, Humanity, Diversity, and the Liberal Arts, 2E. Kendall Hunt Publishing Company, 2015.

    a. describes diversity
    b. explains the pursuit of diversity as political correctness
    c. informs us the importance of diversity in education
    d. persuades us to ensure that diversity is taught in the classroom

_____5. Use a 2 feet by 2 feet paper that can withstand the wind to form the body of your kite. Cut it to the shape of a diamond. Tape or paste a strip of cardboard on each of the four

sides and at the middle to make the kite sturdy. Punch a small hole on top of the paper and attach a piece of string about 36 feet. Cut a piece of paper and tape it to the bottom of the diagonal paper. This is the tail of the kite.
a. narrates what happened to the kite
b. gives instructions on how to make a kite
c. informs what the kite can do
d. tells you how easy to make a kite

_____6. From the bat cave, Batman and Robin zoomed to the town. Blow by blow, they cornered and finished 10 bad guys.
a. describe
b. entertain
c. persuade
d. inform

_____7. If you watch Batman and Robin, you will really be amazed on their speed and precision of finishing their opponents. I think you will agree with me that it is worth watching the movie if you want entertainment.
a. inform
b. persuade
c. entertain
d. describe

_____8. Unlike Robin, Batman is about 6 feet and 4 inches and physically well built. Robin is about five feet. Both wear costumes, so that people will not recognize them.
a. entertain
b. persuade
c. describe
d. compare and contrast

Mastery Test 3

When you read, you do not choose from a list of purposes. You create your own list and decide which makes sense. Study the following passages and identify the purpose. Write your answer and the basis for your answer in the spaces provided. Recall the general and specific purposes. What does the passage generally tell you and do?

Example

Sleep enhances your mood because it activates many chemicals that influence your emotions and mood. If you lack sleep, therefore, you are likely to become irritable, cranky, and unhappy. These situations show that enough sleep is important.

Purpose To prove that enough sleep is important

Reason The paragraph explains the benefits of sleep and the consequences of inadequate sleep.

1. Some researchers, psychologists, and hypnotists tell patients that they are getting sleepy and becoming more relaxed. They also tell them to focus on an object, image, or a given direction.

Purpose _____

Reason _____

2. In order to store this important information in your long-term memory, you have to apply strategies that will help you remember this. You will find these strategies to be effective.

   Purpose _____

   Reason _____

3. We cannot deny that there is a great difference between a person who is intelligent but does not study and an average student who studies diligently. Here are the differences.

   Reason _____

   Purpose _____

4. When you take a long trip, follow the following tips.

   Reason _____

   Purpose _____

5. When you reach your vacation destination, you will notice a fountain at the entrance. The water repeatedly shoots up and down 15 feet. It is decorated with flowers of different colors.

   Reason _____

   Purpose _____

SUSTAINABILITY PROBLEMS AND SOLUTIONS

1Not all problems we face are sustainability problems. Sustainability problems are a special class of problems that pose a particularly urgent threat to human–ecological systems. Their urgency is compounded by their complexity and their involvement of multiple sectors and actors across multiple scales. This complexity means that they are best tackled by using interdisciplinary approaches as diverse as the many systems that affect the problem or by applying new methods to these problems.

2An example of a sustainability problem is urban air pollution. It poses significant harm to the health of many urban residents, and it causes billions of dollars in damage to infrastructure and crops, lost worker productivity, and additional burdens on the healthcare system. It is caused by a complex array of factors: emissions from electric power generation, exhaust from trucks and automobiles, and emissions from construction and industrial sites, among others. Obviously, to tackle such a problem would require understanding of such diverse issues as household energy use, freight logistics, the demand for automobile and air travel, and the technological and regulatory factors governing automobile, freight, industrial, and construction site emissions. It gets even more complex when governments must set air pollution standards, implement strategies to meet these standards, and monitor them. Something as simple as clean air, as we can see, is not a simple matter, but requires a team approach involving efforts from across many different disciplines, such as urban planning, engineering, business, and public policy. Cultural and psychological factors may underlie certain household practices that result in pollution, and these need exploration as well.

Urban transportation and its sustainability problems

3Following from such a definition of a sustainability problem, we can see that urban transportation is not a sustainability problem in and of itself, but it is a significant direct and indirect cause of several sustainability problems. This chain of causation means that focusing on urban transportation is an effective approach to solving those problems it causes. Here, we introduce some of these urgent problems that urban transportation systems cause, grouped into different realms; some, such as petroleum dependence, cause a set of other "indirect"

4Most urban travel in the United States is by automobile; thus, the urgent problems urban transportation systems create here derive from the particular issue of using automobiles for mass transportation. The problems from urban transportation in other countries may relate to different issues particular to systems there. In 2000, 88 percent of United States workers drove or were driven to work, and fewer than 5 percent took public transit. For all trips, not just those to work, only about 6 percent are by human power (biking or walking). Compare this statistic with other industrialized countries like England, where 16 percent walk and bike, or Germany, where more than 34 percent bike or walk. Thus, when we investigate the significant problems arising from our transportation system, they largely result from using the private automobile for mass transportation. Here, we review briefly some of these problems, grouped along social, economic, and environmental realms.

Social problems social disruption from traffic fatalities and injuries

5Around 3,000 people—roughly the same number that perished during the September 11 attacks—die every month on the nation's roadways from traffic crashes. Americans have been dying on our roadways at that rate for the past 700 months. On top of these fatalities are about 200,000 injuries from traffic crashes monthly, resulting in thousands of permanent disabilities and days, weeks, or months of physical therapy and recovery and countless days lost from work or school.

Social inequality, exclusion, and isolation

6Planning a transportation system around the need to own and operate a personal vehicle means that, for those who are unable to do so, the system will be poorly configured. In most metropolitan areas, around 25 percent of the population is too old to drive, too young to drive, or not able to afford an automobile. The dispersion and suburbanization of jobs and housing and the resulting automobile dependence means that those who cannot afford or cannot operate an automobile have greater difficulty finding work, and they can become isolated and excluded from the mainstream of society. In many central cities where low-income populations lack access to automobiles and decent transportation, a lack of access to healthy food and grocery options results in what is known as a "food desert." The reliance on cheaper but less healthy food options has been shown to create health problems, especially in inner-city neighborhoods.

Sedentary lifestyles and detrimental health impacts

7Studies have shown that transportation has a significant impact on how active people are, and in turn, on their health. The lack of "walkability" in many metropolitan areas leads to low rates of cycling and walking, and this inactivity is linked to higher body mass indexes and poorer health. Obesity and diabetes are at alarming rates in many segments of the population, including children.

Ethical dilemmas of petroleum dependence

8The strict reliance on petroleum for the operation of the economy is called "petroleum dependence." Today, U.S. demand for petroleum overwhelms the country's own domestic supply: more than half its petroleum needs are imported from other countries. Ethical problems arise because dependence on oil imports forces the United States to make political decisions that may often betray its own ethics. More fundamentally, however, dependence on oil means we are forced to use it, even if we do not want to. U.S. citizens in several cases were basically powerless to react by choosing alternatives, which were simply not available at any reasonable scale. Examples include the 2010 BP oil spill in the Gulf of Mexico, when the Exxon Valdez oil tanker ran aground in 1989 off the coast of Alaska, and when the government of Nigeria executed indigenous activists in 1995 who were questioning its oil export practices. What is worse is that even these significant spills are dwarfed by the total amount of routine spills that result from the normal operation of the oil distribution system. Petroleum dependence poses a significant ethical dilemma for those urban residents hoping to choose freely how their lives affect the larger world.

Economic problems: Costs of traffic fatalities and injuries, traffic congestion, and petroleum dependence

10Traffic fatalities and injuries impose large financial costs on our society. Some of these costs are borne by car insurance holders, and others fall on society at large. These "externalized" costs are estimated to be between $46 and $161 billion per year. In good traffic conditions, driving is normally the fastest way to travel in U.S. cities, however, during rush-hour, the average traveler can suffer from long delays. At a value of $10 per hour, these delays are estimated to cost between $63 and $246 billion per year. Petroleum

Ververidis Vasilis/Shutterstock.com

dependence imposes several kinds of financial costs on the U.S. economy. Significant costs, estimated to total between $7 and $30 billion per year, result from lack of flexibility in the economy to respond to changes in price. Additional costs result from the non-competitive structure of the oil industry, resulting in prices that are higher than what a competitive market would charge. The sum of these costs since 1970 is estimated to be over $8 trillion. Finally, the United States military incurs costs for its presence in locations of strategic importance to the oil industry, amounting to estimates of between $6 and $60 billion.

Local air pollution

11The Clean Air Act, enacted in 1970 and enforced by the U.S. Environmental Protection Agency, has had a major impact on regulating and reducing pollution emissions from automobiles for more than 40 years. Most pollution is reduced to just a small percent of what it was before regulation. But, large increases in driving and worsening congestion in metropolitan areas means that although each vehicle is cleaner, local air pollution remains a national problem. More than 120 million Americans live in counties that fail at least one of the National Ambient Air Quality Standards that define what levels of pollution in the air are safe to breathe.

Infrastructure barrier effects

12Infrastructure for automobiles, such as freeways and arterial roads, are large, intrusive, and can separate neighborhoods from each other and cause barriers to mobility. Studies show that these "barrier effects" exacerbate automobile dependence because they can deter residents from walking or cycling for even short trips.

Greenhouse gas emissions

13Greenhouse gasses in the atmosphere manage the planet's greenhouse process, whereby temperatures are regulated. Most greenhouse gases are created from the burning of fuels to create energy either in electric power plants, factories, or in vehicles which burn fuels for energy. Overwhelming evidence suggests that the significant greenhouse gas emissions created by human activity, rivaling the amount of gases produced by natural ecological systems, are influencing the

planet's normal climate. Reducing greenhouse gas emissions is essential to avoid the worst effects of climate change. Unfortunately, because human-induced climate change has already begun, we are already too late in avoiding some significant climate change effects.

Production and disposal of vehicle

14Cars and lights trucks use a large amount of non-renewable steel, glass, rubber, and other materials. Data from 1990 showed that automobile production consumed 13 percent

Tamas Panczel - Eross/Shutterstock.com

of the total national consumption of steel, 16 percent of its aluminum, 69 percent of its lead, 36 percent of its iron, 36 percent of its platinum, and 58 percent of its rubber. Around 10 million automobiles are disposed of every year.

Contributed by Aaron Golub. © Kendall Hunt Publishing Company.

Comprehension Check

Choose the best word or phrase that completes each sentence. Write the letter of your answer in the space provided.

_____1. If resources are not sustained, these will become _____.
   a. more   c. scarce
   b. better   d. worse

_____2. Of the following, _____ is not an effect of air pollution.
   a. diseases   c. enough money
   b. lost farmer's income   d. exhaust from vehicles

_____3. With increased air pollution, it is possible that more people will buy _____.
   a. fresh air   c. air conditioner
   b. heater   d. bottled water

_____4. The factor that mostly contributes to the cause of sustainability problem in urban transportation in the United States is _____.
   a. using automobile   c. public transportation
   b. walking   d. biking

_____5. The factor that directly contributes to health problems is _____.
   a. lack of access to healthy food   c. absence of transportation means
   b. being old   d. too young

_____6. The United States relies on _____ of its petroleum resources.
   a. more than 50%   c. 100%
   b. 50%   d. less than 50%

_____7. The Clean Air Act is intended to reduce _____.
   a. local pollution   c. clean air
   b. regulations on automobile use   d. air pollution emissions from automobiles

_____8. Reducing greenhouse gas emissions is essential to _____.
   a. help prevent the effects of climate change
   b. add to the effects of climate change
   c. have no effect on climate change
   d. manage the planet's greenhouse process

_____9. Reports indicate that annual automobile production uses _____ the most.
   a. steel   c. iron
   b. aluminum,   d. lead

___10. The purpose of this article is to _____.
   a. inform us the meaning of sustainability
   b. persuade us to help in the sustainability effort
   c. analyze the barriers to sustainability
   d. explain the sustainability problems, causes, and effects of urban transportation

Answer the following questions.

1. What is sustainability?

2. Why is there a need to regulate vehicle gas emission?

3. How can you contribute to lessen the effect of climate change?

4. What are the three effects of oil dependency?

10

Tone

In literature, characters speak and move to show their emotions or mood. In informational texts, the mood is usually objective or matter of fact. In newspaper editorials, magazines, and other periodicals, the writer's tone may not be objective. Recognizing different tones or attitudes will help you better understand what you read. Like the purpose, the tone is not explicitly stated. In this chapter, you will be able to recognize different tones in reading materials.

Topics

Words That Express Feelings

When you listen to someone face to face, you can infer the person's emotions through the words that are used, facial expressions, gestures, and tone of voice. When you listen to someone without seeing his or her face, you can still sense the emotion through the words used and how these are said. Similarly, when you read, you do not see the writer's face. However, when you read, you only see words and/or pictures and other forms of visuals. Concentrating on the words and visual representations being used and the ideas being presented, you shall be able to recognize the attitude or the tone of the writer.

The following words that express feelings will guide you in recognizing the tone of the characters in stories and the writer.

Words That Express Feelings

amazed	disappointed	hopeless	satisfied
amused	disgraced	horrified	scared
annoyed	disgusted	hostile	self-conscious
anxious	dismayed	humiliated	shamed
aroused	distrusting	humorous	shocked
arrogant	disturbed	hurt	spiteful
awkward	eager	inferior	suspicious
bored	embarrassed	insecure	sympathy
calm	enthusiastic	insulted	tragic
caring	envious	irritated	trusting
cautious	fearful	proud	uncertain
cheerful	frustrated	receptive	uncomfortable
comfortable	grief-stricken	regretful	uneasy
concern	guilty	rejected	worried

absurd, preposterous, ridiculous, ludicrous, farcical, laughable—wildly unreasonable, illogical, or inappropriate

aggravated—made more serious

alienated, estranged—feel isolated or alone

ambivalent, contradictory—having mixed feelings or contradictory ideas about something or someone

anguished, very sad, sorrowful, distressed, heartbroken—experiencing or expressing severe mental or physical pain or suffering

antipathy, antagonism, animosity, aversion—deep-seated feeling of dislike

apathetic, detached—showing no interest, enthusiasm, concern, or care for others awestruck, amazed, wondering—filled with wonder or awe

bitter, hateful, angry, hurt—painful or unpleasant to accept something

compassionate, sympathetic understanding, caring, sensitive—feeling sorrow or showing sympathy for the misfortunes of others or showing concern for others

conceited, arrogant—excessively proud of oneself

cynical—believing that people are motivated by personal gain or self-interest, expecting the worst from people

distressed—suffering strain, misery, or agony

dreading—very afraid or fearful

evasive, misleading—avoiding or confusing the issue

exasperated—angry, annoyed, irritated

formal—using an official style, of a high social class

elated, delighted, ecstatic, jubilant, overjoyed, pleased, thrilled, gladdened, joyous—feeling or showing great pleasure

grumpy—bad tempered

incredulous—unbelieving

indifferent, detached—does not care

indignant, outraged—very angry, annoyed

intrigued—fascinated, aroused, captivated, interested

ironic—stating the opposite of what is expected; saying the opposite of what is meant

irreverent—lacking respect for authority

melancholy, depressed, sad, dejected—having low spirits

objective, factual, straightforward, truthful—using facts without emotions or opinions

optimistic—hopeful, looking on the bright side or hoping for something good for the future

outraged—fierce anger

outspoken—speaking one's mind on issues

pathetic, pitiful—moving one to compassion or pity

pessimistic—looking on the negative side, thinking about the worst to happen

prayerful—religiously thankful

reticent, withdrawn, introverted, inhibited, shy—not speaking out

reverent—feeling or showing respect

righteous—morally correct

romantic, intimate, loving—expresses love or affection

sarcastic—saying one thing and meaning another

satiric—using irony, wit, and sarcasm to discredit or ridicule

scornful—mocking, ridiculing

sensational, overdramatized—causing great public interest and excitement

sentimental, nostalgic—remembering the good old days

subjective, opinionated—expressing opinions and feelings

tragic—regrettable or deplorable

vengeful, vindictive—seeking revenge

Review

Choose five words from the two lists that show positive emotions.

1. _____

2. _____

3. _____

4. _____

5. _____

Choose five words from the two lists that show negative emotions.

1. _____

2. _____

3. _____

4. _____

5. _____

Choose two words from the two lists that show uncertainties.

1. _____

2. _____

Choose two words from the two lists that show no emotions

1. _____

2. _____

Knowing the meanings of words that describe tones will guide you to recognize the mood or attitude that the writer presents in literary and informational texts. The tone may also give you a clue on the purpose of the author or speaker. When you read, imagine that you are the one speaking and reading with expression. This will help you to relate to given ideas or situations.

Example

I have done everything to succeed. However, my time and efforts did not mean anything. I am still a failure.

What do these sentences tell you? In spite of everything that the speaker has done, he or she has not succeeded.

What is the mood or tone? Frustrated

Practice 1

Choose the tone that is best expressed in each statement. Write the letter in the space provided.

a. optimistic	c. matter of fact	e. calming
b. uncertain	d. joyful	f. appreciative

_____1. The criminal justice system, which comprises the police, courts, and correctional facilities, enforces social norms, laws, and justice.

_____2. I am not sure what will happen because one witness testified that he saw someone that resembled my face and built.

_____3. I still think that you will be acquitted because your lawyer presented the DNA test that proved that the blood collected at the crime scene did not match yours.

_____4. After the verdict was read, the defendant embraced his lawyer. "Thank you for everything, you are my hero!

_____5. I am so happy for you, my friend. Finally, you can move on!

Practice 2

Choose the tone that is best expressed in each statement. Write the letter in the space provided.

_____1. I want to know what my grandparents did to help them acquire this beautiful twenty-story building.
  a. admiring   b. doubtful   c. curious   d. excited

_____2. Ten years ago, we were very poor. My mother had to divide a whole fried chicken among the six members of the family for dinner. We went to school with broken shoes that Mom had to keep sewing to prevent water to sip in. Unlike other children, I did not get a new dress for my birthday. It was hard for me to understand that.
  a. objective   c. self-pitying
  b. sorrowful   d. accepting

_____3. I remember those days when my four siblings excitedly waited for Father to come from work. He promised to bring something because it was payday for his doorman job at a hotel. When he came, he was with all smiles.
  a. happy   c. affectionate
  b. nostalgic   d. lighthearted

_____4. After three months, he came like a dying chicken. He broke the news with tears in his eyes, that the hotel would change management. His sadness pierced my heart.
   a. worried
   b. pessimistic
   c. depressed
   d. optimistic

_____5. "I got something good for one month. I do not know how we shall live without food and shelter for the rest," he said.
   a. worried
   b. pessimistic
   c. sad
   d. hopeful

_____6. My mother said, pray and trust the Lord. He will not abandon you. You will get a job.
   a. reverent
   b. optimistic
   c. hopeless
   d. accepting

_____7. I really do not know, my dear. I will keep looking and hope I will get one.
   a. tolerant
   b. optimistic
   c. hopeful
   d. straightforward

_____8. After a month, Dad was shouting with joy and calling my mother's name, then my siblings' names.
   a. bewildered
   b. disbelieving
   c. surprised
   d. uncertain

_____9. My mother immediately rushed to my dad and asked, "What is the matter?"
   a. straightforward
   b. uncertain
   c. surprised
   d. happy

_____10. I could not believe what I heard when he said, "I won fifty million dollars in the lottery."
   a. uncertain
   b. disbelieving
   c. surprised
   d. happy

Usually in textbooks, the writer gives factual information; the tone is objective or straightforward. The purpose is to inform. Use ACTOR to better understand the following paragraphs.

Example

Sociology developed in Europe during the 1800s. Historical events of the Enlightenment, the French Revolution, and the American Revolution shaped the way people thought about issues such as freedom, inequality, power, and progress. The Industrial Revolution was just beginning, and a whole host of social problems emerged as people with different backgrounds, cultures, races, religions, and nationalities merged together in newly developing cities to find work.

Source: Vissing, An Introduction to Sociology, Kendall Hunt Publishing Company, 2013.

What does the paragraph tell you? It presents the start of the field of sociology and the events during that time. The author used factual statements. The tone is straightforward or objective.

Writers use a combination of tones to achieve a purpose. For example, if the purpose is to persuade readers to agree with an idea or make an action, the tone is persuasive and objective or factual. Therefore, there is a combination of facts and opinions and tones.

Example

Although many of us are aware that a healthy diet can prevent diseases, not enough of us know about the healing powers of food. Proper nutrition helps regulate behavior, increase energy and boost mood. With the right vitamins, minerals, essential fatty acids, and amino acids, people can begin to fight all sorts. Since proper nutrition is important, we have to read food labels to be sure that we are buying nutritious food.

> What is the writer's purpose? The author persuades us to read the food labels to find out if the food we buy is nutritious. This is an opinion and the tone is persuasive. The writer also presents factual information regarding the importance of eating nutritious food. The tone is straightforward or objective. There is a combination of straightforward and persuasive tones.

When you use ACTOR, you are able to understand every sentence and connect ideas. Ask, what or who are we talking about? What is being said about to what and who? In using ACTOR, you activate prior knowledge relating to content and or vocabulary, connect this prior knowledge to the new information, trigger strategies to ensure comprehension, organize in your mind the ideas that you get from what you read and respond by reciting or writing it. When you are able to recite the correct information, it means that you understand and remember the important things that you read.

Mastery Test 1

Choose the tone that is best expressed in each statement. Write the letter in the space provided.

_____1. Dance has been used to communicate feelings and covey a message by tribal leaders, professional dancers, children, teenagers, adults, and seniors.
    a. happy   c. admiring
    b. straightforward   d. instructive

_____2. The three general purposes are to inform, to persuade, and to entertain. To identify the purpose, ask yourself about the author's reason for writing the passage. What does it tell you to do?
    a. curious   c. matter of fact
    b. instructive   d. persuasive

_____3. Two major indicators of human-caused global climate change are increase in atmospheric CO_2 concentration and global temperature over the past few hundred years.
    a. curious   c. suggestive
    b. matter of fact   d. persuasive

_____4. People who perform illegal logging do not feel any guilt for disturbing the ecological system and causing unwanted landslides. They should get a stiff penalty for their action.
   a. concerned   c. outraged
   b. tolerant   d. uncertain

_____5. She needs help during this time that she is recovering from the unfortunate situation that came like a hurricane.
   a. pleading   c. sympathetic
   b. objective   d. ironic

_____6. Since she put me down yesterday at the conference, I will throw dirt at her when we meet today.
   a. scornful   c. angry
   b. revengeful   d. scheming

_____7. If you want to be successful in your first business, you have to consider many factors. First, you should make a product that consumers need and want. Second, study all existing products in the market and determine how to make your product better than these. Third, plan how you will design your product. There are many other things to consider.
   a. objective   c. certain
   b. instructive   d. tolerant

_____8. He invented a gadget that would cause a very mild electric shock to an intruder. Five cases of house burglary were reported last month. However, his son was the first victim because he did not turn off the gadget.
   a. sad   c. ironic
   b. angry   d. uncertain

_____9. The protestors against a candidate clashed with others who were in favor of that candidate. This escalated to throwing of stones against each other, burning of cars, and destruction of properties. I am tired of these situations, and the mayor is not doing enough to put an end to this insanity.
   a. depressed   c. detached
   b. discouraged   d. outraged

_____10. We shall show the might of our military. The mother of all bombs in the world will silence all disruptors of order and agitators of unrest in that region. They will think many times before they act because we have the best military capabilities in the world.
   a. ambivalent   c. straightforward
   b. pessimistic   d. superior

Mastery Test 2

Write a sentence or sentences to express each of the following tones. Imagine that you are saying the statements to yourself or someone with feelings.

Example:

Tolerant—It is all right to make a mistake because this is your first time to learn this lesson. I know that you will soon do better because you learn from your mistakes.

1. encouraging _____
   _____

2. self-critical _____
   _____

3. determined _____
   _____

4. defensive _____
   _____

5. apologetic _____
   _____

A HOLE IN MY LIFE

Stterryk/Shutterstock.com

1The living room as big as six classrooms was carpeted from wall to wall. Distinctly expensive paintings and gorgeous statues embellished this room. The sky blue curtains that were embossed with colorful embroidered flowers covered the glass windows. In contrast to these signs of affluence, a lanky man wearing a plain white V-neck shirt and faded jeans stood by the open window. His smooth and pinkish cheeks were partly covered with his long beard. His hair was trapped with a rubber band at the back, so it did not touch his shoulders.

2"Oh, it's another day again!" Sam said to himself. He clicked a button on the wall, and a screen similar to the one found in a movie theater appeared in front of him.

3"The situation here on 55th Street is very tense, Tom. About 100 very determined people are clashing with the New York police officers. They are blocking the street and preventing the cops from getting closer to the dilapidated building," Shellie announced.

4"This is our home! We have been living here for ten years. We fixed this building. Now, you are telling us to vacate this place. Uh . . . uh. . . . We aren't leaving our home," five men yelled in chorus.

5"The people here do not want to leave this building which they call home. The cops won't leave either. We shall take a close watch on this situation, Tom. Reporting from 55th street, this is Shellie Ruiz."

6"Thank you, Shellie," Tom replied.

7Sam felt strong, deep and fast heartbeats as he watched the news. His mouth became very dry and felt a heated balloon that burst on his face. A flash of light cruised his mind. He rushed to the backyard. He rubbed some dirt on his clothes and face. Soon the sound of a fast moving car broke the silence in his mansion. Soon the car found its place on 55th Street. As Sam got off the car, some colorful written symbols caught his attention. He went closer to the building until his curiosity led him inside. He felt the rising and falling of his lungs as he covered his nose and mouth.

8"This is what they call home," Sam uttered in disbelief. He continued walking until his attention was called by a dripping sound coming from a brownish stuff. While raising his head and his eye rolling over the chain of pipes, he suddenly found himself seated on the ground. He took a deep breath, tried to stand up, but his knees appeared to glue together. He closed his eyes with great dismay until he felt two hands holding his left hand and another two holding his right hand. With his arms on top of the shoulders of two men, he was able to limp to the direction that changed the previous scent. The dripping sound was gone.

9"This is our home, and we shall not leave this building," people yelled.

10When he lost sight of the two men who helped him, the things that he saw inside the building flashed in his memory. The damp dirt on his pants reminded him of what happened inside the building. Slowly, he limped to his parked car. Later, he was back to his mansion. As he was taking a shower, the incidents inside and outside the building on 55th Street kept lingering in his memory.

11Sam smiled and called his lawyer. "Attorney, please arrange a meeting with the people living in the building on 55th Street. I have an announcement."

12"Sir, that's dangerous. They don't want to vacate your building." Sam's lawyer cautioned.

"Don't worry about it. I am sure that the people who did not like to vacate the building will stop their chants," Sam responded. For the first time after his parents and two siblings' burials, Sam did not feel a hole in his life.

Comprehension Questions

Choose the best word or phrase that completes each sentence. Write the letter of your answer in the space provided.

_____1. The purpose of describing Sam's attire and hair and the living room in the first paragraph is to _____.
   a. show an example of affluence
   b. express Sam's need to be loved
   c. contrast simplicity and affluence
   d. describe Sam's deplorable condition

_____2. Sam changed his decision to sell the building most likely because he _____.
   a. could not force the homeless to move out of the building
   b. did not like the buyer's suggested price
   c. would allow the homeless people to continue living in the building.
   d. instructed his lawyer to sue the homeless before selling the building

_____3. The 12th paragraph suggests the lawyer's _____.
   a. sadness
   b. admiration
   c. apprehension
   d. ambivalence

_____4. Sam most likely _____ when he met the homeless.
   a. wore nice clothes to prove that he was the owner of the building
   b. wore dirty and simple clothes
   c. came with police officers
   d. came with his lawyer

_____5. The title of the story most likely suggests that _____.
   a. Sam was sad due to her parents' and siblings' deaths
   b. homeless people needed a permanent shelter
   c. the building had to be renovated
   d. the lawyer could not persuade Sam to avoid talking to the homeless

_____6. The italicized word in the sentence that follows most likely means _____.
   Expensive paintings and gorgeous statues *embellished* the living room.
   a. lit
   b. adorned
   c. complemented
   d. scattered

_____7. The story proves that _____.
   a. homeless people need help
   b. everyone has a destiny
   c. true happiness comes after making others happy
   d. money is important

_____8. The third paragraph includes sentences that show _____.
   a. facts   b. opinions   c. facts and opinions

_____9. Sam's change of attitude toward the homeless most likely started when _____.
   a. he could not move his knees
   b. two men helped him to stand up
   c. he entered the dilapidated building in disguise
   d. he reached home

_____10. The overall structure of the passage is _____.
   a. description
   b. cause and effect
   c. time
   d. list

Discussion Questions

1. If you were Sam's sibling, how would you feel after reading the story? Why?

   _____

   _____

   _____

   _____

2. Do you think other people would agree with Sam to talk to the homeless? Why?

   _____

   _____

   _____

   _____

3. What lesson about life did you learn from this story? Explain your answer.

   _____

   _____

   _____

   _____

11

Argument

Every day, you are likely to use arguments to make decisions on how to conduct personal functions, complete work activities, deal with school expectations, communicate ideas during a discussion, or act on different issues. In making an argument, you argue or make a point and give reasons for that point. It provides questions that include what do you think or want to happen and why? In this chapter, you will learn how to present a good argument.

Topics

Point or Position

Supports

Since argument is used in everyday life situations at home, in school, and at work, recognizing and making a good argument is important. Sometimes, persons who present their ideas tend to initially disagree when two opposing sides are presented. There are times when conversations turn into a heated discussion when a point is not clear or the supports are not convincing. If two points of view and valid supports are not presented, the disagreement may prolong. However, if a point of view is clear and is supported by accurate, reliable, related, clear, logical, and adequate information, the disagreement tends to lessen and likely leads to an agreement. Recognizing the elements of a good argument is important for the following reasons.

1. You may be asked to read arguments in editorials, position papers and research rationale, or studies in scholarly materials in your disciplines or major.
2. You may be assigned to write an argumentative essay in some of your courses.
3. In making decisions, you need to give reasons for your actions. Otherwise, the consequence of your decisions may not be pleasant due to hasty actions or thinking.
4. In some fields, the licensure test may require you to write an argument.

The basic parts of an argument are the point or position and supports to the point. The point or position must be clear or not confusing. The supports should be related to the point, accurate or true, clear or not confusing, logical or makes sense, and adequate enough to convince someone to agree.

Evaluating an Argument

1. Is the point clear or not confusing?
2. Are the supports relevant or related to the point?
3. Are the supports clear or not confusing?
4. Are the supports accurate or true?
5. Are the supports logical? Everything fits or makes sense together.
6. Are the supports adequate or enough to move you or someone into action?

Point or Position

A sentence that states a point or a position is the most general sentence that gives what a writer thinks and it is subject to agreement or disagreement. It is open to two points of view, one is for and another one is against. In an argument, the point needs supporting statements that can lead a person to agree or move into an action. For example, a friend invites you to watch a movie and gives you enough convincing reasons to agree to watch a movie. The possible actions are agreeing and watching the movie.

Study the Following Examples

It is raining today. Is it subject to agreement or disagreement? The answer is no because you will know the answer right away by looking outside. It is a fact that is subject to verification to be true or false. It is not subject to agreement or disagreement and will not lead to a further discussion and evaluation of supports.

You should not water the plants. Is it subject to agreement or disagreement? It needs a reason why you should or should not water the plants. Ask why and the answers to this question are the reasons or supports.

Your knowledge of main idea will help you because the main idea, like the point is the most general statement. In a similar way, your knowledge of supporting details will help you because you also need supporting statements to connect or relate to the point. However, the purpose of an argument is to persuade. Use ACTOR to be sure that you understand every given sentence and connect the ideas of all sentences to make sense of what you read.

Practice 1

Identify the point in each item. Write the number of the sentence in the space provided.

_____ Group 1

1Parents should not give their children an access to a joint credit card account.
2They may be encouraged to unwisely spend money that belongs to their parents.
3It is hard to monitor and regulate children's spending.
4Parents will pay for all bills incurred by their children.

_____ Group 2

1Depositors have the options to take a picture of a check and deposit it online by using the bank apps.
2They can use the nearest ATM machine to withdraw money instead of going to the bank.
3Technology has changed consumers' banking practices.
4They can transfer money from their savings to checking bank accounts anytime.
5They can also pay their bills online.
6They can check and print their bank statements anytime from any place.

_____ Group 3

1The marketing message can reach a wide variety of potential customers who use Facebook, Twitter, YouTube, and other forms of online communications.
2To be profitable, business executives should use social media and other creative ways in marketing their products.
3Consumers can be offered discounted prizes for wholesale orders or multiple product orders.

_____ Group 4

1They require special needs that are present in their natural habitat.
2They communicate their needs and feelings in ways which humans many not understand.
3Getting snakes for pets is not a good idea.
4It is expensive to maintain them because you have to buy their food.

_____ Group 5

1In some ways, they think like humans.
2They use tools in order to perform a certain task that humans do.
3Chimpanzees are considered one of the smartest animals in the world.
4They take care of their children.

Supports

Point—You should not water the plants.
Supports
According to the weatherman, it will rain today at 2:00 PM. It will last for three hours.

Notice that the supports give the reasons why you should not water the plants today. The two sentences are factual, accurate, and clear. These are also adequate to convince you not to water the plants. Sentences which do not make sense or sound awkward may not be the supports.

Examples

1. You should not water the plants <u>because it will rain</u>.
2. It will rain because <u>you should not water the plants</u>.

> The first sentence presents a correct point and a correct support. It makes sense and it does not sound awkward.

> An argument is composed of a point and supports. A point is what you think, and it is subject to agreement or disagreement. It is your position or a conclusion on something. There are two sides of a point or two opposing views. If you plan to make a decision, you consider two sides by evaluating your supports or reasons for taking one side. Similarly, during a discussion where there are two points of view or conclusions, your decision to agree and or to make actions is based on the clarity, accuracy, relevance, logic, and adequacy of supports.

Practice 1

Write the number of the sentence that states the point and the numbers of supporting statements in the spaces provided.

Group 1   Point _____   Supports _____

1They look at religious explanations for what happens. 2People consider different factors when they make their decisions and study the things that happen. 3They also rely on the notions of fate or destiny. 4Finally, they consider logical explanations for the occurrence of events whether these bring happiness or sadness.

Group 2   Point _____   Supports _____

1We use symbols all the time to understand the things around us, but we do not necessarily perceive these symbols to have the same meaning. 2For instance, words, body movements, and facial expressions all help us figure out what people mean. 3They have no meaning on their own; they have only the meaning that we attribute to them.

Group 3   Point _____   Supports _____

1Looking at colorful tattoos down a young man's arm and multiple facial piercings may give you an indication of what he is like inside. 2Some people may think he is a "punk" or a "troublemaker," while others may think he looks very fashionable and "cool." 3He could be a criminal, a celebrity, or a CEO—the fact is, you don't know by looking. 4We look for social context and interaction clues to help us make sense of situations and we may not be correct in our conclusion. 5If a store clerk is not courteous with us, this could mean she doesn't like us, that she is angry at her boss, that she hates her job, that she feels sick, or she's not mad at all. 6Perhaps, the trouble at home is preoccupying her mind or that is just her style of interaction.

Source: Vissing, An Introduction to Sociology, Kendall Hunt Publishing Company, 2013.

Group 4   Point _____   Supports _____

1Everyone should treat each other equally and with dignity. 2We breathe the same air and look at the same sky every day. 3We live in the same dwelling place that our parents provide us. 4We have the same wonderful parents and siblings. 5We share the same family goals that bind us together.

Group 5   Point _____   Supports _____

1You can always consult the bibliography on a previous project when you work on a related topic. 2For your research, it is important to plan to include a bibliography. 3It shows your professor that you have reviewed many resources in writing your paper. 4It enriches your resources of information on a project paper.

Practice 2

Write in the space provided the number of the sentence that is not a relevant support in each group. Write the reason why it is not relevant.

_____ Group 1

1It is good to be a member of a union. 2Through the union negotiation with the employer, members are treated fairly. 3Members have to pay annual fees to the union. 4They get more benefits from employers.

Reason _____

_____ Group 2

1Fundraisers after fundraisers that have saved this school for three years are not working anymore. 2It is time to close this school. 3Parents, teachers, students, and alumni's hard work to increase financial resources did not meet expectations. 4The wage freeze that the teachers have accepted did not help. 5Many students will ask for their grades.

Reason _____

_____

_____ Group 3

1You can follow what she has been doing to have a long life. 2She has been eating two eggs every day since she was 17 years old. 3Walking for 2 miles to work, a good exercise, makes her physically fit. 4Her constant prayers gives her peace of mind, strong body, and happy mood. 5She cannot ask for more; she is happy.

Reason _____

_____

_____ Group 4

1In this city, dance is becoming very popular. 2At one corner, on the fifth floor of a tall building, is a dance studio. 3Couples learn how to ballroom dance. 4Among the participants are members of different age groups, including older couples reliving the dances of their youth, gliding effortlessly across the floor. 5There are also younger couples experiencing ballroom dance for the first time, struggling with the elegance and precision demanded of this dance form. 6Across the street, in another studio, is a group of professional dancers taking a ballet class. 7I will ask my dad to build a dance school right away.

Reason _____

_____

_____ Group 5

1Dance is an interesting subject to study, but others do not see it this way. 2It is important to examine how dance continued throughout the ages and to see how dance developed. 3For example, when did it take on shape and form, and begin to hold artistic significance? 4As cultures became more advanced (such as those of Mesopotamia, Egypt and Asia, who began to make significant developments in writing, government and agriculture), people began to become more aware of how dance was presented. 5In other words, people began to pay attention to technique (form, content and style) and also to the appearance of dance. 6Although rituals remained important, many were replaced by ceremonies. 7Ceremonies were more highly structured and stylized than the spontaneous expression of the ritual and the dance, whether serving a spiritual function or done for entertainment, was now seen more as an artistic product.

From *Learning About Dance: Dance as an Art Form and Entertainment*, Seventh Edition.
Copyright © 2016 by Kendall Hunt Publishing Company. Reprinted by permission.

Reason _____

_____

Practice 3

Each group presents three statements, one of which is a point to the supports that follow. Write the letter of the point in the space provided. Write the reason for your answer.

_____ Group 1

    A. There are privileges that many Americans enjoy.
    B. These privileges are subtle and sometimes unconsciously granted to members of the majority group.
    C. A privilege is an advantage enjoyed by a person or group; it can be assigned to selected groups.

Supports—Which statement above is supported by the following sentences?
They can go shopping without being followed.
If they have the money, they are able to buy or rent housing in any neighborhood.
They are allowed to vote for their president.

Reason _____

_____

_____

_____ Group 2

    A. Right-handed people are typically unaware of privileges they enjoy that are denied to left-handed people.
    B. Lefties are still denied access to many tools and societal artifacts.
    C. Historically, right-handedness has always been considered "normal."

Supports—Which statement above is supported by the following sentences?
Power tools and stick shifts in automobiles are designed for righties.
Some classrooms do not provide chairs for the lefties.
Scissors for lefties are difficult to find.

Reason _____

_____

_____

Adapted from Diversity, p. 111.

Practice 4

Support each point with at least four relevant, clear, and accurate sentences. You may use facts, examples, quotations or statements from experts, statistics, common, or established knowledge, cause and effect statements, or personal experience. You may work in groups to share and/or add information.

1. We should use solar energy as a source of electricity.

_____

_____

_____

_____

_____

2. The quest for a healthy body can become unhealthy.

_____

_____

_____

_____

_____

3. The death penalty is a vital tool in the fight against crime.

_____

_____

_____

_____

_____

4. Education is a key to personal success.

_____

_____

_____

_____

As you review your argument, remember that the basic parts of an argument are the point or position and supports to the point. The point or position is clear or not confusing. The supports are logical or make sense, accurate or true, clear or not confusing, and adequate enough to convince someone to agree.

Evaluating an Argument

1. Is the point clear or not confusing?
2. Are the supports relevant or related to the point?
3. Are the supports clear or not confusing?

4. Are the supports accurate or true?

5. Are the supports adequate or enough to move you or someone into action?

6. Are the supports logical? Does everything fit or make sense together?

Mastery Test 1

Write the number of the sentence that states the point in the space provided.

_____ Group 1

1Recent warming of the planet has generated concern among scientists and others. 2In the past, climate changes were caused by natural factors, the current warming trend is primarily the result of human activities. 3If it is not addressed soon, climate change has the potential to disrupt agriculture, water supply, weather patterns, and other conditions essential for our survival.

_____ Group 2

1The vast majority of scientists studying climate change bring no particular political agenda to their work. 2However, because that research is increasingly pointing to the reality of climate change and a major human role in causing that change, it is sometimes dismissed as being motivated by a political agenda. 3Climate change is among the most controversial of environmental issues, and in recent years the issue has become highly politicized.

_____ Group 3

1Human activities cause climate change by adding carbon dioxide (CO_2) and certain other heat-trapping gases to the atmosphere. 2Although global temperatures have varied naturally over thousands of years, natural variability alone cannot account for the rapid rise in global temperatures during recent decades. 3When sunlight reaches the earth's surface, it can be reflected (especially by bright surfaces like snow) or absorbed (especially by dark surfaces like open water or tree tops). 4Absorbed sunlight warms the surface and is released back into the atmosphere as heat. 5Certain gases trap this heat in the atmosphere, warming the Earth's surface.

Mastery Test 2

Write in the space provided the number of the sentence that is not a relevant support to the point in each group. Write the reason for your answer.

_____ Group 1

1Owning a house is not advisable. 2If you lose your job and cannot pay for the mortgage or the monthly payment for a number of months, the bank will foreclose your house—you will not be allowed to live there. 3You are responsible for the repair of your house like leaking roof, malfunctioning heater, or air conditioner. 4I got a discount when a contractor worked on the roof of my house and kitchen remodeling. 5You have to pay for home insurance. 6When there is snow, you take care of removing it in front of your house.

Reason _____

_____

_____ Group 2

1Renting an apartment is not advisable. 2You have to ask permission from the landlord or owner of the apartment in order to paint the walls, place a TV satellite or own pets. 3The landlord can raise the rent every year or at the time of contract renewal. 4I pay $1,500 a month for my apartment. 5You may not be able to live in the apartment as long as you want because the contract lease is usually renewed every year—the landlord decides if you will be allowed to continue to stay.

Reason _____

_____

_____ Group 3

1Cars must pay $15.00 while trucks must pay $20.00 in order to pass this highway going to the next state. 2According to the survey, drivers say that they are willing to pay for the new rate if they find the roads cleaner and safer. 3The money that will be collected will be used to open more lanes to make driving faster. 4It will also be used to promptly clear the highway during the winter storm. 5In addition, it will be used for better regular road maintenance. 6The agency that is responsible for the highway maintenance will be able to pay for existing debts due to the raise of employees' wages and other administrative costs to keep the highway running.

Reason _____

_____

_____ Group 4

1Visual literacy is a pathway to appreciating and contributing to the visual landscape of the workplace. 2It helps people responsible for successfully creating product packaging that consumers will find informative and easy to use. 3It contributes to the design of objects such as computers, phones, and other electronics that end users find intuitive and straightforward. 4Unfortunately, most of our educational experiences keep us isolated from the visual realm.

Reason _____

_____

_____ Group 5

1What you may have missed in the way of visual education has never been more important than it is today. 2Somewhere around the third grade our crayons are taken away from us, and from that point onward, unless one opts to study art or design. ₃Anyone studying business, marketing, or communication must become familiar with the rudiments of visual literacy. ₄All of us need to understand how we see and make sense of the visual flow and flux around us and to learn the intricacies of visual language.

Adapted from Ryan, Learning to See — A Guide to Visual Literacy, Kendall Hunt Publishing Company, 2012.

Reason _____

_____

Mastery Test 3

In each group, a point is stated. Choose the sentences that support each point from the list that follows. Write the numbers of the supports for each group and the reason for choosing these sentences. One sentence is not a good support in each group.

_____ Group 1

Point: People should have a very clear understanding that good nutrition is important.

Supports: Numbers of Sentences _____

Reason _____

_____

₁According to the U.S. Department of Health and Human Services, unhealthy eating and inactivity cause 310,000–580,000 deaths every year, which is similar to the number of deaths caused by tobacco and 13 times more than are caused by guns. ₂Unhealthy eating and physical inactivity are major contributors to reduced quality of life and disabilities. ₃Better nutrition could reduce the cost of heart disease, cancer, stroke, and diabetes by $71 billion each year. ₄Membranes that contain fats surround all the cells of your body. ₅Good nutrition provides energy and muscles.

_____ Group 2

Point: To put a time frame into perspective, very interesting studies that were reported 100 years since 1890 showed a large period of growth of the science of nutrition.

Supports: Numbers of Sentences _____

Reason _____

_____

₁E. V. McCollum (Sommer, 1989) and Adelle Davis (Harper, 1991) discovered fat-soluble vitamin A in butter and discovered water-soluble vitamin B in wheat germ. ₂Axel Holst and Theodor Frolich were pioneers in the combat of scurvy by discovering an antiscorbutic substance (vitamin C) in fresh vegetables (Norum & Gray, 2002). 3By experimenting with fish oils, Edward Mellanby discovered a substance (vitamin D) to prevent rickets (Mellanby & Cantag, 1919). 4By 1920, the science of nutrition was beginning to add reliable information about relationships between diet and health. 5These pivotal "discoveries" set the stage for the next several decades of nutrient research.

From *Nutrition and Health Today*, Second Edition, by Alicia Sinclair and Lana Lewis.
Copyright © 2011 by Alicia Sinclair and Lana Lewis. Reprinted by permission of Kendall Hunt Publishing Company.

TURNING POINT

1Pleasant situations which are followed by unwanted ones appear to occur for a reason that is difficult to understand. In 1989, Nick had applied for a travel grant to attend a convention of the Mathematical Association of America in Chicago, Illinois, USA. Fortunately, he was awarded a grant that could help fund his hotel stay and airfare for the convention. However, after a few months, he received an approval for a possible permanent residence in London. He was bewildered because he also wanted to

Gustavo Frazao/Shutterstock.com

use the travel grant to attend the convention in the United States and to see his brother in New Jersey. After soul searching, he gave up the travel grant. Ironically, he ended up attending the convention after it had appeared that his chance to stay in London permanently would take some time. Also, he became the President of the Math Teachers Association of the Philippines, and he received some funds from the university that he taught.

2He reunited with his brother in New Jersey who had been away for more than thirty years. Although he intended to return to the Philippines, his brother had convinced him to stay in the United States. He said tearfully, "I think I will die without any sibling by my side," Nick's heart melt like a block of ice that slowly turned into water.

3After a month, his brother accompanied him for a job interview. Although he passed the interview for a position to teach in a technical school, he did not get the job because he did not have the papers to work in the United States. The interviewer suggested to him to look for a job in a catholic school. Again, he told his brother about his strong desire to go back to the Philippines because he would lose all his monetary benefits due to possible resignation from his job. In addition, he missed his wife and children. Furthermore, he could not find a job in New Jersey. His brother insinuated to try looking for a job in a catholic school. He followed his advice until he met a very caring principal in a catholic school who accepted him as a teacher and helped him to lawfully work. From an associate professor in a private university in the Philippines to a second grade teacher in a catholic school in Jersey City was a daunting challenge especially that his family was in the Philippines. He had to study how to deal with students who had different characteristics from children in the Philippines. In addition, he felt a need to clearly explain his lessons. Sometimes, he felt that they could not understand him. So, he did several creative things like demonstrating, role playing, using a lot of visual materials, dramatizations, games and other techniques to catch students' attention and to make them more attentive and engaging.

4After a year, Nick was assigned to teach Grade 5 students. Every day, he prayed for the strength and endurance to withstand the challenges of living in another country and to deal with his longing to reunite with his family. To win the confidence and cooperation of his students, he encouraged them to join different writing, oratorical, spelling, math and science contests. As a result, several students won in writing and math contests. One student won first place in the county's spelling bee contest. Another student who wrote an essay won a computer for the school. Parents joined Nick in accompanying students in science and math contests in New Jersey. Parents were happy to see their children explain their science projects to other participants. These situations have inspired Nick to do better in teaching and have helped him to gradually embrace the culture of the new country. Later, his family came to New Jersey. In spite of these positive developments, he still yearned to teach in a university. However, he did not know the right path to reach this aspiration.

5During a casual conversation with fellow teachers in the faculty room, Nick learned that a teacher was completing a master's degree in Math. This prompted him to inquire about this program because he has completed a master's degree in math. Later, he had all his credentials evaluated by the World Educational Services. This office reports the equivalent of the degree that has been obtained in another country to the one that is completed in the United States. When he received the report, he excitedly told his husband that the highest degree that he completed in the Philippines was equivalent to a doctoral degree in the United States. This news strengthened his desire to teach in a university. So, he continuously searched the classified ads in newspapers to determine the expected qualifications of a college professor. He completed all the requirements to enable him to take the test for teachers. Later, he got certified as a math and elementary teacher. This means that he was eligible to teach math to students in grades 4 through 8. Also, he took a math course in a nearby college to acquaint himself on how to deal with college students.

6While learning the possible path to teach in a university, Nick immersed himself in community service, church involvement and different writing contests. Unexpectedly, these have helped him to receive several awards. These have greatly helped him to boost his confidence. He continued to believe that a turning point from challenges to triumphs and happiness was possible. He positively dealt with unexpected circumstances and continued to find ways to reach his aspirations. After six years, he was accepted as an assistant professor in a university in New Jersey. He called his brother right away to share the good news. Several years passed, but his brother could not hear whatever good news came. His brother passed away with a sibling by his side.

Comprehension

Choose the best answer from the list that completes each sentence. Write the letter of your answer on the space provided.

_____1. The sentence in the third paragraph that states Nick's heart melt like a block of ice that slowly turned into water would likely mean that _____
    a. Nick felt that he would like to give in to his brother's request to stay.
    b. Nick's brother was very lonely.
    c. Nick's brother would die very soon.
    d. Nick could not decide what to do.

_____2. A person who has completed a college degree in another country can best prove to the employer that his or her educational qualification is similar to the degree that is earned in the United States by showing a _____.
    a. diploma from the country where the degree has been completed
    b. transcript of records
    c. resume that lists all completed degrees
    d. certification from the World Educational Services of an earned equivalent degree

_____3. Nick completed a course in a nearby school because he _____.
    a. followed a teacher's advice
    b. thought that this could help him prepare to teach in a university
    c. wanted to be a math teacher
    d. believed that this could improve the way he taught students in grades 4-8

_____4. The passage mostly supports the belief about _____.
    a. working for a passion.
    b. continuously finding ways to reach a dream.
    c. remembering that a good situation follows every sad circumstance
    d. listening to people who can help you.

_____5. The word _bewildered_ in the first paragraph most likely means _____.
    a. happy   c. confused
    b. hesitant   d. doubtful

_____6. The word _daunting_ in the sentence below most likely means _____.
Daunting to fail in Math due to failing grades and absences, he pleaded to his professor to work for extra credits.
    a. ready   c. being afraid
    b. hating   d. hesitating

_____7. The most dominant pattern of the selection is _____.
    a. time   c. cause and effect
    b. description   d. list

____8. Of the following statements, the passage that supports the least is _____.
    a. sad things always turn to happiness
    b. inadequacies can be a source of inspiration
    c. no one knows what the future brings
    d. working for your dream is better than dreaming

____9. The last sentence in the fourth paragraph shows a/an _____.
    a. example   c. cause and effect
    b. contrast   d. addition

___10. Nick's long term goal is to _____.
    a. go home   c. teach in a university
    b. reunite with his family   d. attend a math convention

___11. The main purpose of this selection is to _____.
    a. describe the struggles of an immigrant
    b. persuade the readers to work for their dreams
    c. narrate Nick' story
    d. explain how to become certified as a math teacher in America

___12. The italicized word in the sentence that follows most likely mean _____.
    a. questioned   c. answered
    b. indicated   d. praised

His brother *insinuated* that Nick should look for a better job in order to better support his family.

Answer the following questions. Include relevant and at least three supporting statements for every answer.

1. What is your dream job after graduating from college? Why?

I want to _____ because

    a. _____

    b. _____

    c. _____

2. What makes you the most qualified to get that job?

I am the most qualified because of the following reasons.

    a. _____

    b. _____

    c. _____

3. What did you feel while reading this article? Write three sentences to support your answer. _____

   a. _____

   b. _____

   c. _____

4. Why should other people should read this? Write three reasons.

   a. _____

   b. _____

   c. _____

5. How did reading this article change your attitude towards reading inspirational stories or articles? _____

   _____

   Reasons:

   a. _____

   b. _____

   c. _____

Reading Journal Guide (Inspirational Article/Story)

Name _____ Date Due: _____ Date Submitted: _____

Choose any story or feature article that could inspire someone. This may come from any newspaper, magazine, or online source. The article must be two pages or more. Attach a copy of the article. (**5 points**)

Write a report that includes the following: (**5 points**)

Title of the Article _____ Date of Publication _____ Website address or title of magazine or newspaper _____
Summary: Write a summary that is based on the article. The pattern of organization of your summary must be the same as the pattern of the article. There must be 10 on more logical sentences. (**10 points**)

Comments: Answer all of the questions below. Your answer must include a main point/idea and four or more relevant supporting details for each question. (**25 points**)

Write at least one paragraph for the answer to every question.

1. Why did you choose this article?

2. What did you feel while reading this article? Why?

3. After reading this article, is there a change in your beliefs? Why or why not?

4. Do you think other people should read this? Why?

5. How did reading this article change your attitude toward reading inspirational stories or articles? Explain.

The journal report must be typed and must be submitted on time. Use correct spelling, grammar, and punctuation marks (**5 points**).

A report that does not adhere to the guidelines above will be downgraded. The highest grade for an assignment that is submitted after a week is a "70% or C." An assignment that is submitted after two weeks that it is due will not be accepted. The grade is Unsatisfactory.

Total Points _____/50 = _____   Letter Grade _____

Summing Up

In this book, you have learned how to use ACTOR, acquire skills, and apply strategies that can help you better understand what you read. In this chapter, you will use all of these in reading different passages and taking reading mastery tests. Tips on taking reading tests are provided.

Topics

ACTOR

Reading Skills and Strategies

Tips on Taking a Reading Test

Reading plays a great role in life. One way to know what is going on around you is to read the news articles whether online or in newspapers. Through reading, you gain useful information that can help enrich your life experiences. To fill out applications, you must read instructions and questions. In college, you read to acquire information that is related to your field. Assignments, projects, tests, and other tasks require you to read. You also read for entertainment. There are many benefits of reading. As such, you want to be sure that you understand what you read.

ACTOR

You read the material that has been written by an author who uses words that may not sound familiar to you and ideas that may appear complicated. ACTOR, the method that you learned in Chapter 1 shows explicit steps that can help you to become a focused, engaged, and efficient reader. It is important to follow all the steps to ensure that you understand and remember what you read. The steps in ACTOR include **activate** prior knowledge, **connect** to new information in the text, **trigger** appropriate strategies to understand what is being read, **organize** ideas that are generated from the text, and **respond** to what has been read through reciting and writing. In using ACTOR, you choose strategies that work for you or help you to achieve your purpose in reading.

During the *activate* step, you recall prior knowledge by reading the title and headings, asking questions on what the title and headings suggest and thinking about what is known about the expected ideas based on the title and major headings. You also *activate* prior knowledge on content and vocabulary while reading. Then you *connect* previous knowledge (vocabulary or ideas) to the new information to relate or make sense of what is being read. During the third stage, *trigger*, you derive meanings or make sense of printed texts by choosing a combination of strategies from the list below to ensure engagement with the text and comprehension. For example, you break apart a sentence into subject and predicate and think what each part means to you. In the fourth step, you think about what you have read, recall and *organize* in your mind or on paper the ideas that you generate from the text. Finally, you *respond* to what you have read to show proof of comprehension. Answering and asking questions about the texts during class and group discussions or written assignments show the extent of your reading comprehension. Responding helps you to determine if what is read is understood. Independent readers use their own words to recite or think about what has been read.

Reading Skills and Strategies

A reading skill is the ability to understand what is stated in a passage, infer what is not given or read between the lines or ideas, and give conclusions or the results of reading what is stated and the unknown-ideas between the lines or ideas. A strategy is a technique that will help a reader acquire reading skills.

A writer uses prior knowledge that is drawn from personal experience and secondary information and considers writing skills. For example, to write a good paragraph, a writer uses appropriate words, states or implies the main idea, and includes related supporting details. To understand this paragraph, the reader has to apply vocabulary and comprehension skills like inferring word meanings, activating prior knowledge, and identifying the main idea and supporting details. Being able to correctly summarize and sensibly react to the information in the paragraph may prove that the reader comprehends the material. The following skills can help a reader to facilitate and to show signs of comprehension.

Reading Skills

1. Infer the meaning of an unfamiliar word through its surrounding words in a sentence.
2. Figure out the meaning of an unfamiliar word through its prefix, suffix, or root word.
3. Infer the meaning of an unfamiliar word through punctuation clues.
4. Connect ideas in sentences through transitional words.
5. Sense a smooth flow of ideas between sentences.
6. Identify the main idea of a paragraph.
7. Identify details that support the main idea of a paragraph.
8. Connect ideas between paragraphs in an article.
9. Identify the main thesis of an article.
10. Identify the details that support the main thesis of an article.
11. Recognize paragraph patterns.
12. Make an outline of what is read.
13. Summarize what is read.
14. Distinguish between a fact and an opinion.
15. Make an inference.
16. Identify the purpose of a passage.
17. Recognize the tone of a passage.
18. Identify an argument.
19. Identify the point and supports in an argument.

Reading Strategies

A strategy is something that you do to understand what you read. For example, to understand what the paragraph is about, ask yourself what or who does the sentence talk about and what is being said about what or who. Connect the idea of each sentence to succeeding sentences to ensure the flow of ideas or to make things clear to you. To get the main idea or what the paragraph says, ask the following questions: (1) What is the paragraph about? (2) What do all or most of the sentences in the paragraph tell you? (3) What is the most general sentence? and (4) Do the rest of the sentences tell about the most general sentence? Being efficient means that the reader understands what is being read in a reasonable time and shows proof of understanding. After reading, you are able to summarize what you have read. In addition, you do not need to read the material several times to understand. The following strategies can help you acquire the different reading skills and understand what you read. You may use a combination of strategies from the list below before, during and after reading to become focused, engaged, and effective readers.

1. Have a purpose for reading.
2. Read the title and or headings.
3. Think about what the title and or headings in the article suggest.
4. Connect related knowledge about the title or headings to the reading material.
5. Concentrate or stay focused while reading.

6. Use context clues in the sentence or paragraph to figure out the meanings of unfamiliar words.
7. Use the meanings of prefixes, suffixes, or roots to figure out the meanings of unfamiliar words.
8. Use punctuation clues such as commas, colons, parenthesis, or dash to figure out the meanings of unfamiliar words.
9. Use word meaning clues such as is, means, refers to, or is defined as to figure out the meanings of unfamiliar words.
10. Break apart or chunk down ideas in sentences.
11. Ask questions while reading.
12. Say the first sentence without looking at it.
13. Imagine or make a picture of what is being read.
14. Underline or highlight information that is important.
15. Adjust the reading speed or slow down when needed.
16. Study given charts, tables, maps, or pictures in the text.
17. Know if you understand what you read.
18. If you do not understand what you read, change your strategy.
19. Connect the idea in one sentence to the next sentence.
20. Connect all ideas in a paragraph.
21. Recite what the whole paragraph says.
22. Connect the idea in the first paragraph to the next paragraph.
23. Organize in your mind the ideas that you get from the text.
24. Say the information that you understand from the full article.
25. Write about what you understand from the reading material.

Tips on Taking a Reading Test

When you take a reading test, apply ACTOR and the skills and strategies that you have learned. Reading tests usually ask questions that are based on stated as well as implied ideas in literary and informational text passages. You may not be familiar with the content, but applying what you have learned in this book and test taking strategies can help you do well on the test. Sometimes, the passage is easy to understand, but the questions are complicated because it does not ask a simple or straightforward question. For example, instead of asking, what is the transition word in the second sentence, a question may state, what does the third sentence do or how are sentences 1 and 2 related? Another way of asking this question is which choice best describes the relationship between the two sentences? Other times, the questions are easy, but the passage is complicated because it contains unfamiliar vocabulary, complicated and long sentences with major and minor details. The following tips can help you do well during the test.

1. Ask what or who are we talking about in every sentence (subject)? What does it tell about who or what (predicate)? Visualize, ask questions, talk to yourself, break apart the sentence, and use other strategies to be sure that you understand every sentence.

Example

To begin with, our understanding of climate change started with intense debates among 19th century scientists about whether northern Europe had been covered by ice thousands of years ago.

> Who or what are we talking about? [Understanding of climate change]

> What does it tell about it? Started with many debates among 19th century scientists about whether northern Europe had been covered by ice thousands of years ago.

2. Connect ideas between sentences. Use transitions or think about the relationship of the ideas between the parts of the sentence, ideas between sentences, and ideas between passages or paragraphs.

Example

1According to a report, Marie Curie won the prize for Physics after a research on radioactivity. 2Then in 1923, she published "Pierre Curry" with autobiographical notes about her life.

> Sentence 1 states that Marie Curie won the prize for Physics. The second sentence starts with <u>then</u>, a time transition. Therefore, the second sentence tells about the next thing that happened after Marie Curie won the prize for Physics.

Ask, what is the paragraph about? Organize the ideas in your mind and silently recite it to yourself. Doing this helps you to make the passage clear to you.

> You should be able to think about the main idea and major details.

3. Read the question. Ask, what does the question ask or tell you to do? You may choose to read the question before or after reading the passage. Although you will know right away what is being asked when you read the question before reading the paragraph, you still have to thoroughly understand the passage. You can chose any option of reading the question that will help you answer it correctly.

Example

Choose the best meaning of the italicized word.

Since I had witnessed the accident, one driver asked me to *corroborate* his claim that the other driver had gone through a red light.

a. confirm   b. state   c. hide   d. check

> You are asked to choose the best meaning of the italicized word. Any of the four choices is possibly correct. However, the best answer is <u>confirm</u> because the sentence states that <u>one driver asked me to corroborate</u> his claim that the other driver had gone through a red light. Therefore, the meaning of the word should be something that favors the driver who asked to corroborate the claim.

4. Recall prior knowledge on strategies and skills to answer the question. Read each of the given choices carefully. What does each tell you? Which of the choices make sense or connect to what is given in the passage and what is being asked? Your task is to get the

best choice, so avoid questioning the choices and say that the question is tricky or hard. This will make you confused.

5. Use the process of elimination. Sometimes, there are choices that look correct or similar. Read every word and find which choice matches, makes sense, or includes all important information—covers every aspect of the question. For example, which choice best describes the overall structure of the passage? If you see sentences that describe, narrate and compare, and explain in the paragraph, you have to choose the answer that is based on the purpose of the passage because you are asked to give the **overall structure** or paragraph pattern of organization.

Example

1Industrial health professionals are usually the heroes behind the scenes. 2They keep companies in compliance with a variety of regulations, and consequently help save a significant amount of money in the process. 3So what exactly is the difference between public and industrial environmental health careers? 4Well, public health officials are typically the enforcers of regulations set forth by the state and/or federal government. 5They protect the public from environmental influences such as lead, radiation, insect vectors, and disease or illness caused by food, pools, sewage, and the like. 6Industrial professionals protect the environment from the byproducts of manufacturing, assembling, and packaging of commodities we all depend on.

a. description   b. list   c. examples   d. contrast

Sentences 1 and 2 tell about or describe health professionals. Sentence 5 gives examples. However, the overall structure is contrast because the purpose of the paragraph is to show the differences between public and industrial environmental health professionals. Sentences 3–6 show this pattern of organization.

6. Be attentive to words like best, most likely except, not, but, and least likely. Words that include best, most, and most likely usually ask for the correct statement or choice. Words like except, not, but, and least likely ask for statements that are false or suggest a different idea that is stated in the passage. These two guidelines are not always true, so understand what is being asked and given.

Example

The word *copyright* most likely means _____.

According to research, contact is most likely to reduce prejudice under which of the following conditions?

Which of the following is likely the least that the writer intends to accomplish in the paragraph?

7. Using relaxation or motivational techniques before the test may help you. Deep breathing, thinking of the rewards of passing the test, opening and tightly closing your hands, praying, meditating, feeling of preparedness for the test, or any proven helpful approach may help you to focus on the test.

Sample Reading Test Items and Skills

No.	Reading Test Item	Reading Skill
1	It is implied in the passage that _____.	Inference
2	The overall structure of the passage is _____.	Paragraph patterns
3	Sentences 6 and 7 are related through _____.	Transitions
4	The word *copyright* most likely means _____.	Context clues
5	The passage primarily tells about _____.	Main idea
6	The purpose of the second paragraph is to _____.	Purpose
7	Both paragraphs include ____ to clarify given information.	Supporting details
8	The main idea of the passage is _____.	Main idea
9	The topic of the passage is _____.	Topic
10	It can reasonably be concluded from the two passages, _____.	Conclusion/Point
11	The writer adds the second paragraph to _____.	Purpose
12	The writer compares two situations to ____.	Purpose
13	Which of the following is supported by the author's _____.	Argument
14	The purpose of including _____ is to _____.	Purpose
15	The audience most likely feels _____.	Tone

Mastery Test 1

Read the passage and then choose the best answer to the question or the choice that best completes the statement based on what is stated and implied. Write the answer in the space provided.

1The origin of Happy Birthday is a roundabout tale that began with two sisters from Kentucky, Mildred and Patti Hill. 2Mildred wrote the familiar melody that would eventually become *Happy Birthday*. 3Patti, who was an elementary school teacher, wrote a verse of words that would be appropriate for a school teacher to sing to her students at the beginning of each school day—*Good morning to you, Good morning to you, Good morning dear children, Good morning to all*. 4After a few years, this simple greeting was turned around by students into: *Good morning to you, Good morning to you, Good morning dear teacher, Good morning to all*. 5The student-modified version spread throughout the country and became a common morning salutation from students to teachers. 6There is no documented evidence that the now familiar *Happy Birthday* lyrics were actually written by either of the Hill sisters. 7However, Jessica Hill, another sister, recognized the ever-increasing popularity of the song and took legal action to have *Happy Birthday* acknowledged as the creation of her sisters. 8She was awarded the copyright to *Happy Birthday* on behalf of her sisters in 1934. 9Due to several quirks in the copyright laws, the song is still protected under copyright until 2030. 10The performance of the song in a public place or in media of any kind requires that royalties be paid to the copyright holder.

Source: Chiego, The Musical Experience, 3E. Kendall Hunt Publishing Company, 2014.

_____1. It is implied in the passage that _____,
   a. school children can sing "Good morning to you."
   b. anyone who uses "Happy Birthday" for commercial purposes should pay to the ben-
      eficiaries of the sister.
   c. school children can change the lyrics of "Good morning, dear teacher."
   d. Mildred Hill wrote the words that are found in "Happy Birthday."

_____2. The overall structure of the passage is _____.
   a. description
   b. contrast
   c. time
   d. list

_____3. Sentences 6 and 7 are related through _____.
   a. description
   b. cause and effect
   c. time
   d. contrast

_____4. The word *copyright* most likely means _____.
   a. ownership of a song
   b. legal ownership of one's creation
   c. protection under the law
   d. ownership of the "Happy Birthday" song

> According to research, contact is more likely to reduce prejudice under the following
> conditions.
>
>   1. Contact should be between people or groups at equal status.
>   2. Contact should occur between people with common goals.
>   3. Contact should include intergroup cooperation.
>   4. Contact should be supported by the larger social context (e.g., authorities).
>
> Contact has the most positive effect when these conditions are met, but even when
> they are not, contact can still reduce prejudice.

Source: Feenstra, Introduction to Social Psychology. Bridgepoint, 2013.

_____5. The passage primarily tells about _____.
   a. contacts that should occur between people or groups at equal status
   b. contacts that should have positive effects
   c. reducing prejudice through different conditions relating to contact
   d. reducing prejudice even without contacts.

_____6. The overall structure of the passage is
   a. description
   b. cause and effect
   c. time
   d. list

1Although many global civilizations have influenced the traditions and practices of hospitality, the modern business of hospitality developed predominantly in Europe and America during the nineteenth century. 2This period is characterized by a significant acceleration in the pace of technological and economic development, especially in manufacturing and transportation powered by steam. 3The Industrial Revolution created vast new wealth among investors and business owners, resulting in the development of a new managerial class to operate the new huge companies, and contributed to the widespread emergence of an economic middle class. 4These factors, in turn, resulted in a dramatic increase in leisure and business travels.

Source: Brymer et al., Hospitality: An Introduction, 16E. Kendall Hunt Publishing Company, 2017.

_____7. The author connected sentences 3 and 4 through a _____ transition.
   a. description
   b. cause and effect
   c. time
   d. list

_____8. The sentence prior to the first sentence most probably shows a _____.
   a. description
   b. cause and effect
   c. contrast
   d. list

Paragraph 1

Natural disasters and the disasters or catastrophes that result from them, come in a variety of forms. Natural hazards of terrestrial origin can be divided into three different categories: geologic, atmospheric (or hydro-meteorological), and environmental (or biological). These originate from the flow of energy and matter contained on or in our planet. Examples include geologic earthquakes and volcanic eruptions, atmospheric hurricanes and tornadoes, and environmental wildfires and diseases. Natural hazards of extraterrestrial origin include asteroid or comet impacts and solar-related events such as geomagnetic storms.

Paragraph 2

Hazards can also be categorized as rapid-onset hazards which expend their energy very quickly, such as volcanic eruptions, earthquakes, floods, landslides, thunderstorms, and lightning. These hazards can develop with little warning and strike rapidly. These are the hazards we hear about the most because of their violent effects and real-time media coverage. In contrast, slow-onset hazards, such as drought, insect infestations, disease epidemics, and global warming and climate change take years to develop and are usually neglected by the media as not newsworthy until long after the effects have started.

Source: Best/Hacker, Earth's Natural Hazards: Understanding Earth's Natural Disasters and Catastrophes, 1E. Kendall Hunt Publishing Company, 2010.

_____9. Which choice best describes the information in the two paragraphs?
   a. Natural disasters come in different forms and hazards that have different categories.
   b. People get instruction to evacuate before all hazards and disasters occur.
   c. Hazards and disasters bring the same degree of negative effects to mankind.
   d. Natural disasters and hazards are given widespread publicity the moment each one of these develops.

_____10. In the second paragraph, the author's primary purpose is to _____.
   a. explain the two types of hazards
   b. explain how rapid-onset hazards develop
   c. justify the differences in media coverage between the two hazards
   d. contrast natural disasters and hazards

_____11. Both paragraphs include _____ to clarify given information.
   a. examples
   b. cause and effects
   c. examples and cause and effects
   d. comparisons

Paragraph 1

Music plays a very significant role in our lives. The power of music to affect the listener can add joy to a celebration, create a sense of common purpose at inspirational events, or serve as a communal bond when historic events or personages are commemorated. Birthdays and weddings incorporate music as part of the celebration. Political and sporting events usually begin with some type of musical proclamation such as the National Anthem or a fanfare. Parades commemorating national holidays include bands playing marches and other types of inspirational music. National and religious holidays have stimulated the writing of numerous musical compositions, and graduation ceremonies from college and high school always have music as part of the proceedings. Virtually every important event in our lives has a musical component.

Paragraph 2

Other art forms do not play as prominent a role in our celebrations as does music. Occasionally, poems are written to commemorate events or mark a celebration, but the frequency of their inclusion in such events is not as ubiquitous as musical performances. The creation of paintings, statues, or stage plays to mark important events is even less common. A musical performance is an inclusive, communal activity when it is part of an event and as such, it can intensify the emotions of those in attendance.

Source: Chiego, The Musical Experience, 3E. Kendall Hunt Publishing Company, 2014.

_____12. It can reasonably be concluded that the author's point in the first paragraph is _____.
   a. the power of music affects the listener
   b. music affects our experience of important events
   c. paintings and stage plays are less common than music
   d. music plays a very significant role in our lives

_____13. Which of the following does the second paragraph do?
   a. It contradicts the main idea of the first paragraph.
   b. It strengthens the message of the first paragraph.
   c. It weakens the argument in the first paragraph.
   d. It gives examples of common celebrations.

_____14. The word *ubiquitous* in the sentence below most likely means _____.
   a. enjoyed
   b. celebrated
   c. much
   d. dramatic

Occasionally poems are written to commemorate events or mark a celebration but the frequency of their inclusion in such events is not as *ubiquitous* as musical performances.

1The monthly repetition of the phases of the Moon presents the most obvious periodic event in the sky after the daily rising and setting of the Sun. 2Caused by the changing position of the moon while it orbits the Earth, the lunar phases provide a clear basis upon which to base a calendar and to make predictions. 3Lunar calendars are used to this day by many of the world's major religious groups. 4The ancient Babylonian calendar, based on the phases of the Moon, began each month at sundown on the day the crescent moon was first visible in the west. 5Because the time from one new moon to the next is about 29.53 days, the length of the Babylonian months generally alternated between 29 and 30 days. 6The year of 365.24 days contains an average of 12.37 lunar months, so their years had sometimes 12 and sometimes 13 months. 7The ancient Hebrews brought the Babylonian calendar back with them after their captivity, and it forms the basis of the present-day calendar of Judaism. 8Christians use a modified version of this calendar in setting the date of Easter, which was originally associated with Passover. 9The Islamic calendar is also a lunar calendar, and the holy month of Ramadan is linked to phases of the Moon, which is why it occurs on different dates of our Western calendar each year. 10The Buddhist New Year, which is celebrated all over the Far East, is also set by the Moon.

Source: Shawl et al., Discovering Astronomy, 5E. Kendall Hunt Publishing Company, 2006.

_____15. The main idea of the passage is _____.
   a. The monthly repetition of the phases of the Moon presents the most obvious periodic event in the sky after the daily rising and setting of the Sun
   b. Caused by the changing position of the moon while it orbits the Earth, the lunar phases provide a clear basis upon which to base a calendar and to make predictions
   c. Lunar calendars are used to this day by many of the world's major religious groups
   d. The time from one new moon to the next is about 29.53 days, the length of the Babylonians months generally alternated between 29 and 30 days

_____16. The topic of the passage is _____.
   a. Moon
   b. phases of the moon
   c. lunar calendar
   d. religion

_____17. Which choice best describes the tone of the passage?
- a. instructive
- b. persuasive
- c. straightforward
- d. provocative

Paragraph 1

Normally, a scientific theory is a way of explaining how some part of the world works. In most sciences, experiments are used to test the validity of hypotheses. In an experiment, a researcher actively attempts to manipulate a variable in a controlled environment to see if the manipulation has an effect on another variable. But in research that involves people, it is not always possible or ethical to control an environment to the same extent as in a typical laboratory setting. For example, during the 1800s several scientists hypothesized that germs cause disease. Since humans cannot ethically be given diseases, sick people were examined and swabs taken to see if their symptoms were associated with particular bacteria. After many complex tests with people, bacteria, and inoculation, the finding that "germs cause disease" was held to be true and used to build a new theory of infectious diseases.

Paragraph 2

1Or, consider fields such as astronomy. 2Astronomy is a theoretical and observational science in which experiments are almost impossible because we cannot manipulate the movement of heavenly bodies to see what may result. 3Similarly, cultural anthropologists cannot manipulate cultures in an experimental setting. 4It is an observational and data gathering discipline in which theories are evaluated on the basis of their explanatory power. 5The explanatory power of a theory is measured by the extent to which it can link immediate observations or experimental findings to a wider context of knowledge about particular phenomena. 6Newton's theory of gravitation has wide explanatory power since it can be used to explain many characteristics of the natural world, ranging from why you fell when you tripped to plotting the trajectories of planets and spacecraft.

Source: Nowak and Laird, Cultural Anthropology. Bridgepoint, 2010.

18. It can reasonably be concluded from the two passages, that the author believes that
- a. there are things that we cannot manipulate in all experiments.
- b. in research that involves people, it is not always possible or ethical to control an environment.
- c. in some experiments involving humans, astronomy, and anthropology, variables cannot be controlled or manipulated.
- d. in astronomy—a theoretical and observational science, experiments are almost impossible.

19. The writer adds the second paragraph to _____.
- a. show examples that are similar to the dominant situation that is presented in the first paragraph.
- b. compare astronomy and anthropology
- c. contrast experiments in humans and astronomy
- d. explain Newton's theory of gravitation

20. The purpose of including Newton's theory of gravitation in the second paragraph is to show how theories are _____.
    a. evaluated in astronomy
    b. explained in anthropology
    c. explained and evaluated in astronomy
    d. explained and evaluated in anthropology and astronomy

> David Ogilvy's views on marketing apply to many of today's content strategies and presentation—particularly in controlling word and art direction. What follows are some of the most well-known of Ogilvy's quotes that have influenced advertising for the last fifty years. It takes a big idea to attract the attention of consumers and get them to buy your product. Unless your advertising contains a big idea, it will pass like a ship in the night. You now have to decide what 'image' you want for your brand. Image means personality. Products, like people, have personalities, and they can make or break them in the market place. There is no need for advertisements to look like advertisements. If you make them look like editorial pages, you will attract about 50 percent more readers. I don't know the rules of grammar. . . . If you're trying to persuade people to do something, or buy something, it seems to me you should use their language, the language they use every day, the language in which they think. We try to write in the vernacular. Never write an advertisement which you wouldn't want your family to read. You wouldn't tell lies to your own wife. Don't tell them to mine.

Source: Ryan, Learning to See: A Guide to Visual Literacy. Bridgepoint, 2012.

21. The passage will least likely be read in a/an _____ textbook.
    a. science   c. advertising
    b. marketing   d. economics

22. The passage follows a _____ paragraph pattern of organization.
    a. time   c. cause and effect
    b. description   d. list

23. The main purpose of including David Ogilvy's quotes is to _____.
    a. show appreciation of his wonderful ideas
    b. inform students on the influence of his quotes on advertising in half of the century
    c. inform readers on how to make advertisements
    d. explain how to apply strategies in marketing

24. David Ogilvy's views on marketing are shown to be reflected in marketing _____.
    a. at present
    b. fifty years ago
    c. fifty years ago and at present

Mastery Test 2

Read the passage and then choose the best answer to the question or the choice that best completes the statement based on what is stated and implied.

Paragraph 1

Jean Piaget developed his stage theory primarily by observation and three case studies—of his own children. Throughout their childhoods, he carefully recorded their behaviors. He also manipulated the environment and constructed problems—like finding hidden items—that helped him discover the processes underlying cognitive development. Progression through the cognitive stages occurs as a result of both physiological maturation and experience with the environment.

Paragraph 2

Piaget theorized that children and adolescents build mental structures in much the same way that they build physical structures. Both physically and mentally, experiences are *organized* into structures that help children adapt to the demands of the world. **Adaptation** is the process of adjusting to those demands. It is not a passive activity whereby children simply adapt to what is directed at them. On the contrary, Piaget stressed that children actively organize their experiences. For example, infants often find great joy when they conduct experiments from their high chairs. When food is placed on the tray, they like to drop it on the floor, often leaning over the side with interest. They repeat the dropping patterns over and over again. Dropping food may at first be accidental, but it becomes more deliberate as infants organize the dropping experiences into a pattern that makes sense. According to Piaget, infants organize their different dropping experiences into a cognitive structure called a schema. Infants at first construct schemas based on experiences with their senses and motor activity. A "grasp and throw" schema for a 1 year old might include only soft objects like foam balls and banana pieces that can easily mold into a hand. The child soon learns that other small, malleable objects can be grasped and thrown in a similar fashion. Piaget called this process **assimilation**. New "throwable" objects are assimilated into the existing schema.

From *Child and Adolescent Development*, by Ronald Mossler. Copyright © 2013 by Bridgepoint Education, Inc. Reprinted by permission.

_____1. Which of the following questions do the paragraphs leave unanswered?
   a. What is the difference between adaptation and assimilation?
   b. How are children and adolescents similar in learning?
   c. What is a schema?
   d. In how many years did Jean Piaget complete his case studies?

_____2. The word theory in the first paragraph would most likely mean a/an _____.
   a. fact
   b. principle
   c. law
   d. observation

_____3. The word schema is used in the second paragraph to explain a child's _____.
   a. learning experience
   b. learning interest
   c. experiment
   d. behavior in eating

Philosophers use the word **argument** in a somewhat different way, one that emphasizes the idea that arguments put forth reasons to accept a conclusion. A philosopher would call this an argument, although there is probably little passion or a threat of violence involved here—the argument for the transitive property in arithmetic:

$$10 < 20$$
$$5 < 10$$
Therefore 5 is less than 20.

For philosophers, then, the term "argument" doesn't imply the idea it often does when we use the term to suggest anger, emotion, and hurt feelings. Rather, in this context, arguments simply present a conclusion and suggest why certain reasons indicate that conclusion is true, or probable.

Source: Mosser, Philosophy: A Concise Introduction, Kendall Hunt Publishing Company, 2010.

_____4. The given example above is similar to which of the following?
   a. $20 + 50 = 70$, and $30 + 40 = 70$
   b. 5 is more than 1, 3 is more than 1, so 2 is less than 3.
   c. 6 is less than 10, 8 is less than 10, so 9 is less than 10.
   d. 7 is less than 15, 4 is less than 7, so 4 is less than 15.

_____5. The term argument that is used in the passage most likely appeals to _____.
   a. reasons
   b. point
   c. emotions
   d. heated discussions

Paragraph 1

The Sciences discipline includes the hard science subject fields, such as physics, computer science, and medicine. Soft sciences, such as demographics and political science, are parts of the Social Sciences discipline. The Humanities include all the arts—visual, literary, and performing, and other subject fields such as religion and philosophy. It is pretty easy to put some subject fields into their appropriate disciplines: mathematics and biology are parts of the Sciences; sociology and education fit into the Social Sciences; literature, theater, and languages, including English, are considered part of Humanities.

Paragraph 2

There are other subject fields that fit into more than one discipline. One such interdisciplinary subject field is anthropology. Anthropology deals with social and cultural studies (Social Sciences) and with archaeology which may be considered part of history (Humanities). The subject field of Women's Studies, in turn, can be included in either the Social Sciences or Humanities.

Source: List-Handley et al., Information Literacy and Technology, 5E. Kendall Hunt Publishing Company, 2013.

_____ 6. The most appropriate sentence that states the main idea of the first paragraph is _____.
  a. The sciences discipline includes many divisions of knowledge.
  b. The three major divisions of knowledge include sciences, social sciences, and humanities.
  c. All college students are required to take some college courses in the different disciplines.
  d. Hard science and soft science are the two major disciplines.

_____ 7. The word interdisciplinary would most likely involve which of the following examples?
  a. one topic
  b. one discipline
  c. combination of topics in a discipline
  d. combination of disciplines in a subject field

_____ 8. To clarify the main idea that the author presents in the first paragraph, _____ are presented.
  a. lists   c. reasons
  b. examples   d. contrasts

> 1Og the cave dweller comes out of his cave in the morning and sees the sun shining in the east. 2When Og visits the village well later in the day, he and his friends are able to describe what happened. 3"When I came out of my cave, I saw the bright light in the sky!" 4They can all try to agree on the description, and they will all know what happened. 5Over the next several months, When Og and his pals emerge from their caves every morning, they see the sun in the eastern sky. 6They also notice that the sun has moved to the western sky when they return to their caves in the evening. 7After several conversations at the village well, they discover or recognize that a pattern seems to exist in the behavior of the sun. 8In the morning, the bright light is over there. But in the evening, the bright light is on the other side. 9They set up an observational plan to see if their pattern holds up. 10In the mornings, when Og comes from his cave (which faces south), he looks to his left and he expects to see the sun.

*Source: Wallace, et al. **Communication: Principles of Tradition and Change**,*
Kendall Hunt Publishing Company, 2009.

_____ 9. Of the following, which statement does not show what Og and his friends were able to do?
  a. describe what happened in the morning and at night
  b. describe what happened
  c. explain the reasons for the movement of the sun
  d. predict what would happen in the morning and at night

_____ 10. The word emerge in the fifth sentence most likely means _____.
  a. come out   c. enter
  b. stop   d. peep

_____ 11. The organizational pattern of the passage is _____.
  a. description   c. narration
  b. list   d. explanation

The right to express ourselves both orally and in the written word is one of the basic freedoms that separate the United States from much of the rest of the world. Americans can be rightfully proud of their ability to express their feelings without fear of governmental reprisal. Over the years, the U.S. Supreme Court has been very cautious when facing challenges to these basic freedoms. The Court takes many factors into consideration when limiting these rights, including the vagueness of the individual laws and the impact that any restriction will have on our society as a whole. The Court has stated that the government may not restrict speech "because of its message, its ideas, its subject matter, or its content. There are situations where the courts have imposed restrictions on these basic freedoms.

Source: Aberle, The Administration of Justice, Kendall Hunt Publishing Company, 2014.

_____12. Americans have the right to express themselves both orally and in written form, _____.
   a. but in some situations, there are some limits on what they can say
   b. and they can say anything they want to say
   c. and therefore, no one can sue them for whatever they say
   d. and they can also vote

1The *perception process* has three phases: selection, organization, and interpretation. 2The first phase is *selection*. 3Needless to say, at any given moment in our lives, there are many stimuli in our environment that may compete for our attention. 4We simply cannot focus on everything, so we select those stimuli that we feel are significant. 5That is why two people may see the same thing but "see" things differently. 6For example, when two fans watch the same football game, they may have very different perspectives about a controversial play. 7One fan may have focused on watching one player while the other fan focused on a different player. 8Because the two fans selected different things to attend to in the game, they may have a difference of opinion about the outcome of the play. 9Although they have seen the same play per se, they each focused on something different. 10As a result, the selection portion of the perception process will affect how each of them moves through the next phases of the process.

*Source: Chudnovsky, **Communicating in Your Personal, Professional and Public Lives**, Kendall Hunt Publishing Company, 2016.*

_____13. The passage is mainly focused on the _____ process.
   a. perception
   b. selection
   c. organization
   d. interpretation

_____14. Sentences 4 and 5 are related through _____.
   a. time
   b. example
   c. contrast
   d. cause and effect

The word "stereotype" is derived from a combination of two roots: stereo—to look at in a fixed way, and type—to categorize or group together, as in the word "typical." Thus, stereotyping is viewing individuals of the same type (group) in the same (fixed) way. In effect, stereotyping ignores or disregards individuality. Instead, all people sharing the same group characteristics such as race or gender, are viewed as having the same personal characteristics—as in the expression, "You know how they are; they're all alike." Stereotypes involve bias—which literally means "slant," and that slant can be toward the positive or negative.

Source: Thompson/Cuseo, Diversity and the College Experience, 2E.
Kendall Hunt Publishing Company, 2014.

_____15. Which of the following is not an example of a stereotype?
   a. Asians are good in Math.
   b. Germans consistently pursue their aspirations.
   c. Jews are very hardworking.
   d. Some Japanese are technologically smart.

_____16. It is assumed that stereotypes _____.
   a. are always negative
   b. are always positive
   c. can be positive or negative
   d. show bias

1Steve Jobs and Stephen Wozniak were an interesting, idealistic pair who had been tinkering with a computer in Jobs's garage. 2In 1976, they released their computer, called the Apple® I, which soon evolved into the more popular Apple® II. 3This was a personal computer designed for everyone to use out-of-the box, not just the skilled hobbyist geeks who assembled it with their own soldering guns. 4The Apple® II met with a resounding success upon its release in March 1977. 5The company had $700,000 in sales the first year, and $7 million the next. 6Suddenly, a personal computer industry began to flourish, and along with Apple®, other computers hit the market, including the RadioShack TRS-80, the Commodore PET, and later, the Atari™ 400/800 computers.

From Introduction to Digital Literacy, Second Edition, by Mark D. Bowles.
Copyright © 2013 by Bridgepoint Education, Inc. Reprinted by permission.

_____17. The first sentence states a/an _____.
   a. fact
   b. opinion
   c. fact and opinion

_____18. The word evolved in the second sentence most likely means _____.
   a. produced   c. sold
   b. multiplied   d. developed

_____19. The technological impact of the Apple computer _____.
   a. proved that Steve Jobs and Stephen Wozniak invented the computer
   b. narrated how the Apple computer come into reality
   c. led to the production of other computer brands
   d. created more skilled hobbyist geeks

Paragraph 1

A neighbor child comes to your door, collecting money for a well-known charity. Your budget is tight and you give elsewhere, so you are about to respond with a polite no, but the child says, "Even a penny will help." You have a penny, right in your pocket, so you can't really say no to the request. But you don't feel right about contributing just a penny. Reaching into your wallet, you pull out a couple of dollars and hand them over. Congratulations, you have just been persuaded by the technique called legitimization-of-paltry-favors.

Paragraph 2

As the name implies, the *legitimization-of-paltry-favors technique* catches us by making a very small contribution acceptable. It is difficult to refuse when even a very small amount is described as legitimate. But few would give a paltry amount even if it is acceptable, so we give more than just that penny; notice that a penny was not suggested, but legitimized. With this technique it should be clear that while a very small amount is okay, it is certainly not desired.

Source: Feenstra, Introduction to Social Psychology. Bridgepoint, 2013.

_____20. Which of the following is paltry?
   a. donating one's blood
   b. $0.50
   c. $100.00
   d. used car

_____21. The example in the first paragraph supports the point that _____.
   a. a person who does not intend to give money donates when asked to give a specified amount
   b. a person who does not intend to give money donates when asked to give any amount
   c. a person who does not intend to donate money gives as a result of someone's effective persuasive technique
   d. donating a penny is acceptable

Miles repeatedly heard the complaints of the primary tenant on the second floor regarding the noise coming from the first floor of the apartment. She thought that since he was always staying at home due to his medical condition, he became impatient. He complained about routine sounds like vacuuming, chopping vegetables, blending fruits and other everyday chores which he did not notice before when he was working full-time. Miles and her husband called the tenants for a meeting, so that they could understand each other's situation. Both tenants on the two floors had a chance to listen to each other's concerns. The tenant of the first floor mentioned about the noise coming from constant running from a child. Also, this meeting gave Miles and her husband a chance to assess the situation and helped them to determine whose lease contract to renew. For six months, Miles and her husband have not heard complaints from both tenants.

_____22. It can be concluded that _____.
   a. seven months after the meeting, one of the tenants left
   b. after six months, the tenant who was sick left the apartment
   c. the meeting was helpful
   d. the lease of the tenant who complained was terminated

_____23. It can be correctly assumed that the tenant who occupies the first floor _____.
   a. does not have any compliant
   b. has an issue with the tenant of the second floor
   c. mentions something that is not a problem
   d. always complains

Index

CPSIA information can be obtained
at www.ICGtesting.com
Printed in the USA
LVHW01s2251270718
585079LV00002B/2/P